# INDONESIAN CINEMA

## FRAMING THE NEW ORDER

Krishna Sen

Zed Books Ltd
LONDON AND NEW JERSEY

*For my father Sailendra Nath Sen.*
*As the last rites and farewell.*

*Indonesian Cinema* was first published in 1994 by
Zed Books Ltd, 7 Cynthia Street,
London N1 9JF, and
165 First Avenue, Atlantic Highlands,
New Jersey 07716, USA

Copyright © Krishna Sen, 1994

Cover designed by Andrew Corbett.
Cover picture from an advertising poster for *Si Boy II*.
Set in Monotype Baskerville by Ewan Smith.
Printed in the United Kingdom
by Biddles Ltd, Guildford and King's Lynn.

A catalogue record for this book
is available from the British Library.

US CIP data is available from
the Library of Congress.

ISBN 1 85649 123 4 hb
ISBN 1 85649 124 2 pb

# Contents

# Acknowledgements

This book has been a long project. It started as a PhD thesis in the Politics Department of Monash University, and was shaped by my experiences in Jakarta in the early 1980s. Over the years many people in Australia, Indonesia and India, wittingly and unwittingly, have contributed to this work as friends, informants, co-workers, teachers and mentors.

Amongst those who were particularly important in its formative stages are Dr Arun Dasgupta and Dr B. Ghoshal, who first introduced me to Indonesian studies in India, and Dr Herb Feith, who supervised my PhD thesis. Dr Arief Budiman and Professor Ben Anderson's comments on my thesis helped me rethink the subject.

Others in Australia who generously shared their ideas, libraries, time and affection include Barbara Martin-Schiller, Basuki Koesasi, David Goldsworthy, David Hanan, Helen Soemardjo, Ichlasul Amal and his family, Jim Schiller, Keith Foulcher, Max Lane, Pam Sayers, Richard Robison, Tom O'Regan and many students and staff at Monash University's Centre of Southeast Asian Studies and Murdoch University's School of Humanities. The final revisions to the manuscript owe most to my students in the 'Media in Asia' course at Murdoch. They made teaching a wonderful learning experience.

Friends in Jakarta helped me survive various field trips. And this book could not have been written without the support of members of the film community who trusted me with invaluable information and gave me the benefit of their knowledge, despite our differences of opinion in crucial areas. I wish to thank especially Ami Priyono, Anizar Abdurahman, Arifin C. Noer, Asrul Sani, Dr Budisantoso, Eros Jarot, Garin Nugroho, Gatot Prakosa, the late Brig. Gen. G. Dwipayana, Isma Sawitri, Marselli, H. Misbach Yusa Biran, Nasir Tamara, Rahim Latif, Salim Said, Saraswati Sunindyo, the late Syumanjaya, Slamet Raharjo, S.M. Ardan, Teguh Karya and the late Tuti Indra Malaon. Not all who made the field trips in Indonesia valuable in both academic and personal terms would wish to be named. I hope some of them at least will recognize their voices in parts of this book.

I am grateful to the Indonesian Film Archives, Sinematek, Jakarta, for allowing me to use some of their archival film stills in this book, and to Teguh Karya for his permission to include the two stills out of *Nopember 1828*.

To David, who has been my mate through almost the entire life of this project, any attempt to express gratitude would be graceless and downright silly. He and our most important joint project, Su-mita, are ultimately responsible for getting me to finish this book.

# Select Glossary

| | |
|---|---|
| *adat* | tradition, custom |
| AMPAI | American Motion Pictures Association in Indonesia |
| AMPI | *Angkatan Muda Pembangunan Indonesia* (Younger Generation for the Development of Indonesia) |
| Aspri | *Asisten pribadi* (personal assistant to the President) |
| BAKIN | *Badan Koordinasi Intelijen Negara* (State Intelligence Coordinating Body) |
| BAPFIDA | *Badan Pembinaan Perfilman Daerah* (Regional Film Development Body) |
| BPS | *Biro Pusat Statistik* (Central Statistical Bureau) |
| BSF | *Badan Sensor Film* (Film Censorship Board) |
| BUTSI | *Badan Urusan Tenaga Kerja Sukarela* (Board of Volunteer Workers) |
| *dukun* | practitioner of traditional medicine and mystic arts |
| FFI | *Festival Film Indonesia* (Indonesian Film Festival) |
| GASFI | Indonesian Association of Film Studios |
| GASI | Indonesian Association of Subtitlers |
| GOLKAR | *Golongan Karya* (Functional Groups), the government political organisation which contests elections |
| GPBSI | *Gabungan Perusahaan Bioskop Seluruh Indonesia* (All-Indonesia Association of Movie Theatre Companies) |
| G3OS | *Gerakan 30 September* (The Thirtieth of September Movement) |
| *Indo* | People of mixed – Dutch and Indonesian or Dutch and Chinese – descent |
| KFT | *Ikatan Karyawan Film dan Televisi Indonesia* (Film and Television Workers' League) |
| KNPI | *Komite Nasional Pemuda Indonesia* (National Committee of Indonesian Youth) |
| *layar tancep* | temporary, open-air movie screen, literally 'screens stuck in the ground' |
| LEKRA | *Lembaga Kebudayaan Rakyat* (Institute of People's Culture) |

# Note on Spelling
# and Translation

This book uses as its standard the Indonesian spelling system (EYD) adopted in 1972. This system is followed for all Indonesian words, including personal names, and titles of old (pre-1972) films and publications, with three exceptions: old spelling is retained in titles of books and films produced after 1972 which intentionally adopted old spellings (e.g. *Tempo Doeloe, Doea Tanda Mata*) personal names in the Acknowledgements are spelled (wherever known) according to the preference of the person named; Indonesian names of authors in non-Indonesian language publications are spelled in accordance with the publication.

My most sincere apology to people whose preference for pre-1972 spelling for their personal names has been disregarded in this book. However, it was felt that a uniform spelling system throughout would make the text more accessible to those without specialist knowledge of Indonesia.

Indonesian sources are cited in English translation throughout this book. Unless otherwise indicated, the translations are mine.

| | |
|---|---|
| LESBUMI | *Lembaga Senibudaya Muslimin Indonesia* (Indonesian Institute of Islamic Culture) |
| LFI | *Lembaga Film Indonesia* (Indonesian Film Institute) |
| *lurah* | village head |
| NU | *Nahdatul Ulama* (Muslim Scholars' Party) |
| PAPFIAS | *Panitia Aksi Pemboikotan Film Imperialis Amerika Serikat* (Council of Action for the Boycott of Imperialist American Films) |
| PARFI | *Persatuan Artis Film Indonesia* (Indonesian Film Artists' Union) |
| *peranakan* | Chinese, or other non-indigenes, born in Indonesia |
| PERBIKI | *Persatuan Bioskop Keliling* (Union of Mobile Cinemas) |
| PFN | *Perusahaan Film Negara* (State Film Corporation) |
| PKI | *Partai Komunis Indonesia* (Indonesian Communist Party) |
| PNI | *Partai Nasional Indonesia* (Indonesian National Party) |
| PPFI | *Persatuan Produser Film Indonesia* (Indonesian Film Producers' Union) |
| *pribumi* | indigenous Indonesian |
| *priyayi* | Javanese aristocracy |
| PSI | *Partai Sosialis Indonesia* (Indonesian Socialist Party) |
| PUSKESMAS | *Pusat Kesehatan Masyarakat* (Community Health Centre) |
| *rakyat* | the people, the populace, the masses |
| SARBUFIS | *Sarekat Burah Film dan Senidrama* (Indonesian Film and Stage Workers' Union) |
| *satria* | knight, noble warrior |
| *silat* | Indonesian traditional martial arts |
| SOBSI | *Sentral Organisasi Buruh Seluruh Indonesia* (All-Indonesia Federation of Labour Organisations) |
| TNI | *Tentara Nasional Indonesia* (Indonesian Armed Forces) |
| *warung* | small shop, roadside stall |
| *wayang* | traditional Javanese theatre performance |

# Illustrations

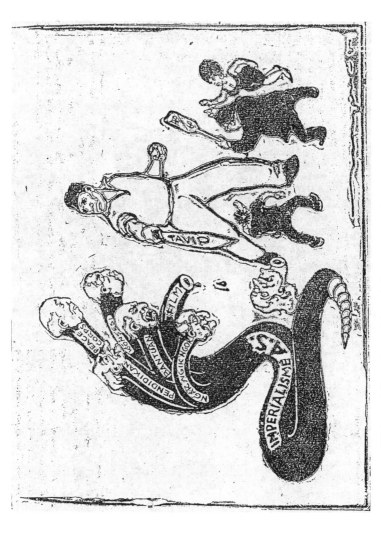

1. US Imperialism, the multi-headed monster, has its film head chopped off. From *Harian Rakyat*, 18 October 1964, p. 1.

2. Actor: 'Yours truly, Overacting'. Producer: 'Me Overbudget'. Director: 'I am Overtime'. And the 'poor fella little worker'. Cartoon on the back cover of the Union of Film and Television Employees' *Bulletin*, September 1981. (See Chapter 3.)

3, 4. From *Nopember 1828* (1978). The Javanese patriot Kromoludiro (3) and the Dutch soldier van Aaken (4), related through casting and camera angle. (See Chapter 4.)

5. Advertising poster for *Janur Kuning* (1980). Suharto is in the centre, flanked by General Sudirman and Sultan Hamenkubuwono. (See Chapter 4.)

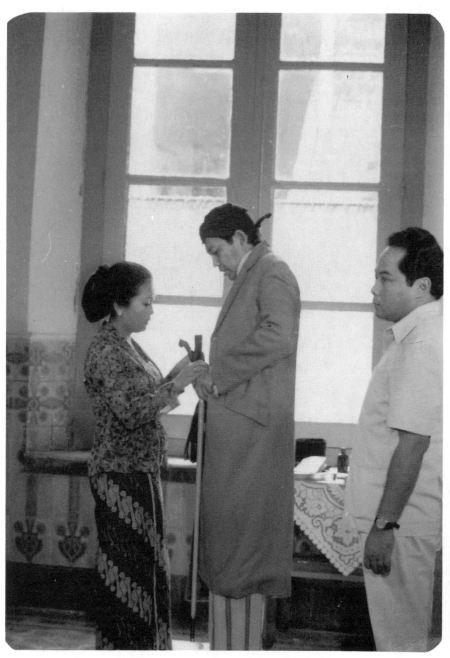

6. From *Janur Kuning*. The ailing General Sudirman leaving the house with his *keris*, followed by his doctor.

7. The cowering *rakyat* and brutal Dutch in *Janur Kuning*.

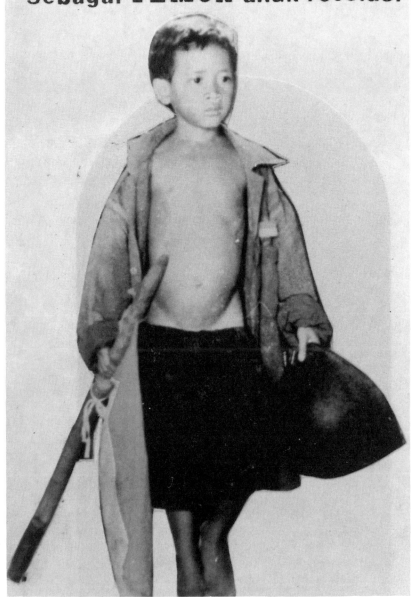

DANI MARSUNI
**Sebagai TEMON anak revolusi**

8. Advertising poster for *Serangan Fajar*. 'Temon the child of the revolution', in a characteristic pose of solitude, searching for his father.

9. From *Nasib Seorang Miskin* (1977). Iwan's days of deprivation are over when he finds his kind, rich uncle.

10. The victim tells her story in *Perawan Desa* (1978).

11. The criminals receive 'the punishment they deserve' in the final sequence of *Perawan Desa* (1978). (See Chapter 5.)

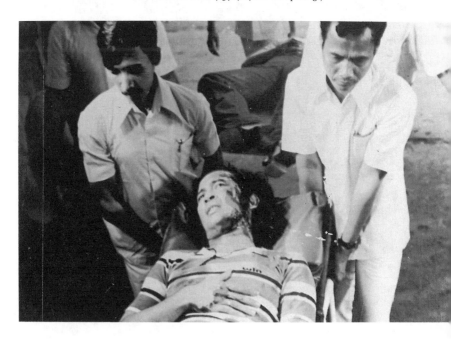

12. Advertising poster for *Si Boy III*. The young teenage protagonists represent a life of boats, bikes, beaches and Hollywood.

13. The unusual black-clad rural hero of modernisation in *Rembulan dan Matahari* (1979). (See Chapter 5.)

14. Lala getting behavioral therapy from the psychologist (left) in *Tangan Tangan Mungil*.

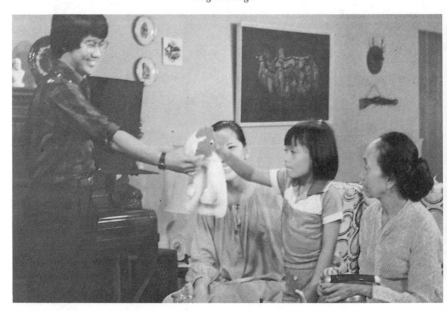

15. Advertising poster for *Bukan Sandiwara* (1980). 'Can a child born of artificial insemination make human beings happy? Or will it in fact be a disaster?'

16. Ayu, the ideal of femininity, in *Rembulan dan Matahari* (1979) represents natural beauty and restraint.

17. Paitun, the prostitute from the city, emotional and demanding.

18. Eros and Suci in *Suci Sang Primadona* (1977). (See Chapter 6.)

19. The dramatic heroine Suci and her clownish lovers.

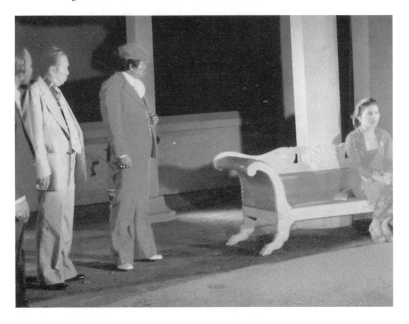

20, 21. Roro Mendut, the heroine who *sees* and uses her sexuality in *Roro Mendut* (1983). (See Chapter 6.)

22. From the cover on the video tape of *7 Wanita Dalam Tugas Rahasia* (1985).
(Discussion in Chapter 6.)

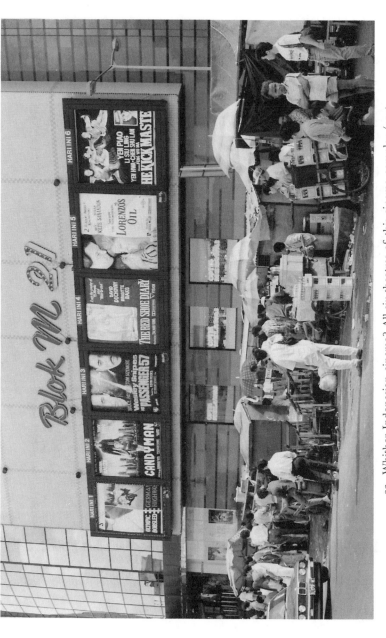

23. Whither Indonesian cinema? All six theatres of this cinema complex (part of the 21 chain – see discussion in Chapter 3) screen foreign films, June 1993.

# Framing the Questions

This book is about the institutions and texts of Indonesian cinema since 1965. It describes how these institutions came into being, and how they operate to produce a particular kind of text with its particular discursive construction of Indonesia – its past and present social relations. The claim to writing a 'descriptive' account is not intended to absolve myself from the responsibility of explaining my political and theoretical positions which motivate this particular account. Yet my hope is that in this very preliminary stage of work on Indonesian cinema,[1] the descriptions here could be appropriated for purposes quite different from my own.

The integration of Asian cinema into the relatively new field of cinema studies, is a recent phenomenon. Only since the 1980s have the cannonical journals of film theory (*Screen* for example) made regular attempts to include papers on Third World cinema. Criticism of the term Third World in other academic disciplines notwithstanding, textual theorists and film theorists in particular have continued to use the term as a heuristic category capable of naming a tri-continental (Africa, Asia, Latin America) phenomenon.

The naming of Third World film as such assumes a certain relationship between it and First World (read Hollywood) cinema and, by implication, First World film theory. Teshome Gabriel, something of a pioneer in Third World film theory has suggested that Third World national cinemas move through a period of mimicry of Hollywood to self-conscious rejection of Hollywood textual practices to a critical engagement with their own national cultural traditions.[2] In an earlier work he elaborated on 'third cinema', which he sees as more or less synonymous with that third phase. The key to the difference between Hollywood and Third Cinema seems to be the explicitness of the latter's socio-cultural messages, as opposed to the hidden ideological workings of the Hollywood text. That difference leads Gabriel to suggest that Western film theory, which is geared to 'find immanent meaning in works whose deeper meaning is concealed', is quite useless in analysing films that 'do not try to hide their true meaning'.[3] While this leads to the argument that these films need to be analysed in their 'proper socio-aesthetic context', that which is worthy of analysis is selected mainly on the basis of its self-aware differentiation from Hollywood.

Julianne Burton has provided a thorough-going critique of Gabriel's notion of ideological transparency and coherence of the so-called 'third cinema'. Her own position shares with Gabriel's, however, that Third World films need to be analysed in terms of their relationship with 'mainstream' cinema.[4] She agrees with Kolker's hypothesis that 'in fact no direct split exists between film-making in America and elsewhere. They are rather an interplay in which the dominant style (or styles) are always present to be denied, expanded upon, embraced and rejected only to be embraced again'.[5] While Burton does refer briefly to the various ways in which films can be 'oppositional' within the context of the particular nation-state, her main arguments remain framed by a conviction repeated in various ways through the essay that 'the film products and practices of the underdeveloped world cannot be understood in isolation from those of the developed world' (p. 10).

Despite the sophistication of this work the basic language and assumptions of this Third World text theorising shares a great deal with dependency theory and the media research done under its influence almost two decades ago. Burton's assertion about the 'development of critical underdevelopment' in the Third World early in her piece is a symptomatic echo of André Gunder Frank's famous 'development of underdevelopment'.

The work most overtly framed in terms of the dependency thesis is perhaps Roy Armes' *Third World Film Making and the West*. Its starting point is 'the fact that the impact of the West was almost universally experienced as a traumatically destructive force by those subjected to it'.[6] In all of this, as in the cultural dependency thesis, the principal target of criticism is relations across the boundaries of nation states, not ones within it.

The second (and older) point of entry of Asian cinema into English language academic work is through Asian studies on the one hand and the international film afficcionados' engagement with Asian films on festival circuits on the other. When Western film critics 'discovered' films from Asia in the 1950s, they initially graded them in terms of the extent to which they revealed some assumed reality of Asian countries. This realist presumption allowed the rejection of both the popular spectacular films of Bombay, and the overtly political films of Communist China. Realism died a slower death in writings on Asian cinema than in film theory as a whole, in part at least because the Asianist scholar's reason for existence is to discover (the real) Asia, simultaneously different from and accessible to the West.

By the 1980s, when realist analysis of films had become unfashionable, the language of what we might call the 'Asianist' discourse on films altered somewhat. For instance, Satyajit Ray's most recent English biographer, Andrew Robinson, writes: 'By the standards of most directors not very much happens in most of Ray's films, and yet each seems to embody a section of Bengali society; together, like Kurosawa's films, they describe a culture.'[7] In much the same way, Donald Richie writes of *Red Sorghum*, that it 'does for Chinese cinema what *Rashomon* did for the Japanese ... it opens a whole world of myth and beauty.'[8] The search has thus shifted from social reality to cultural authenticity. Critical action upon the text no longer seeks the real Asia, but a unique native narrative, shaped by some unique (and pre-existing) culture or world of myth.

There is now a very interesting body of literature analysing Chinese and Indian film texts in terms of the ancient and classical texts of these countries.[9] Vijay Mishra, for instance, starts his reading of Bombay cinema thus:

> In examining the Bombay film as a particular signifying practice and a culturally specific art form we would like to claim that the Indian epics themselves (*Ramayan* and *Mahabharata*) constitute a 'grand-syntagm', a massive narrative form which governs individual segments of the Indian filmic text.'[10]

It seems to me that such readings of films premised on a valorisation of a putative national cultural past has been persuasive in the context of Western academic writing on Asia, partly because it reproduces the construction of the Orient as unchanging, bound by the ancient and the mythic. Moreover, as Trinh Minh-ha has pointed out, analysing texts in terms of their cultural correctness contains an implicit demand that Asians (and other 'natives') remember and reproduce a pre-colonial past consciousness, disenfranchising every other way of constructing national texts and national identities by today's Asians.[11]

We need to ask, too, in what sense is the ancient, pre-colonial available to the popular audience? In India, where new gods are still being created, and in Indonesia, where the ancient demons and god-clown *Punakawan* ride motorbikes and use English or Dutch in the *wayang* repertoire, how useful is it to map the contemporary text on to a pre-colonial, pre-industrial one? This is not to argue that the *wayang* does not enter into the encoding and decoding practices of Indonesian cinema. It does indeed but, as I will argue later in the book, it does so in ways motivated by contemporary political relations. However, to give that relationship (between ancient classics and contemporary film texts) primacy may well mean that we fall into an essentialist (and in this case essentially Orientalist) mistake of emphasising continuities and universalities within a national cinema, so that we miss what is more significant – changes, interruptions and disruptions.

What I have called here the Asianist approach and the Third World text approach, though very different, have as it were a common black hole. In both points of view, the immediate temporal and spatial contexts in which films are produced and consumed disappear as central analytical trajectories – in one case in favour of great traditions of the past, in the other in favour of the great tradition of Western cinema. This down-grading of the national context of cinemas may reflect wider moves, in social and political analysis at large, to see the nation-state as under challenge, on the one hand from the globalising forces of multinational capital and, on the other, through fragmentation by religion, ethnicity and other (generally older – pre-national) identities. It has been argued that the changing technology (such as personal computers and electronic publishing or cable television) of the post-industrial society is increasingly leading to narrowcasting of messages to special interest audiences, rather than broadcasting to mass audiences. The media is not a mass media any more, nor does it address the nation. On the other hand national boundaries are electronically permeable and cannot be defended from media images and messages coming across borders on the parabolas and modems. The two alternative foci of studies of the media in the 1980s thus have been either the globe or the special interest/cultural group.

Against these trends some writers are now beginning to turn analytical attention back upon the nation-state and especially to the power of the state. One useful instance of this is the recent work of media sociologist Philip Schlesinger. Following a Weberian path he defines the state as a 'pacified' social and 'communicative space' that 'the monopoly of force confers within a given territory'. He suggests that we need to focus on 'the permitted range of communicative practices within the territory of a state, and the extent to which official linguistic and cultural norms may be exclusively imposed and resisted'. He goes on to talk about the 'active mobilisation by states against "invasions" of their communicative space from outside ... or "subversion" from within'.

> Notions of strategic and tactical use of communication are far from alien to our understanding of the construction of cultural collectivities and the workings of the media. This is no accident, for the media and the wider cultural fields are indeed conceived of as *battle*fields, as spaces in which the contests for various forms of dominance take place.[12]

In the studies of media in the Third World particularly, the shift away from the globalising framework of cultural/media dependency theories has been quite marked. While recognising 'the limits placed on many nations' media systems by operating within subordinate positions in the world economy', a large amount of research in the media and cultural industries of the Third World now give, according to Straaubhar:

analytical emphasis to the distinct dynamics of each nation's or industry's historical development. Key national issues include conflicts between domestic and transnational elites, interests of key national elites, entrepreneurial competition, the agendas and actions of key production personnel, and the effects of state intervention, particularly as policy-maker, provider of infrastructure and advertiser.[13]

Changes in the direction of Mattelar's work (in the late 1970s), one of the influential exponents of cultural dependency, anticipates this shift from international to national contexts of cultural production. His first major work on Chile emphasised the importance of American input in determining media content and hence values and ideas, transmitted to the Chilean audiences.

> The native ruling class and its lackeys increasingly become mere managers of a body of myths which are not their own. They do no more than mechanically reproduce these myths through the mass media in order to maintain their hegemony. ... The myths being administered are above anything else intended to ensure the hegemony of the imperialist centre.[14]

This generalisation was based on Mattelart's observations, first of the media in Chile's pre-1970 bourgeois democratic state and, secondly, of what he called 'the imperialist cultural counter-revolution', that is the role of media in the US bid to overthrow Allende's Popular Unity government in 1970–73. By the late 1970s, however, he was having to account for the Pinochet government's policy of replacing American media products with local ones. Also, media content in Pinochet's Chile was quite different from what it had been in the Frei government period before Allende. Mattelart thus had to revise his earlier position to argue that 'cultural messages must necessarily be coherent with the state apparatus found in the particular country'.[15]

The problematic relationship between the state and the media text is not raised in this book as a theoretical issue. Rather the concrete historical and political context of post-1965 Indonesia is taken into account in the analysis of the texts and institutions of Indonesian cinema. The first part of the book looks at the structure of the film industry, including patterns of state control, in the changing context of the political economy of Indonesia. Part two, which reads film texts in relation to national politics and often quite specific political movements, is methodologically more contentious. It goes against the grain of theorising about Asian cinema and, more generally, mainstream film theory dominated by psychoanalysis,[16] but also of studies of art and literature in post-1965 Indonesia, based on a notional segregation of social, political, ideological and cultural spheres.[17] However, on my last field trip to Jakarta, the week after the 12 November 1991 killings in Dili, I could not but see *Laut Masih Biru* (The Ocean's Still Blue), starring the daughter of the governor of East Timor, as a confirmation that Indonesian films are about contemporary Indonesian politics.

Two weeks before the Timor killings, *Laut Masih Biru* had been nominated as Best Film at the Indonesian Film Festival. It did not win. But while the year's Best Film was nowhere to be found in Jakarta, *Laut Masih Biru* was playing at several theatres in the city. It would be reasonable to conclude that the Dili incident, not the nomination, helped its release. *Laut Masih Biru* is a Romeo and Juliet story, in which family feuds (and political ones between the rival parties Fretilin and the UDT) split up young lovers. It is also a rehash of Bombay cinema's favourite theme of rich girl meets poor boy. No doubt the protagonists of the film could be made to fit heroes and heroines of some Indonesian mythic typology. But its 'brutal' Fretilin, the 'patriotic' and angry Indonesian soldiers, the almost maternally concerned Indonesian commander ('Don't kill them. They are our children' he sobs before his death), the good (real) governor's daughter as the symbol of integration with Indonesia, cannot be understood without reference to the political conflicts in contemporary Indonesia.

Obviously, only a minority of films will lend themselves to such overt political interpretation. But as this book will demonstrate, especially in Chapters 4 to 6, every film, whatever its overt theme or genre, tells us something about who has the power to speak for and about (that is, to represent) whom and how in New Order Indonesia.

Although there is a break in the book between the focus on institutions in the first part and texts in the second, the argument that binds them together is that Indonesian cinema is political. This book demonstrates that the institutions of Indonesian cinema have been shaped significantly by the political struggles on the national stage, especially the traumatic civil war of 1965–66. Secondly, it argues that state censorship examines each film in terms of the state's long-term interests (for example, maintenance of the nation-state itself) and the (not necessarily compatible) interests of the current government (for example, promotion of the Suharto leadership, suppression of criticism of bureaucratic corruption). All subsequent readings of films take place in the knowledge of this political sieve of censorship through which a film has passed. Ironically, these politicised readings stand in contradiction to the ideal of depoliticised art canonised in Indonesian aesthetics after 1965. (The politics of this depoliticisation is part of the story told in Chapter 2.)

The significance attributed by implication so far to 1965 and to the power of the state after 1965 is most probably unsurprising to students of contemporary Indonesia. Nonetheless something needs to be said about the perspectives on 1965 and the New Order state that are implicit in this book.

In 1965–66, the competition between social forces and ideological commitments that had marked the previous ten years was resolved in a brutal civil war that brought the army under General Suharto to unquestionable domination in the Indonesian political system. Beyond that, however, there is a good deal of disagreement as to who or what was the real winner in the New Order (a name that Suharto's supporters gave to the new government signifying the promise of renewal and change from the Sukarno government, now dubbed the Old Order).

Ben Anderson sees the New Order as a victory for the state itself.[18] In Anderson's terms Indonesian history is the unfolding of the struggle between the representative interests of the nation and the aggrandizing interests of the state. While the years of parliamentary and guided democracy are the unfolding of tensions between an old state inherited from the Dutch and the new nation born out of the independence struggle, the 'New Order is best understood as the resurrection of the state and its triumph *vis-à-vis* society and nation.'[19]

While the theory of the overwhelmingly dominant state, or at least overwhelming dominance of state bureacracies, marks a large amount of research on Indonesian politics, Robison proposed a quite different thesis where 1965 is the beginning of a capitalist revolution (or should it be counter-revolution?), 'the victory of the propertied classes'. According to him, 1965 was the victory of 'a weak but a nevertheless resilient capitalist social order' against the challenge posed by the Communist Party (p. 97) on the one hand and on the other hand over the attempt by the state under Sukarno to mount major social and economic alterations. The structure of class relations which survived became consolidated under the New Order: 'while the New Order may politically exclude dominant social forces from direct access to political power, it rules nevertheless with their general acquiescence and in their general interest'.[20]

Robison suggests that while the politico-bureaucrats who administer the state are themselves becoming an increasingly important section of capital owners, the state does not function exclusively for them, but rather as a mediator between sections of the propertied classes. While this class is identified as consisting of the urban middle classes (including professionals, intellectuals, white collar workers), the large, medium and small-scale bourgeois (both Chinese and indigenous, including the bureaucrat capitalists), land-owning classes, rural traders and finally the lower reaches of the state bureaucracy itself, the actual account in the book demonstrates mainly that the state functions to promote consolidation of the economic position of the large business conglomerates. Robison sees the political life under the New Order as the unfolding of contradictions between sections of the dominant classes themselves, and particularly conflict over direct access to political power between the Suharto regime and sections of the dominant classes.

Within the very limited context of the film industry, as Chapter 3 of this book demonstrates, government policy has indeed promoted the consolidation of monopoly interests of big business. At the wider and more complex level of understanding the politics of textual representation, the notion of the New Order as an alliance of the state and the propertied classes against other subordinated groups in the society has a certain appeal – but with ethnic and gender dimensions added to the equation.

As one reviewer of Robison's book has pointed out, the consolidation of capitalism will not automatically wipe out the vulnerability of certain ethnic groups *vis-à-vis* others, no matter what the purely economic factors may suggest.[21] Burhan Magenda has drawn attention to ethnic factors as crucial elements in relations of domination in New Order Indonesia.[22] He argues that the Javanese *priyayi* (aristocracy) 'has become the main cultural base of the New Order'.[23]

Magenda shows that not only are the Javanese *priyayi* numerically dominant within the Indonesian military, the latter, he argues, has time and again saved the *priyayi* from any challenge to its control of the state, whether from its arch class enemy, the Javanese peasant, or its non-Javanese cultural rivals. In Magenda's view the civil war of 1965–66 cemented the victory of the *priyayi*, which was further reinforced in subsequent years by the increasing prominence of the *priyayi* amongst the capitalist class. After 1965 the *priyayi* was able to establish a cultural alliance with the Javanese masses through their shared Javanese world view, and with some sections of the elites in the outer islands through a shared anti-communism and by playing on the horrible memories of the civil war. Magenda also argues that some sections of the non-Javanese elite are themselves culturally Javanised, through marriage, education in Java and the very fact of the *priyayi*'s domination within the ruling elite.

Critics of the New Order have thus analysed relations of domination and subordination in Indonesia from the point of view of state–civil society, class and ethnic relations. Given that class, ethnicity and gender have been more or less the key words in contemporary social science it is surprising that the gender dimension of the transformations that the New Order wrought have not been systematically analysed. However three aspects of how the New Order affected women have been discussed at some length: (1) the comparative disadvantaging of women in the process of integration of Indonesia into international industrial capital under the New Order;[24] (2) the political disenfranchisement of women by the destruction of the pre-1965 left-wing women's organisations and their replacement by state-sponsored organisations within which the women are ranked in accordance with their husband's position in the bureacracy or the military – in the words of some observers the replacement of women's organisations by 'wives' organisations';[25] (3) the overt ideological definition of women by the New Order government as primarily mothers and wives.[26]

Unlike the state, class and ethnicity analysis of the New Order, however, the gender dimension of the civil war of 1965 itself has not received much attention. Nor is this the place to go into it. It is, however, undeniable that in the myths about the civil war women have a crucial role, since so many of the atrocities against the so-called communists were justified in the name of the cruelty perpetrated on six generals killed in the early hours of the 1st of October 1965. In the military propaganda during and since the civil war that followed not only were women seen as perpetrating the abuses but also the nature of this abuse was sexual sadism involving the mutilation of genitals. 'GERWANI Cabul' (GERWANI Whores) became one of the catch-cries of the anti-communist propagandists.[27] The term continues to be mobilised in the 1990s as abuse against women taking part in mass actions such as student demonstrations and strikes.

Seeing women as sexually threatening is not peculiar to the New Order, nor indeed to Indonesia. Mythology and folklore in Indonesia as in many other countries, East and West, tell numerous stories of the demonic sexual woman. What is interesting about 1965 in Indonesia is the political foregrounding of that male fear of woman's sexuality. In that discourse women's collective, autonomous, political actions become expressions of the dangerous female sexuality. Though men-as-men could not be said to have won the civil war, it may be reasonable to say that women-as-women lost it.

It is not, however, the purpose of this work to decide on any single explanation of domination and resistance in the post-1965 Indonesian society. Perhaps the one common lesson of contemporary social analysis is that no concrete situation, no specific text, can be explained on the basis of a single matrix of power. Global manifestations of oppression such as racism, capitalism and patriarchy, along with other local forms of authority (family, education systems, religion), may be articulated onto each other, but cannot be subsumed under any one. In this sense the foregoing discussion of 1965, somewhat rushed and simplified, can be restated in terms of the New Order signifying the production of certain *systems of domination*, out of a variety of pre-existing struggles for domination.

If 1965 is a victory of the state against the society, and of the capitalist-*priyayi*-male against their 'others' (various and contradictory), that victory is not, however, an ultimate closure. Anxieties anchored in the experience of the civil war of 1965, are not obliterated once and for all by the victory itself, but must be constantly symbolically reproduced in order to be symbolically contained. In that sense this book is about reading the collective fears of the victors of 1965.

# ONE

# Social and Political Context

# 1

# The Beginning: Early 1900s
# to 1956

In the year 1900, moving pictures, a product of the Western technological revolution, came to Indonesia. The first half of the 20th
century was a period of rapid political change which saw Indonesia
move from Dutch colonialism through war and Japanese occupation to
intensified nationalist struggle, the 'Indonesian Revolution' or 'War of
Independence' to the establishment of an independent Indonesian
nation-state. This chapter is a brief sketch of the first 50 years of cinema
in Indonesia in the context of this political transformation, highlighting
certain fundamental developments, such as Chinese financial dominance, the presence of American cinema and state censorship which
became, and remain, the defining characteristics of the Indonesian film
industry.[1]

### Fear of films

In the first two decades of the 1900s American and European films
were spreading in the cities of Java, particularly in Jakarta (then Batavia).
By the middle of the 1920s, when the first film was made in Indonesia,
there were 13 fixed cinemas in Jakarta.[2] But this number does not give
the full extent of the spread of films, since a large number of films were
shown in open air, in temporary tents like circuses by travelling movie
peddlars.

By the early 1920s, the presence of American films was causing
concern in the Dutch colonial circles. In 1926 the Dutch Indies Film
Commission was established, under the Department of Internal Affairs,
to censor every film coming into Indonesia.

The colonial rulers worried about the impact of films on uneducated
natives. In November 1925, *Inter-Ocean*, a Dutch East Indian magazine
covering Malaya and Australia, published from Jakarta, ran an article,
'Films in the Orient', which cited Chinese, Malay and Indian cases to
demonstrate the 'pernicious effect' of some American films.[3] The

following year, an article in *The Times* (London), written by a journalist who had travelled in the Dutch Indies and British India, attracted the attention of the Dutch film magazine *Filmland*. *The Times* article deplored the 'effects of the "pictures" on the prestige of the Europeans in the Far East'. It said that 'the spread of picture houses in remote tropical countries has been remarkable in recent years, and it is now rare to find a town of a few thousand people which cannot boast of its "picture palace".' As a result of seeing movies 'the vast mass of black, brown and yellow people' now saw 'the inner life of the European, and especially that side of it which flourishes in centres of crime and infamy, [which] was unknown until the American films showed them a travesty of it.' The article pointed out that while educated 'orientals' understood and had indeed adopted Western attitudes, it was the uneducated natives who most keenly watched and were affected by films.[4]

The article in *Filmland* in December 1926, titled 'The Danger From Films in the Colonial Areas' quoted a long passage from the *Times* piece to the effect that

> by the unsophisticated Malay, Javanese, or even the Indian and the Chinese, the scenes of crime and depravity [of Westerners] which are thrown on to the screen are accepted as faithful representations of the ordinary life of the white man in his own country. The pictures of amorous passages ... give him a deplorable impression of this morality of the white man and, worse still, of the white woman.

The article also reported that a Cinematography Conference in Paris 'discussed the political and moral danger from some films in the colonial countries'. An ordinance issued by the colonial government in 1940, detailing the structure and powers of the Film Commission remained the cornerstone of the censorship mechanism through the many changes of government even after Indonesia's independence.

### The Chinese connection

About the middle of the 1920s Chinese films arrived in Indonesia. Ethnic Chinese had been involved in the movie business almost since the first films arrived in the Indies. Although the pattern of theatre ownership in the early years of the 1900s is not known, copies of contemporary film advertisements indicate that some of the earliest cinemas were owned by the Chinese. Chinese areas of Jakarta like Glodok, Senen and Pasar Baru and partly Chinese areas like Tanah Abang, Mangga Besar, Kramat and Pancoran, had established movie theatres by about 1910. In 1927 a Bandung paper claimed that 85 per cent of movie theatres in the Dutch East Indies belonged to Chinese.[5] In China, film production had got underway around the time of the First World War.[6]

Within a decade, Chinese in Indonesia were importing films from China as well as producing their own films in Indonesia.

While the first film was made in 1926 in Bandung by two Europeans, the initiative passed quickly on to the Chinese. The first Indonesian–Chinese film was made by the Wong brothers, who had migrated to Bandung from Shanghai in 1928 and started their first film the same year. The Wong brothers had had some film-making experience in Shanghai and brought with them a small amount of equipment.[7] It seems that they received support from a well-established *peranakan* (Indonesian-born) Chinese businessman. The film, *Melatie van Java* (Lily of Java), was a commercial failure, which caused the split between the Wong brothers and their commercial backer and led the brothers to look for a quite different kind of story for their later films.

With their next film, *Si Conat* (character's name), the Wong brothers chose a story that was familiar to the Chinese as well as the ethnic Indonesian population of Jakarta. The story, about an ethnic Indonesian villain and a Chinese hero, was reportedly selected by the Wongs' new *peranakan* financial backer, Jo Eng Sek. *Si Conat* was part of the repertoire of *lenong*, a form of theatre particularly associated with the Betawi people (the local population of Jakarta).[8] *Si Conat* was not only the first Indonesian film set in Jakarta, it was also the first film made in Jakarta – a precursor to the eventual centrality of Jakarta both as the site for the Indonesian film industry and the setting for its narratives. Although the European pioneers of Indonesian cinema, Kruger and Carli, continued to work in Bandung for a few more years, as did the Wongs from time to time, Chinese film companies were being established mostly in Jakarta and to a lesser extent in Surabaya.

*Si Conat*'s success was due as much to the popular knowledge of the fiction as to 'the fighting' in which '*Si Conat* was not to be beaten by cowboy or Wild West films', as a contemporary journalist noted.[9] The combination of traditional, well-known, well-loved fiction with the action and tricks of American cinema became a recipe for success. *Si Conat* was followed by a number of Betawi folk tales like *Si Ronda* and *Si Pitung* where well-known characters performed as well as any unknown American movie hero and, perhaps more importantly, did better than their own stage counterparts, with the aid of film technology.

*Si Conat* was also the first of a number of films with Chinese or Dutch heroes pitted against *pribumi* (ethnic Indonesian) villains. This narrative model was on the retreat by the mid-1930s in the face of the increasing national consciousness among Indonesians, and by the 1940s seems to have disappeared completely.

## Dutch-Indonesian productions: propaganda films?

While the Chinese retained almost complete control of film production in Indonesia until the arrival of the Japanese in 1942, a Dutch government film production company, Algemeen Nederlandsch–Indisch Film (ANIF), was set up in the mid-1930s. This was significant in the history of Indonesian film production for three reasons. First, the company produced a super-hit romantic musical, which was the first film with an all *pribumi* cast and based on a story and scenario written by a native Indonesian. Secondly, ANIF produced the first government propaganda film. Finally, it was to become in 1950 the Perusahaan Film Negara (PFN), the independent Indonesian government's film production unit. ANIF and its precursor, a private Dutch–Eurasian company, Java Pacific Film (in Bandung), between them made only four feature films before the start of the war. ANIF's premises were taken over by Nippon Eiga Sha, the film unit of the Japanese 16th Army, in 1942. In 1946, it reverted to the Dutch government. In 1948–49 its feature film subsidiary, South Pacific Film, became the training ground for Usmar Ismail, who was to become one of Indonesia's most prominent film directors, hailed after 1965 as the father of Indonesian cinema.

In 1936 ANIF produced Indonesia's first propaganda film, *Tanah Sebrang* (The Land Across). Directed by the Dutch documentary maker Mannus Franken, it was a praise for the Dutch government policy of transmigration of population from Java to Sumatra. The film was made for the Central Committee for Emigration and Colonisation for Natives, and funded and supported to different degrees by various government departments including the police force, the railways, and Balai Pustaka (the government publishing house). The *gamelan* (traditional Javanese orchestra) used for the film came from the Sultan of Yogyakarta and the *bupati* of Malang.

The film told the story of a Javanese peasant, Sukromo, and his family, who voluntarily join the programme of colonisation of Lampung in order to improve their standard of living. When they get there they find an already established village community into which they are welcomed and they join in the season's harvesting at once. Having met their immediate needs through helping harvest other people's crops, Sukromo goes on to clear new forest area and establish his own house and rice farm. By the end of the film, Sukromo is not only a successful farmer but has also become the village head.

The second ANIF film, *Terang Bulan* (Full Moon), was made for popular success. It was Indonesia's first sound film. The story line was plagiarised from a recent Hollywood hit. Voicing criticism of traditional values that prevent the marriage between young lovers, the narrative in *Terang Bulan* develops largely in the glamorous, foreign settings of Singapore and Malaya, far from the Javanese village home of the main characters. This was the last feature film ANIF produced until after the war, and has been seen by some observers as the founding model for later popular Indonesian films.

## War, occupation and the politicisation of cinema

The outbreak of the war in Europe in 1939, the accelerated pace of the nationalist movement in Indonesia, and Japanese occupation, affected most facets of Indonesian public life, including cinema. The war in Europe, which disrupted the flow of imports into Indonesia, led to a boom in the Indonesian film industry. From an annual average of one to five between 1926 and 1939, the number of Indonesian films rose to 13 in 1940 and to 41 in 1941. The occupation of Indonesia by the Japanese army in 1942 reduced drastically the number of Indonesian films. The occupation forces banned all private film companies and introduced the first sustained use of cinema for propaganda.

Within a week of the Dutch surrender on 8 March 1942, the Japanese occupied the ANIF studio. The Japanese film production unit, Nihon Eigasha (Nippon Eiga Sha in Indonesian sources), under the control of the Sendenbu, the Propaganda Department of the Japanese army, was the only organisation permitted to produce films. Although Nihon Eigasha's main concern was to make newsreels, it produced eight features, all of them Japanese war propaganda films.[10] In film, as in other areas of life, the exclusion of the Chinese and Dutch gave ethnic Indonesians an extended scope for participation, which was a tremendous learning experience for many. The Japanese had better knowledge of film technique and superior production organisation compared to the Chinese producers in Indonesia.[11] More importantly, the Japanese use of films as propaganda taught Indonesians how they could use films for their cause.

> This new understanding was to be acted upon in the days after the capitulation of Japan and the Declaration of Independence on 17 August 1945. Indonesian film workers took over the film equipment from the Japanese and started to make documentaries of the historic occurrences. Indonesian film workers had finally come to appreciate the meaning of cinema for political struggle.[12]

Japan surrendered on 15 August 1945 and on the 17th Indonesia declared independence. On 6 October, the Japanese transferred the Nihon Eigasha studio to the Indonesians. Its name was changed to Berita Film Indonesia (BFI), and it came under the jurisdiction of the Minister of Information of the Republic of Indonesia, Amir Syarifuddin. As Dutch re-occupation of Jakarta started, the main studio of BFI was an early

casualty on 20 November 1945. But some of the staff members of BFI
had been able to withdraw with some equipment. In December BFI
moved to Solo. There were no feature films made in Indonesia during
1945–47, but the BFI made several documentary films about the activities of the government and armed forces of the Republic. Some of
these newsreels were presented to the allied forces in Jakarta, as part of
the effort to build up international sympathy for the Republic.

A Dutch government film unit, Regeering Film Bedrijf (RFB), was
established in Jakarta in 1946. Initially it only made documentaries and
newsreels. But in July 1948, a subsidiary unit called South Pacific Film
Company (SPFC) started making features. The first of these, *Jauh Dihati*
(Far From The Heart), was directed by Anjar Asmara, a well-known
personality of the modern Indonesian theatre. However, the real director
of South Pacific's film seems to have been Deninghoff Stelling, a Dutch
cameraman who had been a war correspondent. Anjar left the Dutch
company after making only two films and was replaced by Usmar
Ismail.

SPFC provided Usmar with his first experience of film-making.
During the Japanese occupation he had become prominent as a play-
wright. In 1945, after the Declaration of Independence, he joined the
Indonesian Republican Army. Towards the end of 1947 he was posted
to Jakarta as a journalist, but was arrested by the Dutch on arrival.
Soon he was working as Anjar's assistant, and continued to serve in the
Dutch company until December 1949. Usmar's critics, especially the
left-wing writers in the early 1960s, have questioned his nationalist
credentials on the grounds of this co-operation with the Dutch.[13]
Usmar's admirers and all post-1965 writers have ignored, or tried to
explain away, his wartime activities.

In his own writings, Usmar only rarely mentions that he had worked
for the Dutch during part of the nationalist revolution. In one article,
written in 1963, he admits that he was less than free to do his will when
working for SPFC.[14] In an earlier piece Usmar claims that his work for
SPFC brought about marked changes in Indonesian cinema as an art
form. Of his first film, *Harta Karun* (Hidden Treasure),[15] he writes 'this
was the first effort to unite cinema with literature.'[16] His second film,
*Citra* (Image, also the name of the heroine), Usmar says, was the first
film 'to raise the question of national consciousness which was common
in literature for a long time.'[17]

Both these claims, which have often been repeated by his later admirers, are open to questioning. The Indonesian novel *Sitti Nurbaya* (Miss
Nurbaya) had been filmed in 1941. However, Usmar, who according to
close friends never read any Indonesian literature, probably did believe
that an Indonesian novel did not really qualify as literature. And nationalism is so peripheral to the central concern of *Citra* that even long-

time Usmar admirers like Misbach Yusa Biran have interpreted the film as a love story with a background of conflict between urban and rural values.[18]

None of the films made during 1948–49 have survived. But from reviews and summaries of these films it seems that the political implication of Usmar's films with SPFC was not very different from the other films produced by the company. Like the rest of the Dutch-made films of the period, Usmar's work presented the image of a 'zaman normal' (normal time), ignoring the war, conflict and political change that was taking place in Indonesia.

## Independence and cinema: 1950–56

In the film industry the early years of independence were marked by a great deal of enthusiasm about the revolutionary experience of the recent past and about Indonesian cinema itself. Nationalist fervour was reflected in the large number of films dealing with Indonesia's struggle against Dutch colonialism. The industry expanded rapidly from six films in 1949 to 22 in 1950 to 58 in 1955. Mannus Franken observed in 1950: 'After the Second World War, the demand for Indonesian feature films was greater still than before, caused among other things by a rise in nationalist feeling.' He goes on to predict that a large and distinctly Indonesian film industry would emerge out of this support for 'national culture', and that 'the great attention from young intellectuals will ensure this.'[19] The Dutch literary historian, Teeuw, has noted in passing the large numbers of young intellectuals who were drawn to film in the first years of independence. Apart from Usmar Ismail, who came to devote himself completely to cinema, Teeuw writes:

> Rivai Apin, Asrul Sani, Siti Nuraini, Sitor Situmorang, Trisno Sumarjo and many others were fascinated by this new medium which promised so much – especially in a land where for the man [sic] of letters contact with the (not yet) reading public proved to be such a great problem.[20]

The emerging definition of the Indonesian nation affected cinema, too. As Coppel suggests, the nation comprised 'the various members of the indigenous (asli) Indonesian ethnic group' and excluded the Chinese as 'foreign'. Economic nationalism was the 'aspiration for an economy which would be controlled by indigenous (asli) Indonesians.'[21] In cinema this meant not only efforts to set up *Pribumi*-owned film companies but an attempt too to rewrite history with these companies regarded as marking the 'real' beginning of Indonesian cinema.

Two other issues related to nationalism and independence marked these years. First was the question of American film imports. Islamic morality and cultural nationalism led to opposition to the large numbers of American films coming into Indonesia in the 1950s. At the same time there was an artistic admiration for Hollywood cinema in some circles and a more general sense of good relations between Indonesia and America because of American diplomatic support for Indonesia against the Dutch during the last phase of the independence movement. The second issue was that of censorship. There was ambivalence here also, to do with a sense amongst some intellectuals and artists that in independent Indonesia there should be total freedom unconstrained by any intervention by the state, while at the same time most people involved in the debate had a mistrust of the judgement of 'uneducated masses', who were perceived as constituting the majority of the audience.

### 'National' cinema

In 1950 the first indigenous Indonesian-owned companies were established. Usmar Ismail and many of his admirers have regarded Perfini (Perusahaan Film Nasional) as the first true Indonesian film company. But earlier writers more often regarded Hiburan Mataram Stichting, set up in Jogjakarta in 1948, as the first. The organisational leadership of this company lay with a former Japanese official, Hinatsu Heitaro, who took Indonesian citizenship and a new name, Dr Huyung. The funding for the company reportedly came from Bank Indonesia (the National Bank of Indonesia), and one informant suggested that the bank's chairperson, Margono Joyohadikusumo, took an interest in setting up the company. The company's director was Daryono, an official of the Department of Information, Internal Affairs section. The company made only four films and disappeared after Huyung's death in 1952.

Perfini was established with a small amount of capital and ventured into its first production with about half of the funds needed. *Darah Dan Doa* (its English title was *The Long March*) started shooting on 30 March 1950, and would have run out of money had not a Chinese theatre owner, Mr Tong, come to its rescue with a financial advance. This connection with the theatre owner not only ensured that the film would be completed but also guaranteed it distribution in Jakarta. Usmar also notes gratefully the support that he received from some senior officials of the Siliwangi division of the army.

A third indigenous company, Persari, was set up under the initiative of Jamaluddin Malik, a Sumatran businessman who during the war years had invested in theatre companies. Persari quickly became one of the largest producers. In contrast to the pre-independence years when there were no indigenous Indonesian companies, in 1951 four (including PFN) out of the 14 film production companies claimed to be truly Indonesian (in the sense of *pribumi*).

These *pribumi* producers were a new, and in the context of the time exciting, phenomenon. The extent of real change in the film industry was, however, less radical and sudden than this picture suggests. Jamaluddin Malik worked with various Chinese business interests, Indonesian as well as foreign. Hiburan Mataram was led by a Japanese. At PFN many of the Dutch technicians stayed on and exerted a great deal of influence over its productions. And even Usmar's founding of Indonesian national cinema would have been impossible without Chinese financial and marketing support.

On the other hand, the slow growth of *pribumi* Indonesian input into cinema had started as early the mid-1930s. In the late 1930s and early 1940s more and more films were set in the *pribumi* society and used *pribumi* actors. The first film based on an Indonesian language novel was made in 1941. Also in 1940–41 the first *pribumi* film directors started to emerge. Finally the Japanese production of films greatly expanded the *pribumi* involvement in cinema. The Japanese 25th Army in Sumatra also had a film unit, producing non-fiction films in Medan. This meant that for the first time Indonesians outside Java were introduced to movie-making.

Nor did these indigenous companies greatly alter the balance of financial control in the industry. The film industry was no different from the rest of the Indonesian economy where, despite state support, 'by 1956 it was clear that indigenous capitalists had not made inroads into Chinese economic dominance.'[22] Old Chinese companies, banned from film production by the Japanese, quickly re-established themselves. By 1951 there were 12 new or re-established Chinese companies. Although a few more *pribumi* film ventures were founded, the Chinese continued to dominate in the sphere of both production and distribution.

### Censorship after independence

Usmar's nationalist fervour expressed itself not only in the effort to set up an 'Indonesian' film industry, but also in the subject matter of his films. *Darah Dan Doa*, while centring on a fictional school teacher turned revolutionary soldier, was intended to be a historical document recording the Siliwangi Division's suppression of the Madiun rebellion in October 1948,[23] its role against the Darul Islam movement in West Java,[24] and its celebrated 'long march' from Central Java back to West Java after the so-called 'second Dutch Police Action' in December 1948.

The film had cast its net widely over the historical incidents of the recent past. As a consequence it offended a lot of sensitivities. The film was banned in several districts by local military authorities who felt that its emphasis on the Siliwangi division undermined their roles in Indonesia's independence. Some Siliwangi members themselves felt that

the army had been shown as rather weak, given the protagonists' pre-
dilection for 'unsoldierly' emotional responses. By all reports the film
was severely truncated by the censors, but no one has detailed precisely
what was cut out.

Although disappointed with the way the public and the government
had treated the film, Usmar chose another revolutionary episode as the
subject matter of his second film. *Enam Jam Di Jogja* (Six Hours In
Jogjakarta) was about the Diponegoro Division and was even more
emphatically a historical reconstruction since the main characters were
all real people. For a short period during the independence movement,
Usmar had been a major in the TNI (Indonesian Armed Forces) intelligence under the command of Colonel Zulkifli Lubis. Lubis put Usmar
in touch with Marsudi, a key intelligence officer of the Diponegoro
Division around the time of the 1 March 1949 attack on Dutch-held
Jogjakarta. The film focused on the intelligence operations building up
to the March 1 raid by the Indonesian army.

As a result of the problems experienced in releasing his first film,
Usmar was more cautious when he made *Enam Jam Di Jogja*. As a
concession to the sensitivities of the Dutch population in Indonesia,
there was no portrayal of direct confrontation between the Dutch and
the Indonesians. The narrative is set almost entirely in the Intelligence
Headquarters of the army in Jogjakarta. The most visible character is
Marsudi. But the real and invisible hero is Colonel Suharto (now
President), who led the March 1 operation. Throughout the film the
spectator gets news of how Suharto's war with the Dutch is progressing
but never actually sees this war. Even so, the film could not be entirely
protected from the censors' scissors.

Usmar's experiences with censorship were by no means exceptional.
Formal and informal restrictions by the censors were quite common in
the early 1950s. Armijn Pane has detailed the extent to which *Antara
Bumi Dan Langit* (Between Earth And Heaven) was mutilated by the
central Committee of Film Censorship in 1951. The film dealt with the
sensitive question of citizenship of the *peranakan* Dutch and the mixed-
blood people (*Indo*) in Indonesia. Even before the film had been completed, a publicity photograph, showing the heroine Frieda kissing a
long-lost male friend, led to a protest from sections of the Muslim
community. After completion the film was transformed on the basis of
the censors' recommendations to such an extent that Pane, who had
written the screen-play, felt obliged to withdraw his name from the
credit. The title of the film was changed to *Frieda*. The revisions to the
film turned it into a more or less conventional love story.[25]

The main reason for the changes to *Antara Bumi Dan Langit* was the
complaint from the minority community of Dutch-Indonesians, who
objected to the treatment of the *Indo* heroine in the film. They argued

that it was important to show the Dutch-Indonesian community in a favourable light, to show them as supporting the Indonesian revolution rather than acting against it. The censorship committee insisted that some of their objections be accommodated.[26]

The censors were not only concerned about the sensitivities of the minority communities, they seemed to be concerned about any critical representation of any section of the Indonesian society. In 1951–52 there were a number of films dealing with the problem of ex-revolutionary soldiers re-establishing themselves in the post-war society. One of these was *Embun* (Dew) by a new director, D. Jayakusuma. The main story followed the common model of a frustrated ex-revolutionary being brought back to life and society by a woman's love. Unlike other films of its kind, however, *Embun* was set in the background of a village society, with all its 'traditions and beliefs which still existed'. And 'it was in this matter that it had problems with the censors.'[27] The rulers of the newly independent country were concerned that their nation appear advanced and scientific in its self-representation, and were eager to conceal those conventions and traditions that may have seemed to be backward and superstitious.

Both Usmar Ismail and Armijn Pane have emphasised that this heavy-handed treatment by the censors pushed Indonesian films further and further away from real social issues, and more and more into safe formula films. These formula films were often set against the background of the independence struggle or the Japanese period, but the historical setting scarcely touched the characters or conflicts in the narrative.

What is striking about this period is the wide social base of the censoring impulses. Usmar Ismail wrote in 1954:

> The censoring authorities justify their actions on the ground that these are only crystallisations of attitudes that exist among groups within the society itself ... Indeed here lies the danger, that the censorship board is not a balanced institution that is independent, but in fact is tied by every stream of thought existing in the society.[28]

This responsiveness by censors to pressures from a wide variety of the politically vocal sections of the society was, to a large extent, lost after 1965.

When the issue of film censorship was discussed at the Second Cultural Congress in 1952, no one argued that it be ended. Three submissions were put to the meeting of the Film Censorship Section, from Rustam Sutan Palindih, journalist, screen-play writer and an employee of the government film company, PFN; Asrul Sani, a well known literary figure of the 1945 generation; and J.B. Moningka, who was working for the governor of Sulawesi.

Palindih suggested that the only acceptable form of censorship was 'negative censorship', meaning 'Censors may only ban films, or parts thereof, that are dangerous to the society, and in no way have the right to determine whether a film is good or bad as a film.' He suggested that the work of 'protecting cultural values' be left to the people, who could refuse to watch films of which they did not approve.[29] Asrul Sani argued the opposite. He felt that there were certain universal artistic standards and part of the censor's function was to preserve these standards: 'Film censorship is the first and foremost defence of the critical observation of the people.'[30] Preservation of standards included, for him, depiction of social reality in place of artificial glamour. 'There are two important points about censorship. First, it must curb the greed of the producers to deceive the people. Secondly, it must ensure that people can enjoy to the fullest extent the creation of the director.'[31] But through all this argument it is clear that film censorship had become entrenched as an institution. Interestingly, these speakers were asking censorship to perform a policing role, whether ethical or aesthetic, rather than to reflect contradictory concerns at play in the society.

### The American connection

A second concern expressed at the Cultural Congress involved foreign film imports, especially from America. In 1950 there were more American films being shown in Indonesia than ever before. In later years, at the height of Indonesia's anti-Americanism, Bachtiar Siagian accused 'the big monopoly capital of Hollywood, represented by 11 giant companies united under AMPAI (American Motion Pictures Association in Indonesia)' of having imposed an agreement on the young Republic, which would give AMPAI total control of the Indonesian film market through massive imports. 'After the Round Table Accord, the number of American films entering Indonesia rose more than 100 per cent over the preceding years.'[32] The important role of Mathew Fox, who was involved in several Hollywood film companies, in negotiating the first American business contracts with the Republican government gives some credence to Siagian's comment.[33] Some reports suggest that 600 to 700 American films were being imported annually into Indonesia during 1950–55.

Americans were also helping to establish the Indonesian film industry. Under the Technical Cooperation Administration (TCA) programme, in 1950 the PFN received US$500,000 from the American government for new film equipment. In addition the United States government paid for ten American experts to stay in Indonesia for six years to oversee the implementation of the scheme. A number of Indonesians working in cinema, both employees of the PFN and private individuals, were sent to the United States to train in various aspects of film making under the Colombo Plan and TCA.

In the early 1950s, no one questioned the US technical aid and training of Indonesian film-makers. Nor did any one anticipate that American films would come to be regarded as a serious impediment to the expansion of the local film industry. There was a great deal of confidence that, as the number of films produced in Indonesia increased, they would quickly become popular with the large majority of the population which did not understand English. There was, however, some discomfort about the moral and, to a lesser extent, the political content of Hollywood cinema and its impact on the Indonesian audiences. Between 30 and 40 American films were banned from circulation each year during 1950–52 mainly for two reasons. First, some films were deemed to contravene Indonesian moral standards by their depiction of explicit sexual behaviour. Secondly, a number of jungle and adventure movies (including one set in Bali in 1951, *Black Magic of Bali*) were politically unacceptable because they depicted the black and brown peoples of Asia and Africa as primitive or backward. These moral and political criticisms of American films in the early 1950s foreshadowed the strong anti-US film movement led by the left and encouraged by the Sukarno government in the last years of Guided Democracy.

### The shape of things to come

Intellectuals who embraced cinema immediately after independence had been confident that they, and not the producers and importers, would determine the shape of this new and powerful medium. Directors and artists tried to set up their own companies in order to avoid dependence on business people. Imported films were not regarded as a threat. Since India, without even the advantage of a unifying national language, had established a booming national film industry, it seemed reasonable to expect that so would Indonesia. As for censorship, both the censoring authorities themselves and the film-makers hoped that in independent Indonesia censorship would cease to be a repressive government machinery and would become the instrument of aesthetic or ethical protection of the Indonesian people.

By 1956 many of these hopes were somewhat shaken. Contradictions and divisions were apparent within the 'intelligentsia' (*kaum terpelajar*) itself. (That story is taken up in the next chapter.) The artists' effort at autonomy from 'capitalists' floundered. At best they managed only to shift their dependence from the Chinese to indigenous business groups who, no less than their Chinese counterparts, seemed far more interested in commercial success than in the artistic aspirations of film directors. The Indonesian film industry had stopped expanding by 1955 and many blamed this on the hold of imported films on the market. Censorship, a repressive instrument of the state when first introduced, flirted briefly with public opinion in the years of parliamentary democracy, before reverting gradually to its original purpose.

# 2

# Political Polarisation and Cinema: 1956–66

Indonesian film production stopped expanding after hitting a peak of 58 features in 1955. Imports, including about 600 films from the United States and another 100 or so from other, mainly Asian, countries dominated the market. Because it supplied the overwhelming majority of films to theatres, and had resources to provide greater financial incentives to the theatre owners than did the Indonesian producers and importers, the American Motion Pictures Association in Indonesia (AMPAI) was able to exert a great deal of influence on the movie theatres. In 1954–55, while the total ratio of imports to local production remained constant, changes were taking place within the import sector. American imports were declining while the number of Indian films rose from seven in 1952 to 74 in 1954 and 184 in 1955. Indian films, like other Asian films, were mainly imported by Indonesian residents of Indian or Chinese descent, many of whom were also film producers.

As discussed in the last chapter, there had been moral opposition to American films ever since they first started coming into Indonesia. But imports became an industrial issue from about 1956, and by 1964 an important political issue. Different sectors of the industry, particularly the producers' organisation PPFI and the workers' organisation, SARBUFIS, clashed over how the imports should be dealt with. Given the temper of the decade building up to the civil war of 1965, the film industry's problems could be seen as a conflict between the workers and capital owners in the industry.

## The temper of the time

From around the mid-1950s the tiny urban, educated, national political elite, which since independence had been bound by personal ties that bridged 'conflicts of interest and ideology', began to lose its homogeneity and sense of common purpose.[1] The rise of the Indonesian Communist Party (PKI), attempted military coups and regionalist movements increasingly disrupted the national political leadership and ultimately led to the dramatic incidents of 1 October 1965, which changed the face of Indonesian politics.

During 1956 to 1959 Sukarno, with the support of the army, buried the system of parliamentary democracy which despite various challenges had survived since 1950. The Guided Democracy (1957–65) which emerged was marked 'by a particular relationship between President Sukarno and the army, a "stable conflict" relationship characterised by both common endeavour and continuing competition and tension between more or less equally matched partners'.[2] In this balance of power the Communist Party of Indonesia, PKI (Partai Komunis Indonesia) appeared in an increasingly important role on the side of the President and as the foremost rival of the army.

The army made enormous gains, politically and economically, in the early years of Guided Democracy under martial law powers between 1957 and 1963. It secured a large representation in Parliament as a functional group and in the first Sukarno cabinet formed in July 1959. In facing the army, the PKI and the President needed each other. The PKI needed Presidential support for its integration into the existing political institutions of the state. The President, on the other hand, lacking his own organised power base, gained from the PKI's organisational structure which had proved effective in the elections of 1955 and 1957. By 1959 the party had become 'the most energetic and militant supporter' of the President's nationalist creed.[3] Increasingly the PKI's mass base became Sukarno's and their rhetoric and policies became almost identical.

The strategy of a united national front, to which the PKI leadership was committed, allowed the party to operate within the radical nationalist framework of Sukarno's NASAKOM (unity of nationalists, religious elements and communists). Anti-imperialism and anti-feudalism were the key issues on the party's agenda and in this they were keen to make a common cause with the national bourgeoisie and their major political parties, the PNI (Indonesian Nationalist Party) and the NU (Nahdatul Ulama, the orthodox Islamic Party). The party's political work was increasingly based on an analysis of the society which divided it into the Indonesian 'people, on the one hand, and foreign-paid or foreign-inspired enemies on the other'.[4] Even as late as 1964 socialism was not on the party's agenda. Its targets were 'the expulsion of all foreign capital, the elimination of the remnants of feudalism and industrialization.'[5]

Despite the PKI's commitment to the united national front, important political parties and the traditional elite were threatened by the PKI's 'unquestionably modern' and truly egalitarian ideology and 'its obvious concern for popular social and economic interests'.[6] From about

1962 the PKI's conflict with NU over the issue of religion came more and more to the surface and the relationship became further strained over the unilateral action of the PKI's peasant organisation to implement the government's land redistribution programme.

Until 1962 in the uneasy political balance of power between the President and the army, the PKI played the role of a somewhat junior partner. From 1963 onwards there were rapid shifts and changes in that balance. Sukarno took steps to limit the army's role in the government. The army, while giving verbal support to his policy of Confrontation (Konfrontasi) with Malaysia, remained ambivalent about launching a full-scale war.[7] The PKI, on the other hand, embraced the Confrontation enthusiastically and was able to mobilise the masses in the anti-Malaysia crusade, thereby enhancing its own position.

By 1964 many observers were describing the situation in Indonesia as an ideological hothouse. Because Sukarno was the ultimate arbiter in matters of political ideology and foreign policy, and because his power depended on his ability to mobilise the people, by 1963–64 these areas became enormously prominent in the country's political life.

Cinema, as a sphere of both industrial and ideological activity, got caught up in the anti-American foreign policy, and economic and cultural nationalism. In 1964 the film industry became a significant sphere of radical nationalist activity and, as a result, rose to unprecedented political prominence. 'The film boycott became the high point of struggle in the campaign against US "cultural penetration".' US 'cultural imperialism' was an issue 'on which Sukarno and the PKI had long seen eye to eye ... But, from being a mainly propaganda issue, the campaign against American culture was now transformed by the PKI into one of its major agitational platforms.'[8]

### The powers and the passions in the industry

The oldest professional organisation of the Indonesian film industry was SARBUFI, Sarekat Buruh Film Indonesia (Indonesian Film Workers' Union). It was founded in 1951 and immediately joined SOBSI, the federation of trade unions linked to the PKI. At its second Congress in 1953, it was renamed SARBUFIS, the addition standing for 'Senidrama', the dramatic arts. But its main focus remained cinema. It drew its membership mainly from technical workers in movie theatres and studios. Numerically it was one of the smallest national unions within SOBSI. By its own estimate it represented barely 50 per cent of the total number of film workers as late as 1960. But it was prominent despite its numerical weakness.[9]

In 1955–56 a crop of new professional organisations appeared. The most prominent among these were the organisation of producers, PPFI

(Persatuan Produser Film Indonesia), and that of the actors, PARFI (Persatuan Artis Film Indonesia). PPFI remained more or less under the control of Usmar Ismail and Jamaluddin Malik. PARFI was under the strong influence of Suryo Sumanto, whose unchallenged leadership of the actors' organisation is remarkable since he was not an actor at all. Suryo Sumanto (1918–71) had participated in the nationalist movement, had close contacts with senior figures in the military and the Ministry of Defence and, according to his admirers, his 'leadership saved PARFI from the machinations of the PKI'.[10]

In the early 1960s two cultural organisations, linked to political parties, came to play important roles in the struggles and tensions in the film world. These were LEKRA, linked to the PKI, and LESBUMI, linked to the Nahdatul Ulama. In 1959 LFI (Indonesian Film Institute) was formed as a subsection within LEKRA to look after the specific interests of cinema. Largely in response to LEKRA's influence in the artistic community, Nahdatul Ulama set up the Institute of Islamic Culture, LESBUMI, in 1962. Within LESBUMI, the film group was dominant, as Usmar Ismail and Jamaluddin Malik were its first and most prominent office bearers and it included a large number of film directors and other film professionals.

Cinema was more central to LESBUMI than it was to LEKRA. None of the top leadership of LEKRA were film-makers. The only film director to become an important LEKRA office-bearer was Basuki Effendy in 1960, by which time he was not making films any more. Cinema, recognised as the art form most clearly dependent on capitalist financiers, was never regarded as an important instrument of ideological propaganda. LEKRA's ideological interest in cinema was a largely negative one, to keep out undesirable (meaning 'capitalist imperialist' and often just 'American') attitudes and values propagated through foreign films. For the most part LEKRA's policy in cinema, like that of SARBUFIS, was guided by economic nationalism, which sought to expand local film production and to restrict the hold of American importers in the industry.

Soon after its formation in 1956, the producers' union, PPFI, put forward a plan for restricting film imports. But their principal target was Indian rather than American films. While Indian film imports had risen, their number was still well below half that of American films. The PPFI argued that American films drew audiences mainly from the educated urban elite who did not want to see Indonesian films anyway, whereas Indian films, which appealed to the lower classes, took prospective viewers away from Indonesian productions. The opposition to Indian films turned into a rather bizarre episode coloured by rumours, accusations and counter-accusations.

The PPFI's proposals for restricting Indian films were accepted by the government, which agreed in 1956 to impose an annual quota of 30 films from India. However, there was a lapse of months before the regulation came into effect during which time the importers, including some of those producers who were leading the protest against Indian films, built up a large stockpile of Indian imports.

PPFI, under the leadership of Usmar Ismail and Jamaluddin Malik, decided on 19 March 1957 to close all studios, in protest against Indian films' domination of the market. Over the previous two years there had been a number of incidents where AMPAI had been charged with using its control over theatres to block distribution of Indonesian as well as non-American imported films. There were now rumours that AMPAI was behind the PPFI moves against Indian films whose growing popularity threatened American control of the market. A number of producers who did not own studios ignored or opposed the closure. It seems Persari itself continued shooting films while its owner Jamaluddin Malik was leading the protest!

There were suggestions that the studio closure was part of Jamaluddin Malik's business speculations. Jamaluddin Malik, who led the demand for restricting Indian films, was himself an importer of Indian films. Like many other producers, he had turned to imports to offset the frequent losses sustained in producing films. Even his admirers admit that while protesting against Indian films, he was at the same time building up his own supply of them. At the time of the studio closure Jamaluddin was on the verge of bankruptcy. He was arrested in May 1957, a few days after the studios re-opened, and his studio was forfeited by the Bank Negara Indonesia. Post-1965 writers have fabricated more respectable 'political' reasons for his detention but contemporary newspaper reports indicate little apart from bankruptcy.

SARBUFIS opposed the closure, supported by a large number of film artists, causing a split in the artists' union, PARFI. The protesting artists formed the Panitia Seniman Untuk Film which, though started for a limited purpose, remained active until October 1965 and cooperated with SARBUFIS on most issues. This group and SARBUFIS were supported in their demand for immediate re-opening of studios by LEKRA, PKI and a large number of other mass organisations. In an 11-point programme, SARBUFIS demanded immediate intervention by the government to re-open studios and suggested measures for the long-term expansion of Indonesian film production. SARBUFIS demands included the restriction in number of American feature films and the replacement of all American newsreels with ones made in Indonesian.

The government intervened. Quotas were imposed on all foreign films, including an annual quota of 200 for American films. Two important PPFI demands were also met. First, import tax on film equipment was drastically reduced. Secondly, there was to be no further increase in the number of film importers. On 26 April the PPFI re-commended that its members re-open their studios. But the incidents of March–April 1957 demonstrated a degree of division in the film industry along lines of workers against bosses.

## Anti-American moves

SARBUFIS, which had embraced the socialist peace movement, first stated its opposition to American newsreel films in 1955 as part of its anti-nuclear stance. Its Jakarta branch started an anti-nuclear petition and claimed to have collected thousands of signatures. However, the list included only one prominent film director, Tan Sing Hwat, who was a SARBUFIS office-bearer, and only one well-known actor. In 1957, during the studio-closure incident, SARBUFIS argued for a ban on American newsreels on the grounds of the economic interests of Indo-nesian film producers and workers.

In 1958 SARBUFIS demanded a total ban on American films in response to the alleged US support of the regionalist movement in Sumatra. The following year it called upon theatre owners not to show films from Taiwan on the grounds that the Indonesian government did not have diplomatic relations with Taiwan and recognised the People's Republic of China's claim over it. It also called on the government to distinguish between Chinese films from the People's Republic and Taiwan and restrict the latter to ten films a year. In August 1963, in the midst of Indonesia's bitter row with Britain over the formation of Malaysia, SARBUFIS demanded a ban on British films. These moves were related to wider campaigns led by the PKI. None of these calls had widespread support from the film community or from left-wing cultural groups. The 1964 anti-AMPAI campaign under the PAPFIAS (Panitia Aksi Pemboikotan Film Imperialis Amerika Serikat, the Com-mittee for Action to Boycott the Imperialist Films of the United States of America) umbrella, the largest film-related movement in Indonesia's history, needs then to be seen as quite distinct from simply being an outgrowth of the SARBUFIS playing PKI politics.

What was to become PAPFIAS started with the resolution of the first National Conference of LFI (Lembaga Film Indonesia, Indonesian Film Institute) on 3 January 1964. At this much publicised conference, attended by PKI politburo member Nyoto and the head of the Chinese film delegation to Indonesia, Thien Fang, LFI threatened to boycott American films if the Americans insisted on maintaining their Seventh Fleet in the Indian Ocean. Soon after, LFI, along with SARBUFIS and Front Pemuda (left-wing youth movement), called for a boycott of all American films.

The idea of a boycott was given a lot of publicity during the Third

Afro-Asian Film Festival held in Jakarta at the end of April 1964. Under the leadership of Jamaluddin Malik, the film producers' organisation, PPFI, had opposed the Afro-Asian Film Festival. Its earlier suggestion that Indonesia host the Asian Film Festival was rejected by the government because it was to include Taiwan. The PPFI leadership, including a number of prominent film-makers such as Usmar Ismail and Asrul Sani, decided not to participate in the Afro-Asian Film Festival.

During the film festival in Jakarta, there was some discussion of the possibility of exchanging films between the Indonesians and several other participants on the basis of a barter arrangement. The idea of bartering films, particularly with other Asian countries, was an old one which had general support in the film community and had been strongly pushed by the PPFI during its 1957 campaign to restrict Indian imports. At the 1964 Afro-Asian Film Festival support for the idea was canvassed again. Although no deals were struck, after 1965 this policy was cited as an example of LEKRA machinations to bring in films from communist countries.

A week after the end of the festival a 'Committee for Action to Boycott the Imperialist Films of the United States of America' (PAPFIAS) was formed by representatives of 16 organisations. Some of these, for example LKN, SOBSI, GERWANI, Front Pemuda, LEKRA and SAR-BUFIS, were linked to the PKI or the radical wing of the PNI. But there were a number of other groups related to the Indonesian film industry (such as the theatre owners' organisation OPS Bioskop, and the Union of National Importers and Distributors, PIDFIN) which were not overtly linked to any party.

Sitor Situmorang's propaganda verse, which appeared on the front page of the Communist Party daily *Harian Rakyat* (5/7/64) captured the way in which the film boycott had become a key symbol of opposition to imperialism.

ACTION FOR BOYCOTT
*to the supporters of Ampai*

I boycott American films
For the victims of imperialism,
I boycott American films
For South Vietnam,
I boycott American films
Because of interventions
against Asian independence,

I boycott American films
Because the American Negro is my friend,
So that the word solidarity, is not
just a word,

My comrades everywhere,
Whom I defend as an Afro-Asian writer,
I boycott American films
Because I want space
for the films of my country,
and for the good films of the 'new emerging forces'.

Some theatres continued to show American films, leading to outbreaks of violence. The government's position remained unclear for some months with some senior bureaucrats arguing against the ban. One film distribution company, Intrafilm of Widodo Sukarno (who in the late 1970s was to gain virtual monopoly over American and European film imports), threatened to dismiss half of the employees, and refused to discuss the issue with SARBUFIS, unless the latter withdrew from PAPFIAS.

But these were minor problems compared with the sense of victory against American cultural imperialism, especially after August 1964 when the Indonesian government gave PAPFIAS official support. On 16 August the Ministry of Trade instructed AMPAI to cease all operations immediately and announced that the import and distribution of films was to be progressively 'Indonesianised' over the next two years. The ban on American films was seen as one of the earliest and most important successes against the multi-headed monster called 'US Imperialism'. (Illustration 1 from *Harian Rakyat*, 18/10/64, p. 1.)

The film industry itself gained an unprecedented degree of attention because of PAPFIAS. Early in 1965 the most elaborate government policies were drawn up to establish special training programmes for filmmakers, and provide easy credit for national producers. An Academy of Cinematography was planned for 1966 and existing studios were to be upgraded with new equipment. The policies were only in their planning stage when the incidents of October 1965 disrupted the entire radical nationalist political, economic and cultural movement in Indonesia.

In January 1967, after most people with any links to leftist organisations and movements were in prison, underground or in exile, the Department of Information sent out to prominent members of film-related organisations a list of names of film people suspected of involvement in the so-called communist bid to take power through the '30th September Movement' (G30S). The list contained names of some whose only connection with the PKI seemed to be through PAPFIAS. Questions about PAPFIAS were extremely prominent in the interrogations of political detainees with any connection to artistic or cultural work.

But notorious as PAPFIAS became after 1965, during the months that the movement was active there was enormous support for it from most sectors of the film world. This may have been due partly to the nationalist fervour of the time, PKI intimidation or government pressure. But the active support for the boycott of AMPAI was due also to the fact that a break in AMPAI's monopoly over imports was in the best interests of most Indonesians in the film industry. If the political spark that started it off (US Seventh Fleet in Indian Ocean) was unrelated to any interest of Indonesian cinema it was impossible to question the long-standing economic argument against AMPAI's control over by far the largest share of the film market, which was blocking competition from either other importers or national producers. Although PAPFIAS was discredited as a communist conspiracy, no one after 1965 thought of bringing AMPAI back. To that extent the movement achieved its first and most fundamental target. AMPAI has never recovered from its tarnished image; the acronym has become a synonym for unjust monopoly in the Indonesian film business.

In the process of rejecting the PKI, post-1965 commentators have ignored the historical continuities in the conflict of interests between Hollywood suppliers and Indonesian producers, which the politics of 1964–65 had dramatically highlighted. The distortion of the cultural and political role of the left in Indonesian historiography after 1965 is well known.[11] Writing in 1970, Usmar Ismail dubbed the early 1960s the 'Dark Era of National Film History' marked by 'the struggle between the forces led by LEKRA/PKI against the forces of democracy in the film world.'[12] The spirit (and often words) of that title has been reproduced in almost every account of Indonesian film history since.

In the 1980s, as the old battle over the Indonesian audiences between American imports and local productions started being replayed (albeit in very different political and economic circumstances), there was a new ironic twist in the way in which the early 1960s film industrial history was being reworked. In a long article on film history written in 1983, Sumarjono, Indonesia's most senior film editor, mentions the PKI only once. The anti-American film movement, previously condemned as a PKI plot, is credited to Usmar Ismail and Jamaluddin Malik.[13] By 1990 the conflict between American and local business interests in the film industry once again entered the public arena (that story is taken up in the next chapter). In January 1990 an English language Jakarta newspaper ran an article headlined 'PWI [The Indonesian Journalists Union] Does Not Want Ampai Back'. The report quoted a spokesman for a company, which now has virtual monopoly over film imports and distribution in Indonesia, as saying that Indonesia would never allow Americans to dominate the market again after Usmar Ismail and Jamaluddin Malik had fought so hard to resist AMPAI!

As the political-economy of contemporary Indonesian cinema forces another rewriting of history, it becomes urgent that we evaluate the work of the leftist film movement. In the field of literature, Foulcher has

shown 'that there is a history of LEKRA, with its own internal dynamics, quite separate from PKI political history'. He suggests that 'the
proper perspective is to move from the body of ideas and impulses
which formed the core of LEKRA, outwards to the influence and
confluence with the PKI, rather than the reverse.'[14] Similarly, the
dynamics of the film industry were determined by the relations of
production of cinema in Indonesia, which can only be understood in
the context of the wider socio-political turmoil, but cannot be written
off as simply orchestrated by PKI, or even LEKRA, or indeed any
force external to cinema.

### Films and film-makers

The film work of the decade preceding the counter-revolution of 1965–
66 was much less directly related to the day-to-day political moves.
Regardless of the directors' political alignment, the best-known films of
the period, particularly after 1958, contained little direct reference to
the immediate context of political conflict or economic breakdown.
Sukarno's call to 'Return to the Rails of the Revolution', the tendency
towards increasingly vociferous assertion that 'the right to wield govern-
mental power ... lay with those who had led the Revolution'[15] and the
consequent availability of funding for films about the revolution led to
the revolution becoming a popular subject matter for films. Between
1955 and 1964, about half the films directed by Bachtiar Siagian and
Usmar Ismail, the most prominent directors on opposite sides of the
political divide, were set in the revolution.

To the LEKRA film-makers particularly, the revolution came to be
regarded as the most valid subject matter for a film. The left-wing film
critics remained, on the whole, supportive of Usmar's films about the
revolution. Only in the early 1960s did they come to criticise particular
appropriations of the revolution by the liberal intellectuals as a vehicle
for their expression of the 'universal humanist' creed.[16] On the other
hand, those who after 1965 rejected most works of left-wing film makers
as communist propaganda, never identified what constituted that propaganda in the films of well-known directors who were politically committed to various organisations associated with the PKI.

Foulcher partly explains this absence of difference between critics on
the right and left on the ideological implications of films. He argues
that LEKRA never developed radical aesthetic criteria distinct from
the 'bourgeois nationalist traditions' which were shared by the national
intelligentsia as a whole, including the left.[17] But while 'LEKRA critics
failed to confront the theoretical problems' inherent in the bourgeois
nationalist tradition, the 'creative practices' of leftist poets and authors
broke away from many of the established norms of Indonesian liter-

ature.[18] In cinema, similarly, a distinct model was evolving through the works of some LEKRA film-makers, although a clear position on the form and content of cinema had not been formulated.[19]

Any attempt to discuss the leftist 'creative practices' in cinema is necessarily somewhat speculative due to the success with which the left-wing films have been obliterated. Film preservation is a difficult task in any circumstance. Serious attempts to preserve old films started in Indonesia only in the mid-1970s. By this time, neglect and deliberate destruction had ensured that there was almost no trace of films made by directors who had been imprisoned since the late 1960s and whose works had been banned by the Suharto government. The Indonesian film archives, Sinematek, holds only one complete film, *Si Pincang*, directed by a LEKRA figure, Kotot Sukardi.

The absence of data notwithstanding (and indeed, because of it), any analysis of New Order cinema needs to take into account the traditions of filmic practices it inherited and those which it lost in the decimation of the leftist cultural movement. In trying to distinguish the filmic practice that was suppressed from that which was idealised after 1965, I will concentrate on the works of two directors, Usmar Ismail, regarded today as the 'father of Indonesian cinema', and Bachtiar Siagian, the most prolific LEKRA film director and film theorist. This comparison is both essential and impossible, since none of Bachtiar's films are available. Usmar's films discussed in this chapter are held in the film archives in Jakarta. The discussion of Bachtiar Siagian's films, is a (necessarily inadequate) reconstruction from scenarios, reviews, interviews and Bachtiar's theoretical writings.

Usmar Ismail (1921–71) and Bachtiar Siagian (b. 1923) by no means represent the 'average' film directors. Their films are not the typical products of the era, but rather set the standards, and provide the ideals of filmic practice. While their post-1965 position in Indonesian film history is vastly different, with Usmar hailed as the great artist and Bachtiar condemned as a communist propagandist, there is little doubt that they were much more equal at the time when they were both making films. In 1960, the Indonesian entry to the Moscow international film festival consisted of one film each by Bachtiar and Usmar. Bachtiar Siagian is the only Indonesian film director who is mentioned in Usmar's own writings as someone who may have artistic credentials comparable to himself. Their professed artistic concerns (as against political ones) were largely similar, since both sought to make 'good' films as defined by Indonesian artistic discourses and, at the same time, to reach popular audiences. Nor were their films different in the sim-plistic way that distinguishes art from propaganda. Yet their work took Indonesian cinema along divergent paths, because these films were imbued with very different social perspectives, which were vying for position, in an atmosphere of intense ideological contradictions and socio-economic turmoil.

## Usmar Ismail

Usmar Ismail was born into a Minangkabau aristocratic family and received the sort of education to which only a small section of fairly high class Indonesians could aspire (MULO, AMS-A).[20] Of the 15 or so ethnic Indonesians of roughly Usmar's generation who were directing films in the 1950s and early 1960s, only three had comparable Dutch education. Two of them, Asrul Sani and D. Jayakusuma, worked closely with Usmar Ismail in both cinema and politics. Jamaluddin Malik, NU politician and businessman, who also became a close ally of Usmar, shared a similar educational background. No one involved in Indonesian cinema went through higher status or more exclusive schooling (such as ELS) than these people. By contrast all the LEKRA directors, including Bachtiar Siagian, had native school education (as indeed did the overwhelming majority of the native Indonesian school students in the 1920s and 1930s) and on the whole had fewer years of formal education.

Usmar graduated from high school in European classics. His elder brother, Abu Hanifah, medical doctor, writer, Masyumi politician and Indonesia's first minister of education and culture, strongly influenced Usmar's early work. Abu Hanifah notes that European, English and American literature provided most of the scripts for Usmar's early theatrical venture, Maya, a drama group founded in Jakarta during the Japanese occupation.[21] Usmar's early films drew enthusiastic support from Jakarta artists and intellectuals at large. Those who worked with him on his early films included the writer Sitor Situmorang (later leader of LKN, a cultural organisation linked to the left wing of the Nationalist Party PNI), the poet Rivai Apin and the painter Basuki Resobowo (both important LEKRA figures). From the late 1950s, however, these nationalist and leftist intellectuals were to become increasingly critical of Usmar's artistic, political and personal life.

In 1952 Usmar received a scholarship to study cinematography in the University of California. A number of Usmar's close associates, such as Asrul Sani (poet, intellectual and film director), Jayakusuma (academic and expert on traditional theatre), Nya Abbas Acup, Wahyu Sihombing (both successful directors) and Soemarjono (highly respected, and now a very senior film editor), found their way to American academic and professional institutions in the late 1950s and early 1960s. All of them were committed to an anti-leftist, pro-Western position in the politics of the film industry, and since 1965 have held some of the key positions in film schools and professional bodies of cinema.

Despite the suggestions of some later admirers that Usmar's works were influenced by Italian neo-realism, his own writings indicate that since his return from the US in 1953, he was most directly influenced by the working methods of Hollywood directors and actors whom he had observed during his period in America. 'Almost unconsciously', he writes, 'I had taken over the working system of Hollywood'.[22]

In 1954, Usmar and Jamaluddin Malik co-produced *Lewat Jam Malam* (After Curfew) in a bid to make Indonesia a powerful contestant in the First Asian Film Festival, to be held in Tokyo. Usmar does not seem to have had a high regard for Jamaluddin. Distinguishing between his own efforts and those of Jamaluddin, Usmar wrote: 'Persari was established under the leadership of Jamaluddin Malik, whose objective was, also, [like Usmar's company Perfini] to support national culture', but in contrast to Perfini's effort to oppose the tide of commercialism through artistic integrity, Persari 'was drawn into the commercial stream of the Chinese group.'[23]

National-political and film-business interests drew Jamaluddin and Usmar increasingly closer from the late 1950s. The alignment of Usmar, the socialist intellectual, and Jamaluddin Malik, the Islamic businessman, reflects the overt politicisation of Indonesian cinema, where all other differences were overshadowed by considerations of anti-communism. The Perfini-Persari co-production in 1954, *Lewat Jam Malam*, however, predates any visible political alliance between Usmar and Jamaluddin.

*Lewat Jam Malam* is set in Jakarta in 1950, around the time of the transfer of power from the Dutch to the Indonesian government. The hero (or perhaps anti-hero) of the film is Iskandar, a medical student and revolutionary soldier, who finds himself unable to face the prospect of civilian life in post-war Indonesia. He feels guilty for having killed people. He feels betrayed by the leadership because his hopes that the revolution would produce an ideal society are shattered by the rampant corruption and mismanagement which he sees all around.

In the final moments of the film the hero resolves his psychological contradictions and breaks away from Puja, another frustrated revolutionary turned bandit. He is running through dark empty streets to return to the woman who loves him, and to the comfortable wealthy post-independence lifestyle she represents. But the curfew hour has started and he is shot down by the military-police for breaking the curfew.

In 1955 there were at least half a dozen films with variations on the theme of relocation of a former freedom fighter in the post-revolutionary society. In most of these films, which Sitor Situmorang described as 'propaganda for development' (not a disparaging label at that time), the ex-soldier is easily brought into the life and work of peacetime through the new patriotic appeal of national development and/or the affection of a good woman.[24] In *Lewat Jam Malam* the problem is explored much more extensively in personal emotional terms, through a very intellectual and self-analytical protagonist, and ends in a tragedy rather than a successful resolution of the conflict between the individual and the society. Interestingly, the film defines 'normal' and 'correct' social practice through the characterisation of the successful wealthy professionals. It contains criticism of corruption, betrayal of revolutionary values, of a society that pays lip service to sacrifice while protecting the avaricious. However, Iskandar and Puja's verbal criticisms are countered by the characters of Adlin and Karim, who combine goodness with success and a distinctly comfortable life-style, represented in the final sequences of the film by the party at Adlin's house.

The film was about an intellectual, made with the international film critics in mind. The Indonesian intellectuals loved it. In pointing to the uniqueness of the film, Sitor Situmorang wrote, 'I do not agree that it is about the problems of an ex-revolutionary. That is only the background.' The main strength of the film, he said, was that it was a 'modern psychological drama'. He concluded that in its ability to use the distinctly filmic form to explore the 'psychological aspects and contemporary human feelings', *Lewat Jam Malam* was the first film which 'reached the standard of modern Indonesian literature and poetry'.[25] That the film never got to the Asian Film Festival, for which it was meant, was much regretted by Indonesian film critics as a missed opportunity for displaying the nation's artistic achievements internationally.

Usmar's next film, *Tamu Agung* (Honoured Guest, 1955), was a controversial political satire, which is now regarded as a classic Indonesian comedy. The film ridiculed a populist, slogan-mongering politician, and the undiscriminating political attitudes and plain stupidity generated by mass politics. The 'honoured guest' was a thinly veiled caricature of President Sukarno. Released in 1956, at a time when Sukarno was bidding for an enhanced political role, the film echoes the early intellectual criticism of Sukarno's brand of mass mobilisation. The exhortation in the film to attend to the real economic problems of the society and move away from populist movements parallels Vice President Hatta's call to 'dam up the national revolution', in November 1956.[26]

In 1959 with *Pejuang* (The Fighter), Usmar returned to his favourite subject – heroism in the revolutionary war. *Pejuang* is completely dominated by the figure of the hero. Events turn on his personal relationship with two men and a woman. The large number of people whose life and welfare depend on his decisions fade into the background as faceless masses. The film judges the protagonist on the basis of his personal moral actions, the wider historical and social implications of these actions are of little narrative significance.

This was Usmar's first film to win an international award. In 1960 Indonesia's leading star Bambang Hermanto received the Best Actor award at the Moscow Film Festival for his performance in *Pejuang*. When he returned from the Soviet Union, Usmar wrote a long article in the communist party daily *Harian Rakyat*. But, over the next five years, he was to become increasingly associated with national and international institutions committed to anti-Communism.

In 1962 Usmar Ismail became the founding secretary of LESBUMI (Islamic Cultural Institute), the cultural organisation sponsored by the Islamic political party NU. It appears that some time earlier he had become associated with the right-wing international organisation, Moral Rearmament. When in 1962 Usmar made a film, *Anak Perawan di Sarang Penyamun* (Young Virgin in a Robber's Den), based on a novel by Takdir Alisyahbana, he faced a howl of protest from the left-wing press mainly because Takdir was then in political exile and regarded as an 'enemy of the revolution'.

### Bachtiar Siagian

Bachtiar Siagian's film career spanned precisely the decade of the most open ideological conflict in Indonesian society, 1955–65. He was born in the small town of Binjai, North Sumatra, in 1923. His father was a railway worker, his grandfather, in whose care Bachtiar grew up, a plantation labourer (*kuli*). As a young boy Bachtiar worked as domestic help for a Dutch woman who put him through primary school. He had no further formal education. His earliest political and artistic training was among the radical nationalist theatre groups in Medan in the 1940s. His first experience of film-making was in 1943, when his theatre group became involved in a production under the auspices of the Japanese forces. He joined the Medan branch of LEKRA in the early 1950s. In 1954, Nyoto, a leader of LEKRA and a member of the PKI polit-bureau, urged Bachtiar to move to Jakarta and work in the film industry.

Bachtiar's first opportunity to make a film came a year later, provided by Saleh Umar, the radical nationalist playwright with whom Bachtiar had been associated from his youth. Saleh Umar was now a PNI member of the People's Representative Council and working for Muara Film, a film import company reportedly owned by the North Sumatran journalist, businessman and politician (in later years, foreign minister and vice-president), Adam Malik. Bachtiar's and Muara's first film, *Kabut Desember* (December Mist, 1955), was the story of a young woman who becomes a prostitute to put her brother through school. When, on the eve of his marriage, the brother discovers this, he breaks his engagement rather than adopt the attitudes of his prospective in-laws and reject his sister. Bachtiar's treatment of prostitution remains exceptional in the Indonesian context since in much of Indonesian cinema prostitution is seen as a moral problem which needs to be cured (see Chapter 6).

Bachtiar's second film, *Corak Dunia* (The Shape of the World, 1955), adapted from a Saleh Umar play, incorporated a conscious political statement. The film was produced by a recently established Chinese production and import company, Garuda, which funded several other films by Bachtiar Siagian and other LEKRA film directors. In *Corak Dunia* a revolutionary soldier, Johan, finds himself with no meaningful occupation after his discharge at the end of the war. He turns to robbery and crime, until he sees an old woman and her adopted blind daughter trying to eke out a poor but honest living. With their help and support he tries to mend his ways and eventually falls in love with the blind girl. Coincidence throws him into the path of a former comrade-in-arms, now an eye surgeon, who is able to cure Johan's blind betrothed. But when the girl regains her sight she is repulsed by the war wound that has horribly scarred Johan's face. Johan leaves her. His experience leads to a new analysis of the society. He comes to see his misfortune as not a quirk of fate, but the result of war, which in turn is the result of imperialism. He realises that he must fight this political wrong along with other victims of it and decides to join the movement for peace. In keeping with the style of romantic popular cinema, the film comes to a happy ending. Just as Johan is setting off to represent his village at a peace meeting his estranged lover comes back to him.

Bachtiar's first film about the nationalist movement, *Turang* (Beloved, 1957), was chosen as the Best Film at the Indonesian Film Festival of 1957. Bachtiar Siagian sees the critical success of *Turang* as the beginning of a serious interest in cinema among the members of the PKI and LEKRA. Chairman Aidit himself watched the film and there were screenings of the film for the party cadres. The national award and party attention that the film received probably reflect its appeal to mainstream populist nationalism.

From the scenario it seems that *Turang* told a conventional story of the love affair between guerrilla commander Rusli and the village head's daughter Tipi, who nurses him back to life after he has been seriously wounded in battle. Despite the centrality of the hero in the narrative, Bachtiar insists that he was careful to reserve a large part of the film for the 'people in revolt'. This is to some extent confirmed by reviews which saw the film as depicting the 'resistance of the villagers of Kampung Sebaraya (Karo Land) along with the guerrilla forces against the Dutch in the 1945 revolution'.[27] During the revolution Bachtiar had spent some time in the Karo region of North Sumatra. He tried to get that experience of the people and the place to bear strongly upon the film. Seventy per cent of the shooting was done on location in the Karo region, and most of those acting in the film were local villagers. As Bachtiar recalls, *Turang* had no professional film actors, and involved expensive location shooting, and therefore would not have been funded by a private producer.

Funds for this film were raised by the North Sumatran regional commander Colonel Jamin Gintings, a Sukarno loyalist who had more than a passing interest in promoting the revolutionary role of the Karo Bataks, his own tribal group. The support Gintings had from his fellow Karos as well as from communist-organised peasants and workers, had been crucial in his appointment as the North Sumatran regional commander in December 1956 to replace the Toba Batak, Simbolon, who had come out in open defiance of the central government.[28] Both aspects of Gintings' political alliance were served by a film directed by a LEKRA member about the role of the Karo Batak in the making of the Indonesian nation.

Only months before Bachtiar received the award for *Turang*, his film *Daerah Hilang* (Lost Land, 1956) was severely truncated by the Board of Censors. An article in *Harian Rakyat* was headlined '*Lost Land* almost lost in censorship'. Advertisements for the film said 'The Censors were frightened by the honest depiction of social realities'. The film was set in an area to be absorbed into the elite residential Kebayoran Baru of Jakarta. Since the beginning of the urban development project in this area in 1948, initiated by the Dutch, there had been protests from small fruit farmers and traders who lived there. After the transfer of sovereignty, the problem continued, leading by the mid-1950s to conflicts between the Indonesian government and those it regarded as 'illegal squatters'.[29] The film followed the struggles of a villager who had been drawn into Jakarta in the hope of a better life and had built his hut in an area claimed by urban developers.

The political issue at hand was too contemporary and the film was regarded as a challenge to government policy. The censors cut out about two thousand feet from it, that is a fifth to a quarter of the film assuming it was approximately eight to ten thousand feet, which was the average length for Indonesian films in the 1950s.

Bachtiar's next political film got him into conflict with the PKI high command. *Baja Membara* (Burning Steel) was made in 1961 with financial support from an Achenese businessman, Abu Bakar Abdi, who had been involved in several other films by Bachtiar and another prominent LEKRA film maker, Basuki Effendy. Set in Aceh at the time of the Japanese occupation, the film looked at the role of Islam in the birth of the spirit of national resistance against the Japanese. Both Bachtiar and Yubaar Ayub, then head of LEKRA, were taken to task by Aidit himself for the film's positive treatment of religion. But the film was released in its original form. This incident suggests, in contradiction to post-1965 evaluations of LEKRA's film work, that the party had considerably less control over its film-makers than did the state and regional military commands through censorship.

Bachtiar was planning his most ambitious film when he was arrested soon after October 1965. He had begun work on the film with the support of the governor of Bali and of Sukarno himself. In October 1962 Bachtiar submitted to the Balinese Historical Council the concept for a film to be called *Karmapala*. The story that emerges from the draft is about a villager's realisation of the injustices inherent in the society in which he has been born and bred, the deep-rooted inequalities which he has been taught not to question by those he loves and respects, and the painful experience of learning that he must go against those he loves because of his new realisations. There are no heroes in this story and if there is a villain, it is the structured traditional society of Bali, which in the name of religion and tradition perpetrates horrible crimes against human dignity.

The king Cokorde Anom, a benevolent despot, is known to be good to peasants and a strict ruler. He rapes the daughter of a landless peasant, and makes up by giving her family money and marrying her off to an eligible village youth. No one suspects him even when the woman, Ayu, commits suicide, except her brother, Wayan Dipta, to whom she has confided the story of her shame. Unable to bear the guilt of hatred for his king (since he has been taught that even un-expressed anger against superiors is sin), Wayan Dipta leaves his village. In the city he learns about the guerrillas resisting the Dutch. In his interaction with them he acquires a new concept of society, and realises that he should not feel guilty for hating his king, nor be ashamed of his sister for being raped. The conflict between his inherited beliefs and his new awareness persists to the moment he is put to death by the king's soldier.[30]

*Karmapala* is about the making of a revolutionary. It traces the process of a person's conscientisation – from acceptance of established values to rebelling against them. This rebellion is not an angry personal outrage, but organised political action. Though only peripherally, the narrative also traces the process of the spread of revolution. Wayan's awareness arises from a dialectic of his personal tragedy and the in-fluence of the nationalist movement. At the end of the narrative it seems that Wayan's sharing of his new consciousness with the people of his village plants the first seeds of revolution in that society.

While the narrative is set in the background of anti-Dutch national-ism, the planned film needs to be read in the context of the PKI policy popularly known as 'TURBA', an acronym for 'Turun ke bawah' (move down), initiated in the mid-1950s, which required urban cadres to live in villages, simultaneously researching and organising the peasantry. TURBA was to a large extent the cultural counterpart of the PKI's land reform policy.[31] In the second half of 1964 peasants' 'unilateral actions' (aksi sepihak) started with the intent of forcing landlords to implement the land reform legislations passed by the government in

1960. Although *about* the revolution of 1945–49, the narrative's point of reference is the left's thinking in the 1960s about the contemporary class struggle in the countryside and the urban intelligentsia's role in it. In the 'concept' of this film, revolutionary thinking is a strictly one-way movement, from the radical youth through the young villager to the rural community. There is no reference to the other, and unpopular, side of TURBA, requiring young urban cadres to live with and *learn from* villagers.[32]

The elitist implications of the politics notwithstanding, this was a new kind of appropriation of the nationalist movement in cinema, so that the revolution did not represent 'us' the Indonesian nation against 'them' the Dutch, but became a social revolution where the fight against the foreigners included an attempt to identify and challenge the structures of repression within Indonesian society. This was a distinct departure from the standard pattern of nationalist cinema, including the films of Usmar Ismail, which centred on the 'hero-villain' equals 'good-evil' juxtaposition of the *pejuang* (revolutionary) versus *penjajah* (the colonial rulers). Though Bachtiar was not experimenting with film form, his perspective on society gradually moved him away from the common narrative formula in Indonesian cinema.

A very different approach to avoiding the conventional representation of the 'bad' Dutch versus the 'good' nationalist was Asrul Sani's *Pagar Kawat Berduri* (Barbed Wire Fence, 1961). The film was severely criticised by the left because of its 'principle of "Universal Humanism"' which 'ultimately puts the character of Koenen [a Dutch soldier] above all else and makes him a "hero of humanism".'[33] *Pagar Kawat Berduri* received critical acclaim from other sections of the artistic community and today has the status of a classic. It shares with some of Usmar Ismail's films its concentration on the psychological turmoils of the protagonist. This, I think, is the key to the second important difference between Usmar's and Bachtiar's film narratives. In many of his films, which Usmar saw as being innovative (and which were seen as such by his admirers), he attempted to delve deeply into the private psychological world of his characters. Bachtiar, particularly in his later films, tried to explore the historical and social situation of the characters.

The difference is perhaps best exemplified by contrasting Usmar's *Lewat Jam Malam* and Bachtiar's *Corak Dunia*. The films were made within about a year of each other, and both were regarded as innovative treatments of a very common subject matter – the social rehabilitation of a former revolutionary soldier. Bachtiar's film is more generic than Usmar's in that it conforms to the narrative structure of a popular romance. But more importantly there are clearly articulated differences in the way the two films construct post-independence Indonesian society. Much of the world of *Corak Dunia* is made up of the poor and the rural, whereas in *Lewat Jam Malam* the poorer sections of the society are seen either as faceless masses, or as supremely tragic and abnormal, as represented by Puja and his deranged sister. The 'normal' social behaviour is represented in the lifestyle of the wealthy professionals, highlighted in the final moments of the film by the images of the party at the home of Adlin and his sister, which cut across shots of Iskandar's final troubled and unsuccessful journey out of his chaotic existence.

*Lewat Jam Malam* looks at the psychological and intellectual crisis of the sensitive soul. The dramatic conflict is located in the mind of the hero and so is the solution. In *Corak Dunia* the genesis and resolution of an individual's problem is located in wider socio-political issues and mass action. Emotional experiences are important but only in so far as they are elements in directing the protagonist and the fiction towards a political analysis and a course of action that is public rather than private. The binding metaphor of the film is in the title – 'corak dunia', the pattern, the structure of the *political* world – and the narrative explores the protagonist's place within it.

### Legacy to New Order cinema

The New Order inherited a cinema that expressed a highly individualist and elitist approach to society. Usmar's elitism is not only evident in his pillorying of mass politics in *Tamu Agung*, but also in his choice of protagonists in his serious films. Usmar's heroes are successful businessmen (*Citra*), heroic fighters (the historical films set in the context of revolutionary war), intellectuals and professionals (*Lewat Jam Malam*). Characters like the evicted slum-dweller of Bachtiar's *Daerah Hilang*, the prostitute in *Kabut Desember*, and the uneducated, poverty-stricken horse-keeper of *Piso Surit* have rarely been paralleled in heroes of Usmar's films.[34]

One can think of Bachtiar's work as taking Indonesian cinema into what Teshome Gabriel calls the 'third phase' of development in Third World national cinemas, engaged in a critical reassessment of traditional cultures.[35] As mentioned earlier, in Gabriel's model the first phase is one of mimicry of Hollywood, and the second is marked by appropriation from traditional cultural products in terms of both form and content. It is more useful to think of Gabriel's phases as competing patterns of film-making, rather than historical periods that follow one another.

The late 1950s and the turn of the decade were enormously rich in terms of Indonesian film production, not in numbers but in the variety of social, cultural and political perspectives vying for supremacy in the form and content of cinema. Judging by Usmar's own writings, we can categorise his work as belonging to the first stage of Hollywood mimicry in Gabriel's model. Some of Usmar's colleagues, such as D. Jayakusuma

(1918–87) who started his film work within Usmar's Perfini, experimented with various aspects of traditional culture, both in adapting traditional mythological tales to cinema (as in *Lahirnya Gatotkaca*, 1960) and in the self-conscious incorporation of various kinds of traditional cultural tropes into films (such as the traditional martial art 'silat' which constitutes the focus of Jayakusuma's 1953 film *Harimau Campa*). By comparison, a large part of Bachtiar's work is engaged in a complex critique of traditional cultural practices but not from any utopian socialist or developmentalist vantage point. Although Bachtiar had less than a decade of involvement in cinema, his work seems to have taken a direction that was different from that of any other prominent filmmaker of his generation. The suppression of Bachtiar's films then is the end of a form of cultural critique, a reversal from the third and radical phase of Gabriel's model. In the context of Indonesian cultural-politics as a whole it is part of a much wider repression of what Daniel Lev called 'the growth of a forceful egalitarianism' which threatened the pattern of class dominance.[36]

More important than the banning of works of particular film-makers was the destruction of the institutions such as LEKRA, LKN, SARBUFIS, the radical organisations which provided the framework within which works such as Bachtiar Siagian's could be produced. From this point of view LEKRA (and other radical cultural organisations) is not, as it has often been portrayed, an instrument of PKI propaganda or 'a major instrument of intellectual repression' as one historian has labelled it.[37] Rather it is part of a structure that made possible particular kinds of cultural expression. Indeed in the case of cinema, the attempts of LEKRA and other left-wing cultural organisations to oppose particular films rarely led to films being banned. The PKI does not seem to have been entirely successful in keeping control over even the works of the LEKRA film directors. On the other hand, LEKRA directors were by no means immune from state censorship. Bachtiar Siagian's *Daerah Hilang* was heavily censored even in the heyday of liberalism when Usmar Ismail got away with *Tamu Aging*, Indonesian cinema's only caricature (however indirect) of the head of the state. The post-1965 image of the communists as the barrier to artistic expression is, to say the least, inaccurate.

Only briefly, in 1963–64, did the left acquire a share of the state's repressive power over cinema through its influence over the Board of Censorship. Since 1950 the censorship board had been chaired by Maria Ulfa, whose known PSI (Socialist Party) sympathies and supposed leniency in censoring British and American films, led to several calls for her removal. In 1963, she was replaced by Utami Suryadarma, who (along with her husband Air Marshal S. Suryadarma) was close to Sukarno and sympathetic to the PKI. Under Utami Suryadarma, the

BSF threw its considerable weight on the side of the movement against American films. Part of the success of the movement was due to BSF disallowing or delaying release of American films even before the government had imposed a total ban on them.

In May 1965, when Utami Suryadarma had been in office for less than two years, the entire membership of the BSF was replaced by a new team. The reasons for the sudden change are not clear. But the new members were clearly a group that was very acceptable to the new government that would emerge after October 1965. With the exception of the removal of the PKI representative, the May 1965 board remained in office for its full three-year term till May 1968.

The man appointed to chair the board in 1965 was Martono, a professional bureaucrat, and an unknown figure compared to his two predecessors. Since 1965 he has been appointed to more significant positions in the government. In 1969, he became a Golkar member of the People's Representative Council (DPR) and in 1978, the Junior Minister for Transmigration. It would seem the New Order censorship board was established even before October 1965.

## The Establishment of the New Order

A dramatic coup attempt in the early hours of 1 October 1965 set in motion a chain of events which led to the end of Guided Democracy, the fall of Sukarno, the destruction of the PKI and associated political forces, and the rise of the army to a position of dominance under the leadership of General Suharto.

The story of the coup led by Colonel Untung has been told many times from many points of view.[38] The army leadership crushed a coup by junior officers within hours and then proceeded to use the failed coup as their excuse to decimate the PKI, which they presented as the 'mastermind' (dalang) behind the coup. In the months following October 1 there was a gradual erosion of Sukarno's power base. On 11 March 1966, Suharto acquired the authority, for all practical purposes, to govern the state in the President's name. The very next day, he banned the already destroyed PKI. The last cabinet appointed by Sukarno was dismantled and on 18 March 15 of its ministers were arrested.

> During the months after 11 March ... the atmosphere of Jakarta politics underwent a drastic change. The new army-dominated government reversed many of the president's principal economic and foreign policies, and youthful enthusiasts in the Action Fronts that had risen to oppose Sukarno proclaimed the birth of the 'New Order' in place of the discredited 'Old Order'.[39]

The birth of the New Order signified the defeat of the army's opponents, particularly the Communists and radical nationalists. 'At another level', it was 'the victory of the propertied classes over the challenge posed under the PKI umbrella'.[40]

In cinema the casualties of the political transformation included all individuals and organisations that could be remotely connected to the PKI or LEKRA or the movement against US films under PAPFIAS guidance. Directors, technicians and artists with any connections with any of these bodies were detained without trial, some of them for over a decade. Two of LEKRA's best-known directors, Basuki Effendy and Bachtiar Siagian, were arrested and eventually incarcerated on the infamous prison island of Buru till 1979. They were amongst the last groups to be released from there.

All organisations related to film were purged of people suspected of leftist connections on the basis of the list drawn up by the Department of Information. In the post-purge film industry, particularly the producers' organisation, PPFI, seemed anxious to help the army in the destruction of the PKI, not only as an influence in cinema, but in the society at large. The PPFI reportedly supplied to the army 'documentaries' of the communists' culpabilities for use as newsreels. According to one ex-political prisoner, the documentaries included mock-ups of armed rebellion where political detainees were made to act out scenes of PKI misdeeds for the purpose of filming.

In the early 1960s foreign financial domination of the film industry had ended, at least in the short term. But the result was not what the opponents of the American film importer had intended. In the new economic and political conditions after 1965–66, the exit of the big American company left the way open for rising Indonesian big business to take control of the lucrative film import sector. The anti-American film policy was reversed in 1966. In 1967 nearly 400 US films were imported into Indonesia. Hollywood cinema was once again predominant, not only in the Indonesian film market but also as the textual system on which the next generation of Indonesian film-making would be modelled. A significant part of Indonesia's cinematic heritage was destroyed in the civil war and counter-revolution of 1965–66.

# 3

# Institutions of New Order Cinema

As the dust settled on the turbulence of 1965–66, the most immediate transformation in Indonesian cinema was in the restructuring of its institutions. Many of the old organisations were banned and destroyed or had their membership overhauled, and new ones were created. The changes affected the professional organisations, the economics of film production and the workings of censorship. The transformation was not worked overnight and some of the changes had started before October 1965. The new, renewed and recreated institutions provided both new restraints and new opportunities for film-making in Indonesia.

The New Order inherited from the previous government the basis of a tightly controlled medium, under the Ministry of Information. Up until 1964, the responsibility for cinema had been divided between four departments, Education and Culture, Information, Trade, and Industry. By a Presidential Instruction in 1964 the Minister of Information became responsible for all aspects of cinema in Indonesia. Now cinema, like radio and the press, came under the Information portfolio while other cultural and artistic activities such as theatre and literature remained the responsibility of the Minister of Education and Culture. In 1978 the Department of Information was placed under the responsibility of the Coordinating Minister of Politics and Security (Menko Polkam) while the Department of Education and Culture was under the Coordinating Minister of People's Welfare. Thus the positioning of cinema within the state apparatus emphasised the media-information-influence and, hence, security and propaganda dimension of films rather than their 'artistic' dimension.

Despite the constant complaints of Indonesian film-makers about the odious restraining powers of the BSF, there are relatively few cases where the powers of the BSF need to be directly exercised in the form of either excising sections of a film or banning films. The overwhelming majority of films are formed by the prescriptions of other institutions rather than the proscriptions of the BSF. These institutions include the production companies, the professional organisations of the film community, film schools and film festivals. Together these institutions define what constitutes Indonesian cinema and determine who becomes a filmmaker. These cinematic institutions are, of course, themselves shaped by the economic and cultural institutions of the society (such as education and religion). Who has access to literacy, schooling and urban life limits the group of people who will ever come into contact with a film studio and have the option of becoming a film-maker. For example, deep-rooted social convictions about cinema and about women's work exclude women from many aspects of film work. In the 60 years of Indonesian film there have been only four women film directors, all of them related to prominent male members of the film community.[1] There have been no women photographers or music directors. Questions such as why men control, almost exclusively, the most valued aspects of film work are related to social and cultural phenomena that are wider than the subject of this discussion. However, focusing on film institutions (keeping in mind the wider social and historical conditions shaping and sustaining them) allows the identification of special characteristics of these and the specificity of cinema as a medium.

## Corporate and professional bodies

Included under this heading are three sets of organisations: successive Film Councils, advisory bodies providing linkages between government departments and the film community; the annual film festivals (Festival Film Indonesia, henceforth FFI) which judge the films produced each year; and representative organisations of particular professional groups in the film industry. These corporate and professional bodies, though nominally autonomous, are authorised by the government and have specified places in the government's programme of 'guidance and development' for the national film industry. With the exception, to a limited degree, of the professional organisations, these organisations have no coercive power over any sector of film-making. But they all have a degree of influence on cinema as forums of group pressure.

### The film council

Of all the institutions of Indonesian cinema the successive film councils have been most involved with the government's rhetoric of developing Indonesian cinema as an art form. By the time General Ali Murtopo became Minister of Information in 1978, some people in the industry had come to regard the institution as part of the ministerial publicity machinery, having a high profile but no real control over any area of film-making.

The first post-1965 film council, Dewan Produksi Film Nasional (National Film Production Council, henceforth DPFN) was set up in 1968 by the Minister of Information, the long-time newspaper editor, businessman and PNI (Nationalist Party) supporter, B.M. Diah. It was expected to facilitate the production of quality films which would at once be examples to commercial producers and raise audience appreciation of Indonesian cinema. These productions were to be funded by a levy on imported films introduced the previous year, commonly known as 'Dana SK 71' (Ministerial Decree No. 71 Fund). In these early years of the New Order, when industry was trying to re-establish itself in the new political and economic circumstances, it was hoped that improvement in the quality of Indonesian films would make them competitive with imports. The DPFN consisted of nine members selected on the basis of their 'expertise, experience, education and dedication to national cinema, from ... the private and the government sector, *not representing organisations nor because of official position*' (my emphasis).[2] This 'expert body', representing (purportedly, at any rate) the interests of Indonesian cinema as a whole, was given the responsibility of judging any planned production presented to it, on the basis of which the film might receive financial assistance. Also the council could itself assume the responsibility of producing films.

This DPFN depended more on the expertise and goodwill of its constituents than on a clear hierarchical structure and lasted for only a year in its original form. In 1969 the new Minister of Information, Air Marshal Budiarjo, restructured the organisation, now called Dewan Film Nasional (henceforth Film Council). The council's membership was nearly doubled to 17, with seven members drawn from government departments. This move towards bureaucratic interference in the Film Council paralleled other changes going on within the Department of Information at the same time. The writer and academic, Umar Kayam, and Moscow graduate of cinematography and later prominent film director Syumanjaya, whom Minister Diah had appointed to top positions in the Department, were replaced by career bureaucrats early in Budiarjo's period in office.

The Film Council's role in the production of films was now swamped by its role as advisor to the Minister of Information on matters of policy. During 1968–69 a fairly successful programme had seen the DPFN produce four films, including *Jampang Mencari Naga Hitam* (Jampang in Search of 'Black Snake') which was a box office hit, and *Apa Yang Kau Cari, Palupi?* (What Are You Searching for, Palupi?) which won an award at the 1970 Asian Film Festival. After 1970, the Film Council stopped producing films and thus ceased to be a factor in the film industry as a source of support for film-makers, offering a possibility for autonomy from commercial considerations.

The next minister to hold the Information portfolio, Mashuri (1972–77), revoked the SK 71, the regulation which had been the Film Council's financial base. The Council's advisory function was taken over by a much smaller body, the Institute for National Film Development (LEPFINAS), made up principally of leading artists and film-makers, while the older Film Council lived in limbo. LEPFINAS lasted for just over a year, when it was abandoned by the next Minister of Information, General Ali Murtopo (a powerful figure with a major role in New Order intelligence activities), who reconstituted the Film Council on a vastly grander scale. It had 49 members with the Minister of Information as its *ex-officio* chairperson. Six of its members were from the Information Department, and one each from six other government departments. Sixteen members were drawn from various film organisations. The remaining 18 were representatives of religious and social organisations, including several GOLKAR-affiliated ones, and individual intellectuals and academics.

Very little changed under the next (and current) Minister of Information, Harmoko. In 1986, when appointing a new Council, the minister described its function simply as making recommendations to the minister about promoting the film industry of the country.

The first film council had been an attempt to provide a forum and an organisation for film-makers which would be independent of the bureaucratic and financial interest groups. By 1979 it had become a body reflecting the same bureaucratic and business interests which controlled the industry. Increasingly its policy declarations came to contain the same instructions for film-makers which were emerging from the various government departments, particularly the Board of Censorship. But its veneer of independence gave these policy declarations the appearance of being the free choice of representatives of the film community and the society at large. Its much talked of *Ethical Code of Film Production in Indonesia*, published in 1981, was no more than a setting out of practices already in operation in the censorship system, and is best discussed in that context.

### Film festivals

The Indonesian Film Festival, FFI, has been a regular annual event since 1973. These festivals are held in the different provincial capitals and the national capital in turn in cooperation with the local governments. The organisational structure and scale of the festival has changed from year to year. Some see them as publicity campaigns for the successive information ministers and provincial governors.

The festival is also the single biggest publicity event for Indonesian cinema itself. It focuses enormous media attention on Indonesian cinema and is the only occasion when most major theatres in the festival city show Indonesian rather than Chinese, Indian, Italian or American films. This is, however, less true for Jakarta than for the festivals held in the provincial capitals. The three successive festivals I attended were in Semarang, Surabaya and Jakarta (1980–82). Unlike the two provincial capitals, in Jakarta a number of major theatres continued their normal pattern and did not go out of their way to screen Indonesian films. In 1991, the week after the festival in Jakarta, it was difficult to find any Indonesian films except in the cheap theatres of the distant suburbs.

Indonesian cinema really comes to town when the festivals go provincial. At the Semarang festival in 1980 and the Surabaya one in 1981 thousands of people turned out to see the 'procession of stars' through the main city streets. Throughout the night huge crowds turned up at every station to meet the special train that carried hundreds of Jakarta film people to Semarang. Dozens of people on the streets of Semarang and Surabaya told me that they would go and see this or that film now that they had touched the hand of a star or had a brother who had kissed an actress through a glass pane of the train. Elderly trishaw pullers and *jamu*-sellers (traditional herbalists) who had never seen a film, stopped to watch the stars' processions, simply because it was *ramai*, crowded and festive.

The more formal aspect of the festivals is the handing down of the annual film awards by a jury panel. The jury members are selected by the festival's organising committee and appointed by the Minister of Information. The jury changes each year, but some senior journalists and academics have been repeatedly appointed.

Citra (the Indonesian equivalent of the Oscar) are given out for 12 categories of film work in addition to less important awards. Although ticket sales figures from major cities indicate quite clearly that a Citra does not make a film popular with the audiences, over the years winning a Citra has become an increasingly important goal for directors, actors, editors and others working in the industry, especially since the late 1970s as Indonesian films started to seek stature in the international film world. Like a film that does well in the box office, one that wins a Citra is likely to be followed by other films made to a similar formula.[3] Award-winning directors, writers, technicians and actors are more likely to find work, although clearly not to the extent of those who are involved in box office successes. Nonetheless, the award system is part of the selective process determining who participates in Indonesian film-making.

On the whole, the jury's opinions have run very close to those expressed in the film reviews of such elite national publications as the weekly *Tempo*, and journalists from prestige magazines and dailies are regularly included among the jury. The Film Festival award can be seen to represent the values, ideals and interests of the urban intelligentsia, of which the film-makers themselves are a part, as against those of the bureaucrats and financiers. The festival award system operates not by punishment (like censorship), or through exclusion (like the market), but through the privileging of certain films and their makers, and by extension of certain perspectives on art and society.

## Professional organisations

After 1965 three very important organisations of cinema, SARBUFIS, Lembaga Film Indonesia and Panitya Seniman Untuk Film (mentioned in Chapter 3), were destroyed. The remaining professional organisations, instead of protecting the interests of their memberships, cooperated with the New Order government to identify film people who were in any way associated with the supposedly communist, banned organisations and movements. Most of the organisations, split to some degree during the last turbulent years of Sukarno's rule, were purged of members suspected of communist sympathies. As a result, in some cases organisations which used to be recognisable bastions of anti-communist politics were now reconstituted as apolitical 'functional organisations'.

The clearest case of such transformation was that of Ikatan Karyawan Film dan Televisi Indonesia (Union of Film and Television Employees, henceforth KFT) which became the only organisation for the technical, artistic and unskilled staff of the film industry, after the banning of SARBUFIS. KFT had been set up in March 1964 to speak for the *karyawan* (employees) rather than the *buruh* (workers) of the film industry, whom the much older SARBUFIS represented. SARBUFIS organisers had directed themselves towards the unskilled and semi-skilled workers in studios and production companies (technical assistants, script boys, set-makers and others who do not usually rate a mention in the credits) and the movie theatres (projectionists, menial and clerical workers). KFT, by contrast, was organised by the most highly paid and highly skilled professionals, the 'creative forces' as distinct from the lower echelons of the industry's workforce. The 18 founding members of KFT were, with one exception (who was a bureaucrat in the State Film Production Company), all directors, editors, and cameramen,[4] that is, the elite of film workers. One KFT founding member said its purpose was partly to challenge the influence of the PKI Trade Union movement in the film industry.[5] Another, in his tribute to the organisation noted the founders' determination not to commit themselves to the 'political concept of NASAKOM' (i.e., Sukarno's left-wing nationalism).[6]

After the banning of SARBUFIS in 1965, KFT inherited the constituency of the very organisation with which it was set up to compete. The distinction between the *buruh* and *karyawan* was suppressed in the new political discourse, so that KFT could incorporate all levels of the industry's workforce. In 1976 it was officially designated as the only legal organisation for all those employed in film production (excluding actors). While membership of KFT now became compulsory for anyone wishing to work with the film studios or production units, the leadership of the organisation remained largely with the so-called 'creative forces'. A cartoon on the back cover of a KFT bulletin in 1981 referred obliquely to the difference between sections of the organisation's membership, between the film directors and the 'little workers' (see illustration 2). The discrepancies in the pay structure of KFT's membership were enormous by the end of the 1980s when, according to reports, established directors were earning about 30 million rupiah (about $20,000) and the average crew member was earning Rp.600,000 (about $400) per film contract (four months of work on an average).

Also in 1976 five other organisations were officially endorsed as the only lawful organisations for particular functional sectors of cinema. These were Persatuan Artis Film Indonesia (Indonesian Film Artists' Union, PARFI) for actors, Persatuan Perusahaan Film Indonesia (Indonesian Film Producers' Union, PPFI) for producers, Gabungan Perusahaan Bioskop Seluruh Indonesia (All Indonesian Association of Movie Theatre Companies, GPBSI) for theatre owners, and two smaller and less significant organisations for the half-dozen studio owners, GASFI (Indonesian Association of Film Studios) and those working in subtitling, GASI (Indonesian Association of Subtitlers). Their central function, as stated in the ministerial decree endorsing the organisations, was 'to aid in the execution of every policy formulated by the government for the development of cinema in Indonesia'.[7]

No one can take any part in the making of a film without prior approval of the functional organisation of which he or she is a member. Therefore these organisations can prevent any individual from working in the film industry. Although only used infrequently, their power of exclusion has been part of the process of keeping out film-makers who were allegedly associated with the PKI before 1965.

While some of the industry's professional organisations have, to an extent, acted as lobby groups, most have been ineffective in influencing government policies that affect their members' work conditions.

### Production, import, distribution

In a dramatic reversal of policy after October 1965, the film market was thrown open to foreign imports. By 1967 the number of imported films rose to pre-PAPFIAS levels of about 400 and then nearly doubled in 1969. In the 15 years prior to its banning in 1964, when AMPAI (American Motion Pictures Association in Indonesia) had dominated the market, it had been able to set up a chain of local distributors and theatres. Once it became possible to import again, the former local agents of the big American company were able to re-establish themselves as importers. At the same time the removal of political constraints on business relations with Hong Kong and Taiwan allowed the Chinese business contacts to be revived so that Chinese films (from these two countries) became a major part of the import sector for the first time since the 1930s. At this stage the local industry was struggling to produce five to ten films a year.

The local industry's struggle to survive against a much stronger import sector had a long history. But PAPFIAS had become such an anathema that in 1966 an open door policy of importing films could be introduced with almost no resistance. But within a year several factors were pushing the government towards intervention on behalf of the local industry. First, during this period the New Order government was generally responsive to the ideas of the intellectuals and professionals who had supported its ascendance to power. The film industry that emerged out of the political battles, like other professional sectors, had demonstrated its support for the new regime by purging itself of the left's influence. Some of its members had cooperated actively in the construction of the myth of communist atrocities. As before 1965, film professionals started arguing against unrestricted imports. The young film-maker Syumanjaya, appointed head of the Directorate of Film, strongly pushed for protection for the local film industry. Finally, B.M. Diah the Information Minister, a long-time cultural nationalist, was sympathetic to these demands.

Towards the end of 1967, in response to proposals coming out of Syumanjaya's directorate, Diah decreed steps to 'rehabilitate national film production' by 'giving protection to artists and workers so that they may commit themselves to the field of cinema' and 'improving the standard and technology of national cinema'. The new measure, frequently referred to as SK 71 (Ministerial Decree No. 71, 1967), imposed a flat levy of Rp.250,000 for each film imported into Indonesia. That amount was then to be made available to a local production and the funding import company regarded as a coproducer. The fund was to be administered by an autonomous Film Foundation, on the basis of recommendations from the Film Council (DPFN). The system remained in operation, with minor changes, until early 1976. In 1970 film production began to rise. Twenty-two films were produced that year, equalling the average of the early 1960s. In 1971 the number of local productions rose to 50, and their share of the audience to about 20 per cent.

Despite the initial enthusiasm for SK 71 among film workers, the rise in production, by all accounts, had little to do with it. The scheme was fraught with corruption, the accounting system was in disarray and years after it had been abandoned some of the money was still un-accounted for. The rise in the number of films produced is perhaps best explained by the general expansion of the Indonesian economy in the early years of the New Order. The increase in Indonesian films in 1970–71, however, made very little difference to the volume of imports, which remained at around 750.

Producers of Indonesian films had two main complaints about their position in the film market in the early 1970s. First, importers had more films to offer to theatres than did individual producers. As principal suppliers of films to the theatres, importers had preponderant say on when, how many and even which Indonesian films would be shown. This power seemed more odious as importing became concentrated in fewer and fewer hands since each importer came to have a vastly greater number of films to sell than the producers. The establishment in 1975 of P.T. Perfin, a single distribution agency for all national films, did not substantially improve the situation. Secondly, while the total number of theatres was rising, the expansion was disproportionately greater at the top end of the market. The expensive urban cinemas in Indonesia have historically catered for a section of the society which can pay high prices and is mainly interested in Western films. These up-market cine-mas automatically favour the importers.

The recovery of the film production sector and the resulting rise in confidence of producers and workers on the one hand and the growing political importance of criticisms of foreign cultural and economic influence from around 1972–73 combined to bring pressure on the government to take steps to protect the developing film industry. Soon after the Malari riots of 15 January 1974, which prompted the go-vernment to accommodate economic nationalism, a programme of progressive reduction of imports was started.[8] From 1974 the government decided to cut imports by 100 films each year. Imports were down from 600 in 1972 to 300 in 1976. It was projected that by 1979 there would be no imports, except for a select few exceptionally good films.

Hardly anyone in the industry, including, one suspects, the Minister of Information Mashuri, trusted that projection entirely, since even as he was cutting imports, he was taking steps to shore up the position of Indonesian importers in relation to foreign film sellers. Acting on the advice of some importers that the competition among Indonesian buyers was artificially raising the prices of foreign films, Mashuri decided that importers should form themselves into buying units for negotiations with the foreign film dealers. The argument was in tune with the national economic policy formulated under the influence of the govern-ment thinktank, the Centre for Strategic and International Studies (CSIS), which was promoting the 'building of "national giants" in an attempt to counterbalance the power of the "foreign giants".[9] There was also a security or censorship interest, particularly with regard to Chinese films. The government was worried not only about the possibility of PRC films containing communist ideas being smuggled in, but also that films from Taiwan and Hong Kong might encourage feelings of Chinese ethnic identity. A single agency responsible for the buying of all Chinese films could be held accountable more easily than a large number of small buyers.

The idea of large import monopolies had been broached several times since 1965. The first steps in favour of the bigger companies had already been taken under Minister Budiarjo early in 1972 when he made it necessary to import at least ten films a year to qualify for an import permit. In October 1973 all importers of Chinese films were grouped into a single 'consortium', whose elected leadership would negotiate the buying and then hand the films to the member companies for distribution. It soon became clear that political connections were going to be crucial in the internal organisation of that and all future consortia. In March 1976, despite opposition from many importers, the consortium system was extended to all imported films.

Four consortia were established: one each for Chinese films (Mandarin Consortium) and other Asian films (Asia Consortium), and two for European and American films (Euro-America I and Euro-America II). The government insisted that it was acting with the support of the majority of importers and that the companies themselves chose the consortium they wished to join. The latter claim at least is implausible as the three newly constituted consortia had exactly 21 members each, whereas the Mandarin Consortium, which had had the time to squeeze out some of its initial members, had only eight. Some importers have claimed that they only had the option of joining a particular group or giving up importing.

The Minister authorised four companies to head the four consortia. These arrangements lasted, with one exception, until 1982. Suptan Film under Sudwikatmono, foster-brother of President Suharto, was appointed coordinator of the Mandarin Consortium. Suptan became part of the Subentra group, established in 1980 by Sudwikatmono and Benny Suherman, a major Chinese Indonesian businessman.[10] Euro-America I was headed by Widodo Sukarno and his Archipelago Film. Widodo Sukarno had been involved in film imports since 1960 through a company called Intrafilm, an AMPAI agent, and had stridently opposed the anti-American films campaign in 1964–65. By the 1970s Widodo Sukarno's business had expanded greatly, partly, it seems, through his access to the presidential family. The Asian Consortium was headed by Adhi Yasa Film, a company owned by a number of senior Air Force officers and their wives and controlled by one of the most prominent Air Force businessmen, Air Marshal Suwoto Sukendar. Suptan, Archipelago and

Adhi Yasa gained increasing monopoly control over the import of Chinese, Euro-American and Asian films, respectively.

The fourth group, Euro-America Consortium II, lasted less than two years. It was headed by a Japanese-trained lawyer from East Java, Herman Samadikun, on behalf of Jati Film Jaya, with mainly Chinese shareholders. Jati, which like Suptan was a newcomer to the film industry, owed its position to Samadikun's friendship with Mashuri. The adviser to the consortium was Lieutenant General Suryo, a prominent military-businessman, and former member of the president's personal staff, representing Dharma Putra Jaya Film, part of the Kostrad Group's (Army Strategic Reserve Command) business interests.

Three important developments occurred in the first year of operation of the consortium system. First, Euro-American Consortium II got involved in a series of corruption charges, which were widely reported in the press, involving particularly Jati Film and some middle-ranking bureaucrats in the Department of Information. Asia Consortium was also reportedly involved in corrupt dealings with its own members as well as with government officials. Second, the total quota of 228 films for the year, divided equally between the four consortia, was seen as favourable treatment of the one controlled by Suptan Film since the Suptan Group with eight members had a quota of 57 films while the other three groups with 21 members each also had the same quota. Finally, and most importantly, the number of companies in each group dropped rapidly. The heads of groups treated the entire consortium's quota as their own and employed various means to squeeze out other member companies. In the early years of the New Order most producers had also been importers. But by the late 1970s the exclusion of companies from the import sector re-established a clear demarcation between the producers and importers, such as had existed before the demise of AMPAI.

Soon after becoming Minister of information in 1978, Ali Murtopo reorganised the consortium system, now renamed 'associations'. There were now three of them: Mandarin headed by Suptan, Euro-American headed by Archipelago and Asia-Non-Mandarin headed by Adhi Yasa. The Suptan group now had six members, Archipelago fifteen and Adhi Yasa five. Mashuri's plan for progressive reduction of imports was abandoned and the annual total was fixed at 260 films with 150 from Europe and America, 60 Mandarin and 50 other Asian films (i.e. ten for each member company of each group).

Ali Murtopo's period witnessed a further strengthening of the import sector over the production sector by the removal of the last of the pre-1965 restrictions on imports by which only two copies of a foreign film could be brought in. Mashuri had raised the permissible number to three. Ali Murtopo raised it to six, then to nine and finally to 15 in

1982. The original restriction had meant that the imported films could play in only two (later three) theatres at the same time and copies normally became unusable by the time they had done the run of the major cities. Indonesian films therefore had an advantage in the smaller towns and second-run cinemas. The changes significantly reduced the unit price per imported film, since the largest element in the cost structure, the royalty, remains fixed regardless of the number of copies bought. The changes Ali Murtopo effected thus meant that imported films could now occupy a greater share of the market at a smaller financial outlay than they had even in the days when over 700 films were coming in each year.

Mashuri had also imposed a requirement on importers to fund the production of at least one film for every three films they imported. As a result, in 1977 a record number of 122 films were produced. But the measure was opposed by importers and producers alike. Importers were unwilling to be forced to spread their resources into the riskier area of production. Producers were worried that if the powerful business groups were forced to take part in production, they would eventually squeeze out the small producers, just as they were excluding weaker competitors from importing.

While the majority of film workers remained in support of compulsory production, the industry's financiers were able to orchestrate an argument that compulsory production was leading to a decline in the quality of films. The argument cannot be supported on the basis of the films produced by importers in 1977, some of which received Citra awards. However, within weeks of Ali Murtopo becoming Information Minister the compulsory production legislation was replaced by a flat levy of Rp.3 million (about a tenth of the production cost of a low-budget film in the late 1970s) on each imported film. Despite his rhetoric in 1981–82 that films must become one of Indonesia's main non-oil export commodities, local production declined during Murtopo's ministry from a high of 122 in 1977 to 52 in 1982.

In 1983 Ali Murtopo, the most powerful Information Minister since 1965, was replaced by Harmoko, a former journalist and editor with financial interests in the press. The replacement of a military strongman by a former journalist, known to many in the film industry as a colleague, has prompted comparatively open conflicts in the film industry, where the minister has been unable or unwilling to act against a powerful business group's increasing monopoly control over import and distribution. While Harmoko returned to Mashuri's policy of progressive reduction of import quota (which was down to 160 in 1990), there were no new legislative initiatives at a time when dramatic new developments were changing the parameters of the contradictions in the Indonesian film industry.

*Establishment of a monopoly*

As mentioned above, in line with the government's 1970s economic policy, state-protected import monopolies had started to be established in the film industry. From the very beginning, Suptan, under Sudwikatmono, was the most successful in controlling its Mandarin Association. Increasingly, through the second half of the 1980s distribution of all imported films throughout Indonesia was channelled through Suptan's agents, who had formerly distributed only Chinese-language films. Eventually even the offices of the other two import associations were moved to the Suptan building, so that by the end of the 1980s Suptan was, to all intents and purposes, the only film importer.

Suptan's monopoly was made possible partly through political manoeuvring, but also in large measure through investments by its parent company, Subentra, in an entirely new development in the Indonesian film market. The first 'sinepleks' or cinema complex, that is theatres with multiple screens, was constructed by Subentra in 1986. Only a major conglomerate like Subentra could enter into such a bold new venture at a time when audience numbers, especially at the upper end of the market, seemed to be declining. The experiment worked. The plush new carpets, comfortable seats, clean toilets and the most advanced projection and sound system brought back some of the dwindling audiences.

Subentra's rapid expansion in the film industry needs to be seen in part in the context of the changes unleashed in the Indonesian economy as a whole in the mid-1980s as a result of the collapse of oil prices and recession. Robison suggests that the government, under pressure from both international capitalists and domestic producers to move away from the system of protection and state-allocated monopolies, started liberalising some sectors of the economy.[11] In the media, however, where ideological considerations of message and content have always been paramount, the old structures remained firmly in place. Subentra was thus well-placed to take advantage of its protected monopoly in film import, while at the same time moving into the deregulated banking sector which, according to some observers, provided the large business conglomerates with 'the licence to print money'.

In the two years after the establishment of the first cinema complex, Subentra invested heavily in renovating older theatres into new style multi-screen cinemas, initially in Jakarta and then in the other major cities. Typically Subentra entered into partnership with the existing owners by providing the finances for the renovations. By 1989 Subentra owned some 10 per cent of all screens in Indonesia (estimated at about 2,500 in all), but a far larger proportion of the top quality theatres in major cities. Some of these cinema complexes are located alongside supermarkets of the Golden Truly chain also owned by a company headed by Sudwikatmono. While by most accounts cinema does not constitute a major part of his empire, it seems to be integrated into the overall structure of his corporate network through linkages with banking, real-estate and construction and retailing. While denying charges of creating a monopoly, Sudwikatmono has indicated in published interviews that he expects to expand his interests in cinema to as much as 30 per cent of an 'integrated film industry' including production.

Producers of Indonesian films have been vocal in their criticism of what they see as the effective control of Subentra over the entire system of film exhibition in Indonesia. In the early 1980s, when the idea of cinema complexes with their small, intimate screening facilities was first broached, there was considerable enthusiasm about these amongst the artists and workers of the film industry. Some expected that this would provide for non-mass appeal films and eventually encourage the growth of an Indonesian art film circuit. As the Indonesian 'sineplexes' emerged, linked to big business interest in import monopolies, not only did that hope prove to be false, the new style cinemas further disadvantaged Indonesian films in comparison to imports.

A 1975 decree, issued jointly by the Minister of Information and the Ministers of Internal Affairs, and Education and Culture, had made it obligatory for every theatre to show at least two Indonesian films every month, one starting on the first Thursday of each month and a second on any following Friday of the same month and showing for at least two days each. This secured Indonesian films some 10–15 per cent of the total available screen-time. Since the quota referred to each theatre, given that the legislation had no way of anticipating the multi-screen theatres more than a decade before their establishment, the new cinema complexes could stay within the law by screening Indonesian films on only one of the three to six screens of the theatre, thereby giving local productions proportionately less screen-time.

But by the late 1980s, Indonesian cinema's industrial politics could no longer be framed entirely in terms of the old contradiction between imported films and local production alone. Since 1972, when the government started legislating single film import agencies into existence and establishing import quotas, the Motion Pictures Export Association of America (MPEAA), which represents all of the major Hollywood studios (MGM, United Artists, Warner Brothers, Universal, Disney and 20th Century Fox), had periodically expressed its concern over its reduced access to the Indonesian market. In 1988–89, for the first time since the expulsion of the American export agency in 1965, the MPEAA openly entered into the fray.

Factors in the international film market may have partly determined MPEAA's latest interest in its Indonesian market. But a number of developments within Indonesia made MPEAA's interventions economically interesting and politically possible. In terms of the overall Indonesian economy since the mid-1980s, various factors had rendered the government more malleable to pressures of international capital and less able to protect state-allocated monopolies of its client conglomerates.[11] With many of the monopolies being dismantled, international (particularly American) interests were able to put pressure in areas where state support for monopolies continued, such as in rattan (controlled by another presidential crony, Bob Hassan) and in film. Also, by the late 1980s the Indonesian consumer market had grown large enough to generate a rise in American interest in it.

The MPEAA blamed the lack of competition for the reduced prices that their films could now command. And, for the first time since 1965, American films were facing serious competition from other imported films, particularly from Hong Kong and Taiwan. Traditionally, while Chinese films had a substantial following, they played mainly in what was classified as 'B' class cinemas, in the Chinese quarters of the large cities. But as Subentra came to acquire the newest and best cinemas in greater numbers, Chinese films imported by its subsidiary, Suptan, found a new place in theatres where previously only American and European films would have played. American films seemed to be adversely affected by this competition. In most years since 1985, the number of European and American films imported has been well below what the quota allowed. Available statistics, undependable as they are, indicate a slow rise since 1986 in Hong Kong films' share of the total audience and a corresponding fall in that of American films.

The resentment of some Indonesian producers and directors against Sudwikatmono's politically protected monopoly was so great that by around 1988 they were willing to make common cause with the American agency against Subentra. Some contacted MPEAA offices in Singapore secretly to negotiate various ways of dealing with Subentra. Others took a public stand in favour of MPEAA's demand for 'the right to distribute directly to the cinemas without a middleman'.[12]

In 1989, at the instigation of the MPEAA, Indonesia was included in the US Trade Department's 'watch list' for unfair trading practices. In June 1991, after three years of intense negotiations involving US diplomats and various Indonesian ministers, MPEAA dropped its demand to distribute directly and agreed to work through two Subentra subsidiaries.

Cinema is only the first and most intensely controversial of the media monopolies of the Suharto family. Private television, established since 1989, is entirely in the hands of presidential relatives. Reportedly similar incursions into the press are starting as well. Film-makers and other media workers fear the potential of these monopolies to dictate media content in the interests of particular political and economic lobby groups, without even the modicum of accountability to the society that state censorship has historically required.

*Production*

Of the three sectors of the film market – production, import and distribution – production is the most difficult to discuss as an institution. Although some major New Order business groups have had film production companies, most producers are comparatively small-scale entrepreneurs. Nor do producers necessarily have financial control over any particular production since many films have invisible financial or political backers, who are not named in the credits. On the other hand, businesses or individuals who have not contributed financially to the film are sometimes named because, as one producer said, it seems 'advisable' to do so. After the banning of television advertising in 1981 this was further complicated by national and international advertisers with consumer products to sell 'sponsoring' films to carry their messages.[14]

The financial insecurity of the producers makes them sensitive to the slightest hint of government disapproval since they cannot afford to have their films held up by the censors. Mostly of Chinese or Indian descent, many of them are insecure about their status as Indonesian citizens.

Ever since the 1950s government departments and sections of the military had used selective funding of films as a means of propaganda. In the 1970s two companies, closely associated with state functionaries, were set up. The first of these was PT Safari Sinar Sakti Film Corporation which grew out of a group of performers who went on the Golkar (the government party in the Parliament) campaign trail for the first post-1965 general election in 1971, helping to attract crowds with entertainment. Although no prominent Golkar politician is directly involved in the company, most people working in the film industry regard it as a Golkar company. The second company, Metro 77, started as a film unit of the Jakarta Metropolitan Police under the initiative of Colonel Abbas Wiranatakusuma in 1974.

The most overt use of films for government propaganda has been through the Perusahaan Film Negara (PFN), the State Film Corporation. PFN (whose early history was discussed in Chapter 1) had stopped producing feature films in 1962. After 1965 it operated mainly as a film processing studio, and produced a few newsreels and documentaries. In 1978 PFN was given new tasks and resources. During a brief period when Secretary of State Sudharmono was *ad interim* Information Minister, he installed Brigadier General Gufran Dwipayana as head of PFN. Dwipayana was a member of the personal staff of the President (Aspri), especially responsible for matters relating to the mass media. He was, in effect, the chief presidential image-builder. Under him PFN was committed, for the first time in its history, to big budget feature films about the head of the state.

The three most expensive films made in Indonesia in the early 1980s were produced by Metro 77 and PFN. Given the small size and financial weakness of the production sector, film-making by groups closely associated with the government became, in the early 1980s, a significant factor in Indonesian cinema.

## Government censorship

Censorship is the most visible aspect of government control over the form and content of films. Until the mid-1980s when attention shifted to import monopolies, censorship was the most intensely discussed aspect of cinema in Indonesia.

Pre-censorship as a condition of production distinguishes Indonesian films not only from their imported counterparts but also from all other local private sector media. Inherited from the Dutch era, the Board of Film Censorship (Badan Sensor Film, BSF) is the oldest and most persistent of the institutions of Indonesian cinema. BSF, however, is only part of the story of New Order censorship. The scenario of a film requires approval from the Directorate of Film of the Department of Information before shooting can start. At the completion of the shooting, the rush copy (unedited prints) needs to be submitted to the same authorities for guidance about what may need to be edited out.

Since the abolition in the early 1970s of the government subsidy programme for which the submission of scenarios was originally required, the official justification (which film producers largely accept) for this first step in censorship is that it protects financiers against investing in a film that will ultimately be banned by the BSF. In some instances a scenario may be referred on to other departments with responsibility for issues and subjects contained in the film, as an attempt to make pre-production censorship less arbitrary and more responsive to specialists. It works as a discreet kind of censorship which affects fewer people, causes little open friction between the government department and those involved in the industry and rarely gets into the press.

Both before and since 1965, local military commanders and local governments have, from time to time, arbitrarily stopped films, passed by the BSF, from circulating in their areas. In the mid-1970s attempts were made to regularise these regional interventions. In 1975 Regional Film Development Bodies (BAPFIDA, Badan Pembinaan Perfilman Daerah) were set up at the provincial level. BAPFIDAs were appointed by the governor, headed by the regional chief of the Department of Information and made up entirely of government department representatives including some from the security agencies. The *raison d'être* for their establishment was to ensure that Indonesian films secured a fair share of the market in the provinces. But in 1977 the BAPFIDAs were also made responsible for censoring films to be screened in their provinces. Unlike the BSF, they cannot cut or in any way change a film, but they can ban it in their provinces or areas thereof. In practice, this power has been used only sporadically and often ineffectively. Nor has the formalisation ended arbitrary bannings by local military authorities. But it has acted to caution film-makers about offending the sensitivities of regional authorities.

## The Board of Film Censorship

The Board of Film Censorship (BSF) is in law the only agency of film censorship. Every film produced in or imported into Indonesia must be presented to the BSF, to be seen by a committee usually made up of three members. If this committee cannot arrive at a common position on a film, it is presented to the full membership of the board. The producer or importer of a film that has been rejected by the initial three-member committee can also request that it be reassessed by the plenary board.

Boards of censorship, with different names, have existed as long as there have been Indonesian films. The first one was set up by the Dutch in 1925. Even in the time of the revolution (1945–49), the Republic had its own film censoring body in Jogjakarta, though it looked at only two films in four years! Under the Dutch, censorship, primarily concerned with security, was under the Department of Internal Affairs. After independence censorship was placed under the Department of Education and Culture reflecting a new attempt to take cultural and social factors into consideration. Until the early 1960s, the censorship board was responsive to socio-cultural sensitivities and popular pressure. Through the 1970s, however, the BSF's openness to the society at large and its willingness to accommodate pressures, apart from those coming from important state functionaries, declined markedly.

In 1971, some of the members of the BSF made an attempt to open the institution to the wider public. In August 1971, the BSF started a monthly bulletin called *Berkala BSF*[15] intended to allow the public access to the internal workings and discussions of the BSF. Arief Budiman, a 1966 student radical appointed to the board in 1968, wrote the introduction to the issue. He distinguished between censorship in a democratic society and in an authoritarian one and expressed the hope that the bulletin would allow the society to understand as well as direct and influence censorship policies.[16] The bulletin's first and only issue reported in detail the discussions about three controversial films censored in the preceeding few weeks. Had the periodical not died in its infancy through lack of interest and funding, it would presumably have been abolished or unrecognisably altered in 1973, when measures were taken to make the internal workings of the BSF strictly confidential, so that meetings were no longer minuted but taped and the tapes held at the BSF. Access to them required the special permission of the Director General of Radio, Television and Film.[17]

The changing composition of the BSF since 1965–66 indicates its transformation, to all intent, into an arm of the government's security apparatus. For 15 years, from June 1950 to May 1965, the chair of the censorship board was held by two women. Significantly, since 1965 all four heads of the BSF have been men. On a board of 22, later 37 members, women have rarely filled more than the two, later three, positions reserved for women's organisations.

As recounted in Chapter 2, the New Order BSF actually came into existence before October 1965. This board, convened in May 1965, was made up of 24 government representatives and nine from the political parties. The government departments most heavily represented were Information, and Culture and Education with ten members each. When Budiarjo became Minister of Information in 1968 he replaced that board with a much smaller one with a substantially reduced government representation. Three years later, in tune with the growing weakness of parties in the Indonesian political system, political parties were excluded from the BSF. The board of 1971–72, which included well-known intellectuals and artists, has been seen in retrospect as the most liberal and open since 1965.

The relative autonomy of the BSF was eroded quickly after 1973 and the ideal that Budiman expressed in the 1971 *Berkala BSF*, that the institution should represent various social interests and not just those in power, was replaced by an increasing emphasis on the interests of key government departments. The BSF was put under the control of the Director General of Radio, Television and Film (Dirjen RTF), who was its *ex-officio* chairperson. The Executive Director, responsible for the day-to-day working of the BSF, was also drawn from the Department of Information. The 1973–74 board had 20 other members, two each from seven government departments (Information, Interior, Religion, National Defence and Security, Foreign Affairs, Education and Culture, and the Attorney-General's Office) and two each from three non-governmental groups, namely the journalist's union (PWI), women, and the nationalist 1945 Generation (Angkatan '45).

Representation of government departments and especially security agencies was further increased by Ali Murtopo in 1979. The number of members was raised to 37 including the chair and executive chair. The other 35 members were divided into four sections, responsible respectively for Indonesian, European and American, and Asian films, and video cassettes. The heads of these made up the 'core group'. Indonesian and European and American films were under two representatives of the Department of Information, Asian films under BAKIN (the intelligence coordinating body), and video cassettes under the attorney-general's office. BAKIN also had two other representatives on the board, the attorney-general's office had three others and the police department a total of four members. Government departments thus made up more than two-thirds of the BSF, over a third of those from its security arm.

### Censorship criteria

Through much of its history, censorship was based on a 1940 Dutch ordinance, promulgated to 'fight the dangers to morality and dangers to society that are related to the screening of films'.[18] This ordinance laid down that every film had to be examined from three perspectives: morality, public security, and whether it was 'coarse or could be deleterious from any other perspective'. These very general criteria were interpreted to exclude quite different kinds of discourses in different political circumstances. Immediately after 1965 they meant excluding any hint of atheism and flags of socialist nations.

In 1977 the *Censorship Guidelines* (*Pedoman Sensor*) were laid down in a ministerial decree. Further guidelines were drawn up in 1980, by the BSF itself, in the *BSF Ethical Code* (Kode Etik Badan Sensor Film, henceforth *BSF Code*), which were further elaborated, as mentioned earlier, in the Film Council's *Code of Ethics* (Kode Etik Produksi Film Nasional, henceforth *DFN Code*) in 1981. The attempt to publicise and standardise censorship rules is in part the result of the insistence of the industry, particularly the producers, to gain access to the BSF standards, in order to avoid making films which will be truncated or banned by BSF. The government also has an interest in reducing cases of overt intervention, since every such case is an acknowledgement of conflict between the authorities and a section of the community.

While the BSF's public relations pronouncement emphasises censorship of sex and violence (and the *BSF Code* does have a section on what constitutes pornography and what is consequently not permissible), most of the regulations relate to the security of the state and the nation as well as its current rulers. Both the BSF documents (the *Guidelines* and the *Code*) instruct that films are to be banned if they are deemed to be able to 'destroy the unity of religions in Indonesia', harm the 'development of national consciousness' or 'exploit feelings of ethnicity, religion or ancestry or incite social tensions'. *DFN Code* recasts the BSF proscriptions as positive prescriptions. Accordingly Indonesian films need to express 'the harmonious co-existence of religions' and 'mutual respect for the practice of faith in accordance with the religion and belief of each person'. Films are also urged to show 'how Indonesian people put unity, unification as well as the well-being of the nation and the state above personal and group interests' and particularly to include episodes 'which emphasise the values of ... national unity'. Further, films are forbidden to 'project scenes which show the conflict of one religion with another'.[19]

The political section of the *Censorship Guidelines* sets down the ideo-logies not to be expressed in any form. This includes colonialism, imperialism and fascism along with all manifestations of communism. While it is hard to think of any film banned since 1965 for containing ideas of imperialism, colonialism or fascism, films have been banned for directly or indirectly containing what the BSF regarded as Marxist ideas. (However, *Max Havelaar*, discussed in the next chapter, was banned for ostensibly being both Marxist and imperialist.) At the Seminar on the Ethical Code of Indonesian Film Production (1981), General Sutopo Yuwono, a former head of BAKIN, explaining the nature of sectional conflicts not allowed in films, started with conflicts between 'the rich and poor'.[20]

The political section of the *Guidelines* also states that films are to be banned if they are regarded as harmful to 'Indonesia's internal or foreign politics' or 'in conflict with policies of the government'. Further, crimes can only be depicted if they were shown to be punished. The *BSF Code* adds to the list of prohibitions anything that could cause damage to persons or institutions associated with the state. The *DFN Code* points out the responsibility of films to exclude 'any statement which may lead to the decline of the community's trust in the organ-isations of justice' and specifically forbids mocking of the 'upholders of law and order', and showing police officers being killed at the hands of criminals. It provides that in stories involving kidnapping, the child must be returned unharmed by the end of the film!

I will have occasion to discuss the interpretation of some of these regulations in relation to particular films in the next section of the book. What is clear is that films are not only expressly banned from criticising any aspect of the state's function or power, but also barred from discussing many aspects of social conflict. The latter restriction relates to a general understanding throughout the media that religious, ethnic and other collective identity conflicts can only be talked about with the greatest caution.[21] By 1980 censorship regulations had become detailed, comprehensive and public, contributing to the increase of self-censorship in the film industry and increasingly reguiarised government censorship that was less and less affected by the arbitrariness of its functionaries. At the same time the clarity of the restrictions also identified for film-makers the spaces where dissent was still possible. Ironically, as later readings of film texts will show, censorship does not only restrict, it also creates the conditions for film-makers and audiences to experiment with form and meaning to get around the spirit of the censors, without seeming to contravene their words.

## The audience

The audience is not an organised entity like the institutions discussed in this chapter so far. At one level, it is a collection of disparate and unpredictable individuals. But at another level the audience is a structure in as much as the concept of an audience affects not only the textuality of each film, but is fundamental to the construction of cinema as a public sphere to be culturally, politically and economically controlled.[22]

Wilbur Schramm, in his influential work on the mass media, wrote that:

> the citizens of the developing countries, for the most part, are meeting radio and film before they are exposed to print, and therefore we can reasonably expect that both these media will have an importance and a vividness for such countries that they have never had in a country where printed media were highly developed before the audio-visual ones appeared.[23]

Successive Indonesian governments have justified censorship on the basis of a similar view, that cinema reaches the non-reading, illiterate, and therefore unsophisticated and easily influenced, masses. So who watches movies, particularly Indonesian movies? And more importantly, who conceptually conjures up this audience and its characteristics?

Undependable as statistics are, data from the Indonesian Statistical Bureau (BPS) provides the first construction of the audiences. During the 1980s the total number of film audience was at around 130 million a year, having reached over 144 million in 1980. Figures from 1987, relating family expenditure to film-watching, indicate that those most likely to go to the movies are those whose family expenditure is over Rp. 100,000 per month (i.e. that section of the population considerably better off than the average worker, on a daily rate of Rp. 2,647).[24] However, movie-going drops dramatically for groups with family expenditure over Rp.300,000. From 1970 to 1982 Jakarta accounted for about a fifth to a quarter of the annual total theatre audiences, and in 1981–82 over a quarter of the revenue from the sale of tickets.[25] In the late 1980s Jakarta's share of the total audience had declined to about one-sixth. Somewhere between 30 and 40 per cent of the spectators overall watched Indonesian films in the 1980s. No statistics are available as to what economic group the Indonesian movie-goers come from.

Statistics, however, do not correspond exactly to the film industry's own construction of its audiences. The BPS numbers which come from regular theatres in the cities and larger towns exclude the seasonal theatres, popularly known as *bioskop misbar* (that is, *kalau gerimis bubar*, literally 'disperse if it rains'). They ignore, too, the audiences of mobile cinemas (*bioskop keliling*), which since 1974 have been obliged to screen only Indonesian films.

No figures are available regarding the numbers of people who see films on these temporary screens, *layar tancep* (literally 'screens stuck in the ground'). Occasional, open-air screenings, organised by the mobile cinemas, are largely a rural phenomenon. However, even in the *kampung* areas of Jakarta,[26] which are within easy reach (15 minutes on a motorbike) of three or four movie theatres, one occasionally sees hundreds of people gathered around a *layar tancep* show, put on to celebrate anything from the election of a *lurah* (head of the *kampung*) to weddings of its more prosperous residents. One sample survey of 13 provincial capitals in 1971 showed that 11 per cent of those surveyed had seen films through *bioskop keliling* and that about 40 per cent had seen films in situations other than established movie theatres.[27]

In rural areas, where there are no established theatres and where the mobile cinemas operate on a regular basis, these serve the overwhelming majority of the audience. Those involved in the mobile theatres say things have come a long way since the 1950s when villagers were so unfamiliar with the film medium that some used to run away during shots of approaching cars or trains thinking they would be run over! In the early 1960s there was one mobile film company with three units (car, screen, generator and projector) in Java. By the mid-1970s this company had around 20 units and there were dozens of other smaller companies throughout Indonesia.

By 1980 the success of the mobile theatres was so evident that the police-department-owned film company, Metro 77, was considering setting up its own fleet of *bioskop keliling* in its bid to carry its propaganda films down to the village level. While this indicates that the rural audience has greatly expanded, the actual number of villagers who watch these screenings is virtually impossible to estimate. Often the screenings are paid for by a sponsor whose goods are advertised at intervals during the show. Even when tickets are sold, open-air screenings are inevitably watched by many more than those who pay for them. An office-bearer of the union of mobile cinemas (PERBIKI) estimated that by the late 1970s mobile cinemas were regularly visiting at least 80 per cent of villages in Indonesia.

While this seems unlikely to be the case in the remote areas of the country, audience surveys conducted in Java indicate that Indonesian films are indeed reaching large sections of the rural population. A 1979 sample survey in nine villages in three provinces of Java indicated that over 90 per cent of the villagers between the ages of 17 and 60 had seen at least one Indonesian film in their lives.

Conventional wisdom within the film industry is that foreign, particularly American and European, films cater for the comparatively prosperous and well-educated sections of the big city population, while Indonesian films are watched by the working classes of the big cities and people of small towns. One can readily observe in any major city in Java that American films, and since the mid-1980s Mandarin films, run in the most expensive theatres which cater for the wealthy. In Jakarta the most expensive theatres, which are located in the elite residential areas of Menteng and Kebayoran Baru, generally show Indonesian films only for the minimum obligatory period. The most expensive half-dozen Jakarta movie theatres have constantly sought to be released from any obligatory screening on the grounds that their clientele does not watch Indonesian films. Producers and distributors suggest that Indonesian films run longest in the cheapest theatres in Jakarta. In small towns, where there are only one or two theatres with little or no price discrepancy, local and foreign films run in the same place. Here the *becak* driver and the local government official go to the same hall. In small towns, therefore, it becomes even more difficult to surmise what sections of the population see Indonesian films.

BPS figures for 1984 indicate that the largest segment of audience for all films is drawn from the 15–24 age group, followed by the 10–14 and 25–29 age groups. Figures from 1987 suggest an older audience with the 30-pluses watching almost as many films as the 15–24-year-olds and considerably greater than the under-14s. Producers as well as censors seem to believe that largest section of the Indonesian film audience is made up of teenagers. Since the mid-1970s, the large number of films with teenage protagonists, based on novels that had sold successfully to young readers, demonstrates a recognition by the industry of its young audience. New female stars who have appeared since around 1976 have been very largely young fresh-faced women who made their initial impact playing the roles of urban high school kids. In the late 1980s the top grossing films, the Si Boy series, were based on a popular teenage radio programme and dealt entirely with lives of late-teenagers.

On any Friday afternoon or Saturday evening near the old Rivoli theatre (opposite Proyek Senen) or the somewhat more up-market Megaria (on Jalan Proklamasi), small motorbikes and *bebek* (motor-scooters) are far more evident than cars. Many more films screened in these theatres are Indonesian compared to, say, New Garden Hall, Kebayoran Baru's most expensive theatre, which screens Western films 90 per cent of the time and whose parking area has more cars and taxis. Rivoli and Megaria cater for the expanding urban middle class, sons and daughters of largely white-collar workers in the government and private sector, or small-scale business people. This is not the Menteng crowd or the fashionable set of Kebayoran Baru, but the sort of people who live in the new housing estates mushrooming all around Jakarta.

The phenomenon of pop novels and comic books being made into films also indicates a substantial overlap between some sections of the reading public and film audiences. Kimman (1981, following Eapen and Gunawan Mohammad) suggested that the total reading public is about 10 per cent to 15 per cent of the population (although nearly 85 per cent of the population under 30 is statistically literate). He argues that the overwhelming majority of these live in cities in Java and up to half of them in Jakarta. He distinguishes between four categories of readers: occasional readers, pictorial readers (that is, those who read pop novels and comic-strips), newspaper and magazine readers and, finally, book readers.[28]

Newspapers, both tabloids and serious dailies such as *Kompas* or *Sinar Harapan* (renamed *Suara Pembaruan* in 1987), regularly carry film reviews and other articles about cinema, particularly Indonesian cinema. The popular tabloid paper *Pos Kota* carries advertisements of Indonesian films every day and has for years run a special weekend issue on films, *Pos Film*, which carries pictures and gossip, largely though not exclusively, relating to Indonesian films. Its non-Indonesian component consists mainly of news about 'kung-fu' movies and sometimes photographs of voluptuous heroines of Italian 'spaghetti westerns'. *Tempo* (perhaps best described as Indonesia's *Time*) gives roughly equal space to Indonesian and Western (mainly American) films, and almost never reviews Indian or Mandarin films. The popular women's magazines include coverage of Indonesian stars and starlets in almost every issue and some run movie-star fan-mail columns. But the serious dailies which cater to the educated carry regular advertisements of Chinese and American, rather than Indonesian, movies. Certainly *Kompas*, the most prestigious daily, carried far fewer ads for Indonesian films in 1991 than it did in the early 1980s, suggesting that movie owners and distributors do not regard the *Kompas* readership as the target audience for Indonesian films.

Those who read pop novels, comic books and subscribe to popular tabloids are the prime target for the first run of the Indonesian films in the second ranking theatres, where tickets cost around Rp.2,500 (well over the minimum daily wage of Rp.1,600, which many workers still do not get). By the time a film reaches the villages, three or four years after it has been made, and earns Rp.50 per spectator, the return on the film is economically insignificant. It is the aesthetic and social values of the urban, largely middle class, and 'reading' public that must be taken into account by the producers and directors in making films.

This is the 'significant' audience from the point of view of those who make and market the films.

The top margin of this significant audience is marked by the more sophisticated, more highly educated sections of the urban community. They are on the fringes of Indonesian cinema's viewership, and the effort of film-makers to reach them is evidenced in the more complex and experimental films as well as in the attempts of some film directors to open up contacts with universities.[29] At the bottom margin of this audience are large sections of the urban poor, the unskilled industrial workers, pedicab drivers, footpath traders, domestic servants and so forth. Efforts to reach this group are seen in the film versions of the cheap, roughly produced comic serials like *Si Buta* and *Tuan Tanah Kedaung*. These films generally play at *kampung* theatres, where tickets are under Rp.1000. These, unlike the pop novel films, do not get into the more middle class theatres like Megaria.

The government's censorship rhetoric may emphasise the importance of shielding the illiterate masses, who are the potential audience of Indonesian films, from undesirable influences, but the practice of censorship seems to recognise the appeal of films to the urban middle class. That is why *Di Bawah Lindungan Kaba'h*, a film based on a novel by the Islamic leader Hamka, and deemed by the authorities to be a pro-Islamic political film, was not allowed to be circulated in Jakarta before the 1981 general election. That is also why *Petualang Petualang*, a film exclusively addressed to the rich and young of Jakarta, was unrecognisably altered by the BSF. In 1982 I sat through some showings of censored segments organised by the BSF. None of the cut films were the cheap productions aimed at the bottom end of the market which is the mainstay of the rural and *kampung bioskop misbar* and *layar tancep*.

What relationship any real audiences bear to the audiences conceptualised in the state bureaucratic, market capitalist and film aesthetic discourses cannot be resolved easily, certainly not without much greater empirical research into audience behaviour. Nor is it essential from our point of view to find the 'real' audience. What is important for the analysis that follows is that every film is made, and therefore needs to be read, in relation to the hypothetical practices of a hypostasized audience.

# TWO

# Society and Politics in Film Texts

# 4

# Narrating the Nation for a
# Military State

[A] historical film is for today's audiences. Therefore, historical interpretation must take into account attitudes that are present now and this includes the mission for the future.[1]

The above excerpt from an interdepartmental report encapsulates the objections of the Directorate of History and Traditional Culture of the Department of Education and Culture to the scenario of *Perang Padri* (Padri Wars). The script was forwarded to it by the Directorate of Film in 1981 for expert advice. Permission to film was eventually refused.

*Perang Padri* was to be about the history of the Islamic religious wars in West Sumatra around 1800 to 1837. Neither the production company, Rapi Films, nor the scenario writer, Arto Hadi, had a reputation for making controversial films. As far as Rapi Films was concerned, it was trying to cash in on what it saw as growing audience interest in historical films.

The planned film took its name from the battles of the leaders of the Minangkabau Islamic reform movement, the Padri,[2] against the traditional Minang rulers and the Dutch. The hero was the most famous Padri leader, Tuanku Imam Bonjol, who built and lost the principality of Bonjol. The narrative opens with the young Tuanku Muda (later Imam Bonjol) arriving at the court of his father's old friend and ally, Tuanku Nan Renceh. There he trains in the martial arts and the study of Islam. The scenario then follows Tuanku Muda on his holy wars against the neighbouring regions, and his establishment of the fortress of Bonjol. The dominant discourse of the film supports unequivocally the hero's perception of the neighbouring areas against which he carries arms as 'other countries'. What unifies Imam Bonjol and his allies is their shared faith and it is for this religion that they attack and pillage the neighbours who formally follow Islam but still live by their old *adat* (traditional social laws/customs). The scenario presents these people as unkempt and dirty. Their *adat* allows them to gamble and smoke opium, and their women to go about with their limbs and faces uncovered.

After a period of peace with the Dutch, the Imam recieves the news that the Dutch have violated the agreement with him. His anger is more against the *adat* leaders than against the Dutch:

> This is all the fault of the *adat* leaders ... because they are so easy to bribe with opium and the opportunity to gamble ... yes, things that are prohibited by Islam. Their self respect is taken away and they are set to fight against each other ... . We shall not stand by and watch the unbelievers (*para kafir*) trample underfoot our honour and our faith.[3]

From this point on, the campaigns are mainly against the forces of the Dutch and their allies. Among the latter is the famous Sentot, hero of the Java wars, who has been tempted by the Dutch offer of territories to support the Dutch war against the Sumatran Muslims. Not quite sure about presenting a man regarded today as a national hero as a land-grabbing foreigner in alliance with the Dutch villains of the film, the scenario indicates that there are doubts in Sentot's mind even as he fights the Imam's forces. Having occupied the fort of Bonjol, Sentot verbally asserts the unity of Islam that he feels with the Padri warriors and claims that he has asked the Dutch to appoint Imam Bonjol's son as Regent, 'because we are all of the same religion of Allah ... we shall always defend Islam'. The statement does little to mitigate the fact that the Javanese aristocrat has been an instrument of the hero's defeat.

It is only in the last quarter of the scenario that Dutch misdemeanour leads to the breakdown of their alliance with Sentot and finally awakens even the traditional *adat* communities to the wisdom of supporting the forces of Islam against the Dutch. The narrative ends with the defeat and death of the Imam. The role of the villain is shared by the Dutch and the *adat* leaders. Also Sentot and the 'other dark-skinned soldiers of the Dutch' are not quite clear of blame as agents of the Imam's tragedy.

As mentioned at the beginning of this chapter, bureaucrats from the Department of Education and Culture who read the script judged its merits not on grounds of historical accuracy, but on political efficacy. One report, signed Sukisno Kutoyo, argued:

> Religion is a sensitive issue, and was particularly so during the period 1803–1820 when it caused war within the nation. But our need is to unify the nation. Thus it is better not to extensively expose that period; it would be better just to deal with the period 1830–37, that is the war between the Dutch on one side and the unified forces of the Padri and the *adat* community on the other ...

> Perhaps one could choose the post-1820 period, or the period 1830–37, wherein the supporters of *adat* and the Islamic forces had already united to oppose the Dutch, when the war of the Padri had in fact become the war of Minangkabau.

The second (unsigned) report made explicit the need to tailor historical discourse to fit the nationalist one:

> Seen from the point of view of history and anthropology such indeed was the situation. Perang Padri took place due to conflict of interest between the *adat* chiefs who were established and the religious groups who brought reform. However, the film-maker must have a specific mission, in the very least s/he would not wish to rake up old sores or revive old problems, to say nothing of inciting hatred. If necessary – make the Dutch the scapegoat for having cleverly set up the religious side against *adat*. There is no need to discredit the *adat* followers who are supporters of Indonesian culture.

Even in the writings for internal official consumption *Perang Padri* is deemed, anachronistically, as showing a 'war within the nation', even though the film is about a time well before the birth of the idea of an Indonesian nation, or even the word Indonesia. That assumption and the motivated obliteration of known 'facts' is not surprising if, as Ben Anderson suggests, while 'nation states are widely considered to be "new" and "historical", the nations to which they give political expression always loom out of an immemorial past.'[4]

The nation is not inscribed exclusively or perhaps even primarily through state intervention. Nor is history the only location for imagining the modern Indonesian nation.[5] But to cite Ben Anderson again 'History is the necessary basis of the national narrative.'[6]

## The New Order's historical films

Historical films in the New Order have generally ignored pre-Dutch history of the communities of the Indonesian archipelago. Discussion of the immediate past, the periods of Parliamentary and Guided Democracy, has also been conspicuously absent in New Order cinema. The silence about the events of 1965 seems especially surprising in the face of the massive anti-communist rhetoric in other mass media, such as the press and television. Until the PFN production of *Penghianatan G30S* (The 30th September Movement Treason) there was only one film set in the context of the fight against communism. Called *Operasi X* (Operation X, made in 1968), it was directed by the devoutly Islamic and anti-communist Misbach Yusa Biran and funded by the Pusat Rohani Islam Angkatan Darat, the Islamic chaplaincy for the army. It was a spy story with a historical flavour, but without the mention of any specific historical incidents or characters whose presence defines the historical genre in official and popular categorisation of films in Indonesia. The film got very little exhibition and was never released commercially.

The wariness of producers and directors regarding government sensitivity to any 'incorrect' interpretation of the coup and countercoup of 1965 would no doubt have dampened interest in the subject. A newspaper article published on 30 September 1973 offered more interesting reasons as to why there were no films about this Indonesian historical watershed. First, the article suggested, the Indonesian government's foreign policy was one of friendship towards communist nations and, therefore, overt anti-communism in films might be unacceptable to the government. But a more important reason was that 1965 was a 'family quarrel' (*pertikaian saudara*) 'in contrast to the '45 revolution where we together confronted opposition from other nations.'[7] When, in 1981, the PFN decided to make the first, and so far the only, 'historical' film about the coups that brought Suharto to power, PFN head G. Dwipayana was convinced that this was a subject matter which should only be filmed under close government supervision.

The concern not to depict 'family quarrels', which made *Perang Padri* unacceptable, and silences discussions about 1965, explains why pre-Dutch political history, a history of conflicts, defeats and conquests of one regional entity by another, is very rarely the subject matter of a film. Almost by definition 'historical' implies films set in the colonial period, usually with some reference to the resistance to Dutch rule, to Japanese occupation, or both.

Even this history was absent from films in the early years of the New Order. In the 1950s, enthusiasm for the struggle for independence made the 'revolution' of 1945–49 a popular subject for films. In the early 1960s particularly, there were a number of films funded by different military divisions depicting their role in the Indonesian 'revolution'.[8]

Directors of both right- and left-wing political persuasion made their services available to military financiers (some of those films are discussed in Chapter 2). After 1965, these factional military propaganda films disappeared for some time. Between 1965 and 1972, as far as I can tell, there were no films that could be categorised as 'historical'. The struggle for state power having been settled in favour of a particular army faction, there was no longer a place for public debate on the historical role or nationalist credentials of the various contenders. At a more general level, there was a degree of rejection of the constant nationalist and revolutionary rhetoric of the last years of Sukarno's rule. And the new legitimising rhetoric of the New Order concentrated on the present need for stability and future promise of development, rather than memories of the past.

Nationalist history re-emerged in films in the early 1970s, first as settings for war, spy or adventure movies, but increasingly in later years as the central thematic concern of films. This can partly be explained by the expanding film industry's need for greater variety in themes and plots. But the specific interest in history was related too to the rekindling in the early 1970s of the interest in Indonesia's emancipatory nationalism of the 'revolutionary' era. This was part of the student criticism of the Suharto government's policy of development with massive foreign aid. James Schiller, in his study of the critics of New Order development ideology, suggests that 'national autonomy' was a major concern of the student critics of the early 1970s. 'Critics could and did trace their concern about autonomy to the principles of the 1945 constitution, to their [students'] "struggle bodies" of the revolution.'[9] At one level, the industry was simply cashing in on the younger generation's interest in the Indonesian struggle for independence. But more, the return of history to cinema signifies an acknowledgement of the importance of national cinema to national politics after its temporary relegation in the early years of the New Order to the 'entertainment only' zone of cultural discourse. (This banishment was precisely due to the medium's radical politicisation in the build-up to the civil war of 1965. See Chapter 2.)

The political content of the students' concern with nationalism could not be privileged in a severely government-censored medium such as cinema. But the past that is narrated in cinema is inevitably marked by present divisions, including the anger of the younger generation of the 1970s against the ageing military rulers. As we will see, the nation is narrated in New Order cinema through a process of writing over – and containing (both in the senses of holding and limiting) – the differences of region, class, generation and so on, *within* the imagined boundaries even while appearing to underline the boundaries between Us– Indonesian–Nation and Other–Dutch–Colonialists. To a large extent this shift of serious concern away from the outsider, the colonial, distinguishes the hisorical discourse of New Order cinema from that of pre-1965.[10]

## The nation in history

The two most talked-about historical films until the making of the 'Suharto films' (discussed later in this chapter) were *Nopember 1828* (November 1828) and *Max Havelaar*. Directed by Teguh Karya in 1978, *Nopember 1828* swept up the overwhelming majority of the annual film awards for 1979, including Best Film and almost immediately achieved the status of a classic. By contrast *Max Havelaar*, the Dutch–Indonesian co-production of 1976, was released in Indonesia almost a decade later after numerous deletions and revisions.

*Nopember 1828* is set in the second stage of the Java Wars led by Prince Diponegoro.[11] Historians have pointed out the regional (rather than national) and conservative character of Diponegoro's struggle. Ricklefs concludes that 'the Java war was the last stand of the Javanese aristocratic elite ... a conservative movement to turn back the colonial tide.'[12] John Legge argues that Diponegoro's resistance against the Dutch was a 'local movement reflecting local discontent' which was very different from the twentieth century nationalism.[13] It would be foolish of course to search a fictional film for historical accuracy. What is interesting is how this 'local' and 'aristocratic' comes to be identified with the national and popular in the film, without ceasing to be either local or aristocratic.

A film of epic proportions, considerably longer and twice as expensive as the average Indonesian film that year, the story of *Nopember 1828* unfolds in a central Javanese village which Dutch troops have occupied on suspicion of its collusion with the forces of Sentot Prawirodirjo, one of Prince Diponegoro's principal lieutenants. The greedy opportunist village head Jayengwirono turns Dutch spy in return for money and accuses Kromoludiro, the highly respected village elder, of colluding with the rebel Prince. Kiai Karto Sarjan, the revered Islamic teacher, sends some of his students to inform Sentot of the presence of the Dutch army. Meanwhile the Dutch commander Captain de Borst tries to extort information about Sentot from Kromoludiro. In the midst of his torture of Kromoludiro, de Borst's immediate subordinate, Lieutenant van Aken, reveals himself as a supporter of Diponegoro and declares that he has been informing Sentot about Dutch military strategy. Kromoludiro is killed and van Aken put under arrest.

Eventually, de Borst is beaten by Sentot. An advance army of the Javanese commander enters the Dutch fortress under the guise of a dance troupe. Attack is launched suddenly and simultaneously by the frenzied dancers inside the fortress and masses of villagers at its gates. Before the Dutch army can recover from its confusion the bastions of the fort are broken and villagers pour in with their bamboo sticks and bows, laying down their lives in the face of confused Dutch firing. Just as the Dutch seem to be establishing their superiority, Sentot rides in, noble and resplendent on his white horse, heading a well-armed battalion. The Dutch are beaten. The village is restored to the villagers. Sentot leaves, along with the village boys who have been wounded in war, promising to return them to the village as soon as they are healed.

The story of the village becomes, in the film, the Java War in microcosm. But more than that. The language of nationalism is explicitly inserted into the film turning the struggle of the village into a struggle for the nation. At the end of the battle, as Sentot's troops are clearing away dead bodies of their comrades and taking away Dutch prisoners, one Javanese soldier in the Dutch army asks another: 'How come we weren't taken prisoners? Though we're not dead!' The other responds: 'We're of no account. Dead or alive. ... That's the way for people *without a nation*' [my emphasis].

The director Teguh Karya thinks of films as having an important 'national function' in 'a country of many islands with many diverse cultural traditions' and as 'a medium for expressing his feelings inspired by the call of his motherland'.[14] Yet his most overtly 'patriotic' film (and described as such by the film's producer) is constructed without any *real* Dutch characters (or actors) taking part in the conflict. The Dutch soldiers are not distinguished from the Indonesians in their physical racial characteristics. Ethnic Indonesians are cast in every role of the combatant Dutch, and without the kind of theatrical make-up that turns Indonesians into red-faced foreigners in folk theatre (with the exception of Slamet Raharjo playing De Borst with noticeably tinted hair and beard). The two key characters on the colonial side, the only two of whom we know something apart from their membership of the colonial army – are both *Indo*, that is part-Indonesian. De Borst, the fanatic Dutch commander, and his lieutenant van Aken, the partisan of the Indonesian side, have exactly the same ethnic and class background. In successive flash-backs we find out that both men spent their childhood in opulent mansions with loving Dutch fathers and Indonesian mothers. The child de Borst declares playfully that he wants to be a general, while the more reflective van Aken asks, 'Are the Javanese really evil?' To which his Dutch father replies, 'There are no evil people. There are only greedy persons, also amongst the Dutch.' The ambitious boy becomes a repressive colonial while the other one, by choosing to be human, becomes Indonesian.

A remarkable piece of casting establishes a visual continuum between the characters Kromoludiro and van Aken. The actors, Maruli Sitompul who plays Kromoludiro and El Manik who plays van Aken, are of the same ethnic extraction – Bataks from North Sumatra. After the execution of the (Sumatran) Javanese Kromoludiro, his visual and narrative space is taken over by the (Sumatran) Dutch van Aken. Stripped of his Dutch official uniform, tied to a pole in the same room, in the same posture as Kromoludiro, he engages in the same moral arguments with de Borst as Kromoludiro, while the camera angles collude to emphasise the similarities in their facial features (see illustrations 3 and 4). Both visual and verbal discourses then literally 'relate' the warring sides.[15]

Teguh Karya himself sees the film as primarily a story of a 'family facing disaster', and the sacrifices it makes.[16] While Teguh is referring to the family of Kromoludiro, given the comparatively small segment of the diegesis taken up by members of that family, the statement is only understandable if we think of all the other diegetic Indonesians including Sentot and his armies, as parts of a family extending out of that nuclear one at the centre of the village saga. This family is bound together by a perfectly harmonious hierarchy of age and status, where authority flows from the invisible but omnipresent (since he is constantly talked about) Diponegoro, through Sentot to the village elders, with the village youth carrying out the actual struggle. Generations are bound together in the cause, as are classes. The peasant masses and the princely army are brought together in the final assault on de Borst's forces.

'Family quarrels', so unacceptable as a subject for films, is neatly deflected on to the side of the colonials in the de Borst–van Aken conflict. There is of course division on the Javanese side as well, represented by the greedy, weak and utterly isolated Jaengwirono. But he functions only as a representation of moral degeneration making absolutely no impact on the rest of narrative and does not breach the fundamental unity of the family/nation.

The emphasis on war is noteworthy too. The war, though not visible, is present from the opening moment of the film. The village is occupied as part of the Dutch battle strategy against Diponegoro. The village youth go to one of the war headquarters when they carry messages to Sentot. The Islamic leadership supports the war in the person of *Kiyai* Karto Sarjan, who is killed by Dutch fire. The 'artists', represented by the dance troupe, join the Javanese resistance. The arrival of the dance troupe brings closer to the village the Java war that had so far been the background rather than the actual subject of the narrative. Finally, with the arrival of Sentot, the resistance in the village finally becomes one with the great cause of Java's liberation from foreigners.

With every advance in the story the war moves closer into view. The liberation of the village, the microcosm of the nation, comes as a result of the military defeat of the Dutch at the hands of an Indonesian army. The nation is thus born out of the war under the leadership of military heroes. In the spirit of official New Order historiography, national liberation becomes a 'war of independence', rather than a 'revolution'.[17]

This reading of *Nopember 1828* provides some of the clues to the furore in Indonesia over the Dutch–Indonesian co-production *Max Havelaar*, based on Multatuli's celebrated 1859 novel,[18] two years earlier. After the film was released in Holland, Lieutenant General Sutopo Yuwono, Indonesia's ambassador to Holland, reportedly wrote to the Department of Information requesting that special attention be paid to the censorship of *Max Havelaar*, since there were elements that could 'damage Indonesia'.[19] As a result, a particularly high-powered team, including the executive director and the deputy director of BSF, reviewed the film and refused to release it because 'this film humiliates the Indonesian nation'.[20]

The film deals mainly with the part of the novel that tells the story of Lebak, Banten in Java, after Havelaar has been appointed as the assistant resident. Havelaar is idealistic and committed to doing what he sees as his duty, to serve the people of the Indies in the name of the King of Holland. He attempts to curb the misuse of power by the *bupati* (the highest native official in Java under Dutch rule) and other nobles, first with gentle persuasion and then increasingly by asserting his official authority. While the exploited peasants bring him stories of their misery, they do not dare to give evidence openly against the chiefs.

Havelaar takes the matter to the resident of Banten, who is himself corrupt. All this eventually leads up to Havelaar's resignation and his desperate and unsuccessful bid to see the governor general. In the final scene he stands before the portrait of the King of the Netherlands shouting bitterly: '30 million natives persecuted, oppressed, exploited, left to die of starvation and murdered! And all this *in your name*! In *your name!*'

Into Havelaar's indictment of the Dutch colonial administration is knit the story of Saija and Adinda, an illustration of repression and resistance amongst the population of Lebak. Saija's father is one of the many victims of the *bupati*'s arbitrary and predatory power. Time after time the *bupati*'s men seize the farmers' water-buffalos. Saija and his beloved Adinda, encouraged by the *jaksa* (native legal officer working in a residency) bring to Havelaar the proof of injustice, but to no effect. In a final desperate bid to survive, Saija's father plucks up enough courage to ask to be paid for his confiscated bullock and is beaten to death. Like other young people of Lebak, Saija and Adinda eventually leave for Lampung where rebels are contesting Dutch authority. Their purpose is not to join the anti-Dutch rebellion, but to search for lost friends and family. Both die at the hands of Dutch soldiers.

What is of interest here is the reception of the film, which although technically a co-production and substantially using the Indonesian language, is, like the novel, a Dutch work on Indonesia, addressed principally to a Dutch, and by extension a liberal Western, spectatorship. The Indonesian co-director dissociated himself halfway through the shooting and increasingly in the debate that ensued in the press *Max Havelaar* came to be seen as part of a colonial imagination of Indonesia, even though there was little support for banning a film based on a novel 'which was so frequently praised by our nationalists in the past'.[21]

In a long interview, the head of the BSF gave five reasons for the banning. First, the impact of a book was not as great as that of a film. If 'the film was seen only by the small group of educated people (*kaum terpelajar*), there would probably be no problems.' Secondly, the film was too critical of the *bupati*'s abuse of power, 'giving the strong impression that the real cruelty was from the *bupati* of Lebak and the Dutch came to protect the people'. Thirdly, the role of the anti-Dutch rebellion in Lampung, which affected the people of Banten, was inadequately dealt with. Fourthly, there were unacceptable segments in the film which were not there in the officially approved scenario. The example Sumarmo gave was a scene where Havelaar jumps into shark-infested waters to save a puppy and then declares that he cannot die because he still has the '*tugas suci menolong para pribumi*' (the sacred task of helping the natives).

This, Sumarmo said, made Havelaar, a Dutchman, the 'saviour' of Indonesians. Finally, the Indonesian title, *Saija dan Adinda*, had to be changed, because the film did not explore their story except as 'appendages to the Dutch hero'.[22]

The puppy saving scene did have the potential to give offence to many Indonesian nationalists. When rebuked by his wife for foolishly jumping into the shark-infested waters, Havelaar says: 'Me dead! I've too much to do in the Indies. I've a mission to fulfil.' And the melodrama of the statement is somewhat mitigated by the response of the ship's Indonesian captain: 'That's true. But do the sharks know that?' When I watched the film in 1979 in a restricted screening for film directors and critics, the scene produced an audible disapproval from an otherwise sympathetic audience, offended at the analogy between a drowning dog and the 'natives' who were to be the target of Havelaar's mission in the Indies. However, the words in the scene are identical to those in the scenario approved by the Information Ministry.

Many of those who attended the special restricted screening suggested in private conversations that the film was not being released because the story of feudal exploitation was too much like contemporary Indonesia. The earliest article in *Tempo* about the controversy over the film hinted at this, saying Multatuli's work was 'earlier famous as an attack against imperialism and (do remember) feudalism'.[23]

Undoubtedly the depiction of vicious exploitation of the peasant masses by the aristocracy caused some concern in government circles. Even the then Vice President, Adam Malik, who favoured releasing the film and recommended it as one that should be seen by the younger generation of Indonesians, was disturbed by the representation of the *bupati* of Lebak 'because I knew *bupati*'s children too. And they were not oppressive'.[24] Although the alterations that the BSF proposed to the Indonesian producer of the film to make a release possible were never made public, it was well-known that one suggestion was the deletion of some of the scenes showing the excesses of the *bupati*.

But that did not alter the fundamental problem that made the film an 'insult to the Indonesian nation' – the absence of any notion of Indonesia in the film. The Javanese peasants and the Javanese aristocracy are presented in the film as just that – peasants and nobles with no social relation between them apart from exploitation on one side and desperate acts of individual resistance on the other. The Javanese *jaksa* who might mitigate this division cannot do so as his relation to the other natives is mediated by his location in the colonial system. In other words, though Javanese and virtuous, the *jaksa* owes his existence to colonial administration, not national spirit.

The one fundamental way in which the banned film deviated from the approved scenario was in the presentation of the character of *Kiyai*

Jufri who in the scenario attempts to rally the exploited villagers in Lebak against the 'Dutch infidels' and encourages them to join the rebellion in Lampung. In leaving out the *Kiyai*, the one symbol that made possible the imagination of a national in opposition to the colonial, the film unacceptably wiped out the idea of Indonesia. The only nation that is addressed by the film is Holland.

In the film, as in the book, the flight from Lebak to Lampung is caused by popular desperation rather than Islamic nationalism. The censors required the *Kiyai* Jufri scene to be restored to the film. Although only a brief episode, it significantly alters the reading of the Saija and Adinda plot of the film. Without the rallying cry of opposition to the Dutch, Saija and Adinda's flight to Lampung is the final act in the dispossesion of the peasant youth by the corrupt aristocracy. Saija and Adinda are driven out of their home, and finally to meaningless death. The call to arms against the Dutch dramatically changes the meaning of the departure from Java. It is no longer a *flight from* Lebak, but more an *arrival in* Lampung. Their travel links Lebak to Lampung, Java to Sumatra, against the Dutch, under the unifying banner of Islam.

It was almost a decade before the film was released, no longer just the story of class and colonial exploitation, but now containing the symbol of nationhood, in the aspirations of *Kiyai* Jufri and the martyrdom (not just death) of Saija and Adinda. The problem with *Max Havelaar* was not so much that it had good Dutch and bad Indonesians, there are plenty of those in other Indonesian films too; the problem was that it provided no space for imagining Indonesia at all.

Born out of a civil war, symbolic threats to the New Order arise not so much out of questions of its autonomy from others outside, but more from the painful memory of a blood-bath that resulted from differences within. Historical cinema thus needs to be not only cautious in the actual representations of that particular civil war, but to empty these contradictions out of all of history. With the making of the Suharto films we can see the beginning of the efforts of the regime not only to claim a role in the nationalist struggle, which is the ostensible purpose of the films, but more than that to inscribe itself into the nation's 'immemorial past', and at the same time ascribe the unity of the nation to itself.

## All the president's films

The Siliwangi Division of the Indonesian Army was the first after 1965 to sponsor films about its role in Indonesia's independence with *Mereka Kembali* (They Have Returned) in 1972 and *Bandung Lautan Api* (Bandung a Sea of Fire) in 1974. In these films the leadership of the nationalist war is clearly in the hands of identifiable sectors of the armed forces, particularly the army. By an unwritten, but never ignored, convention all films relating to military history must have their scenarios checked by the Armed Forces History Centre (Pusat Sejarah ABRI) and by the division or command to which the film refers. Not only do these films emphasise 'war' over other efforts towards independence, they all incorporate an argument against the efforts of the civilian leadership of the nationalist movement, even while acknowledging the symbolic importance of Sukarno and Hatta. The rules of the game of making films about the coming of independence are well understood, and there have been few public controversies.

The majority of these military-history films are not, of course, *about* Suharto. But the general inconspicuousness of other historical figures in these 'historical films', is in sharp contrast with the overwhelming presence of Suharto in the Presidential propaganda films.

*Janur Kuning* (Yellow Coconut Leaf), the first film with Suharto as the historical and narrative hero, was made in 1979 and released the year after. Its director, Alam Surawijaya, had made two films about the army previously. A big-budget film ('*kolosal*', that is colossal, was the description frequently given in the press), *Janur Kuning* cost an estimated Rp.385 million, almost twice as much as the average film (which at that time was about Rp.200 million), and was almost twice as long. Of the three companies originally involved in the production, only PT Metro 77 was a film company (owned largely by senior members of the Jakarta police, discussed in Chapter 3). Of the other two, PT Daya Karya Mandiri, owned by Marsudi, ex-colonel and former political prisoner[25] was responsible for the historical material in the film since Marsudi had been a close associate of Suharto during the independence movement. The third partner PT Oceanic, owned by the state-owned PT Berdikari, was to provide the funds. However, Oceanic withdrew funding about halfway through shooting. The production was bailed out of financial crisis with funds from the president himself, though this was never publicly acknowledged. Nor was it acknowledged that the state oil company Pertamina, with whom Metro 77 had a long established contact, was a major source of funding.

*Janur Kuning*, set in the context of the Dutch recapture of Jogjakarta from the republic in December 1948 and centred on *Serangan Umum 1 Maret* ('General Attack', the six-hour penetration of Jogjakarta by the Indonesian forces on 1 March 1949), is first and foremost about Colonel Suharto (see illustration 5). The film opens with a seriously ill General Sudirman, the commander of the Indonesian Armed Forces, being carried back to Jogjakarta by a contingent of boisterous, singing troops. Following closely the instructions in the scenario, the film sets Suharto out from the mob. He 'is not singing but his face looks brighter (than the rest). His demeanour is gentle and calm. He is energetic and with an easy smile.'[26] In all battle scenes he is distinguished by his calm courage and his special weapon, the Owen gun. His superior physical endurance is emphasised when, after a week-long march, the troops 'look tired, apart from Colonel Suharto, who still walks energetically'. As the men are falling behind, shifting their load from shoulder to shoulder, Suharto's superiority is acknowledged by his subordinates, as Lieutenant Suhardono says: 'Walking seven days and nights! This Suharto never seems to tire.' And Suharto's example keeps his men going.

Suharto has a paternal concern for his soldiers. When the army, resting in a village, is offered food, Suharto makes sure others have received their share before he accepts his. Suharto's concern for others is contrasted with that of the average officer, like Lieutenant Sugiono, Suharto's chief-of-staff, who eagerly receives his portion and starts eating immediately. In return Suharto's men look up to him in child-like dependence. When Suharto reappears, after he is thought to have been killed in battle, one soldier, Sudarso, runs 'like a child, rushing to its mother' (scenario) and weeps loudly on the commander's shoulder. Sugiono, who has also returned with Suharto, after being similarly presumed dead, is largely ignored by the people ecstatic over Suharto's return. The focus of the camera and the conversation is on Suharto. Several important members of the New Order government, like Suparjo Rustam, governor of central Java at the time of filming, later Minister of Internal Affairs, and Cokropranolo, governor of Jakarta 1977–82, appear as 'Suharto's men', extending their current relationship with the President into the nationalist past.

Suharto's historical importance is established at the expense of well known nationalist figures. Most leaders of the independence movement are either absent or mentioned only in passing. The roles of General Sudirman and the Sultan of Jogjakarta, Hamengkubuwono IX, received a good deal of publicity during filming but in the final product they too are peripheral figures.

General Sudirman is an ailing man, punctuating his lines with consumptive coughs, too feeble to walk without help (see illustration 6). He is a religious, God-fearing man, praying for his men at all times but never taking any strategic decisions. That he is guided by Suharto in important matters is established in the opening dialogue of the film when he is being escorted into Jogjakarta by Suharto and his Brigade X. Sudirman: 'To [diminutive for Suharto], actually I am still hesitant about entering Jogja ... This current Rum-Royen pact could be another one like the Linggarjati or Renville peace. We should keep up our guerrilla actions until they [the Dutch] have left the land of Indonesia.' Suharto argues that the situation has changed and the Dutch could not go back on their promises again. He concludes, 'Believe me, Sir.' Sudirman: 'If I refuse?' Suharto: 'The government will seem lame. The

President and the Vice-President have returned to the capital. Only the Indonesian National Military leadership has not returned to provide security.' Sudirman: 'Okay, To. I trust you.' Sudirman's faith in Suharto comes through again at the first critical moment in the film. Colonel Latief brings news of the Dutch attack on Jogjakarta on 19 December, 1948. Sudirman's first query is, 'How is Suharto doing?'

After this point Sudirman has nothing at all to do with the planning and execution of the war. Even the weapon he carries, a *keris*, is a ritual rather than a real weapon. In almost identically constructed scenes, immediately following the Dutch occupation of Jogja, Sudirman, setting out from his house, asks for and is handed the *keris* by his wife; and (in the following scene) Suharto leaving his house is handed the real weapon, the Owen gun, also by his wife. Sudirman's authority is thus spiritual and symbolic rather than real and military. But his central position in the existing popular memory and history (and mythology) of the 'War of Independence', means that his support for Suharto's every move adds to the nationalist role that the film ascribes to the latter.

The role of the Sultan of Jogjakarta, while substantial in the original scenario, was cut down to that of a passive if concerned and sympathetic observer of the army's anti-Dutch activities. In the scenario, just before the launching of 'General Attack', Suharto has a meeting with the Sultan. Marsudi, who was intelligence officer under Suharto at the time of the battle, and was the producer responsible for the historical material in this film, remembers that such a meeting did take place. The Sultan has also asserted that he met Suharto *before the attack*.[27] But the film presented the version that the President favoured – that he met the Sultan only after the attack. This ordering of events takes away from the Sultan any claim to initiative in the political strategy of planning the attack.[28]

In the film, the only pre-March 1 contact between Suharto and the Sultan is a letter sent by the latter after hearing a Dutch radio broadcast denouncing the freedom fighters as mere bandits. 'The Dutch are forever telling the world that our national resistance is in total confusion. That our national army does not exist. Only thieves and extremists remain. What is your opinion?' For all the secrecy and trouble involved in delivering the letter, its content is entirely pointless in the development of the story. Its only point is to show the Sultan as bewildered by Dutch propaganda, looking to Suharto for guidance.

Suharto stands alone as the man of action. Very early the senior civilian and military leaders are discredited for failing to come up with any definite response to the Dutch attack on Jogjakarta, the seat of the republican government. As the Dutch mount an attack on Jogjakarta's Meguwo airport, Suharto receives a message that 'a meeting is on ... the Sultan, Hatta and General Sudirman are at the meeting'.

Suharto: 'No decision yet?'

An aide:'Not yet, sir.'

Suharto 'sighs deeply ... looks disappointed' (scenario) and, despite the indecision of the higher authorities, rushes off to take action against the Dutch. This is about 25 minutes through the film. No civilian leader is mentioned again apart from the Sultan (and he in only three short sequences).

Nasution, one of the best-known military leaders of the 'war of independence', is conspicuously absent and his famous Siliwangi Division is disposed of in a single one-minute sequence. Suharto asks Zulkifli Lubis (head of Military Intelligence in Jogja): 'I hope the Siliwangi division will help in the defence of the capital of the Republic?' Lubis: 'Unfortunately the Commander of Java and Madura has given instructions for withdrawal.'

Given the extent to which Suharto and his Brigade X of Diponegoro Division are idealised in their effort to maintain a military presence in Jogjakarta, the Lubis sequence amounts almost to a betrayal by Siliwangi for moving out of the Jogjakarta region. Nasution (commander-in-chief of the Java Command in Jogjakarta 1948–49) is damned without even being mentioned by name.

The Dutch recognise Suharto as the real leader of the guerrilla movement. In a discussion regarding the success of the Indonesian army a Dutch military officer says, 'This is definitely not Sudirman's planning because we have been after him constantly ... . The action is well-organised and coordinated ... . There's got to be someone behind this ... .But who?' The answer is in the next scene. A spy brings the news that 'the name is Suharto.' Sudirman is mentioned only to deny him any credit for the guerrilla resistance to the Dutch.

The interpretation of the events of 1948–49 in this film has shifted in Suharto's favour even compared with the version presented in the Armed Forces Museum opened in 1972. A series of dioramas in the museum depicts the history of modern Indonesia. The period dealt with in the film, 1948–49, is shown in a set of three dioramas, noting the high points of the nationalist movement in that period. The 1 March 1949 diorama, the last of the set, stresses the importance of the six-hour 'occupation' of Jogja by Suharto's brigade, and the political and military significance of the event, in terms that are very similar to those of the film. But the diorama for 19 December 1948, the date on which the film's narrative starts, relates to Nasution. Titled *The Siliwangi Long March*, the caption reads:

> Once more the soldiers and the Indonesian people underwent severe trials during the Second Dutch Military Action, 19 December 1948.
> Because a *Dutch attack was expected* [my emphasis], Col. A.H. Nasution as the commander of the army and territory of Java issued an order known as

the *Strategy Number One*. One of its main points: the duty of the Indonesian troops to penetrate behind the enemy lines and to form force pockets so that the whole island of Java would become an extensive guerrilla field. One of the elements involved was the Siliwangi unit. They marched from central Java to pre-determined places in West Java ... the well-known Siliwangi Long March.

This interpretation clearly denies the existence of any plan to defend the capital, which in the film Suharto calls upon the Siliwangi to do. The Dutch attack was expected, rather than unexpected as the film would have us believe. And what coordination of guerrilla actions there was, was due to Nasution's strategic planning rather than Suharto's tactical actions. The film by contrast suggests that the capital should have been defended and perhaps could have been but for Nasution's mistake in ordering most of the troops away from Central Java, thus leaving Suharto who heroically, if hopelessly, tried to defend the city.

While the Siliwangi's move away from Jogja is criticised in *Janur Kuning*, a 'long march' is created in the film for Suharto and his men. Once Jogja is definitely lost, Suharto organises a nocturnal guerrilla presence in the city and then leaves with some of his close associates on a seven-day march from Jogja to Gondok to Godean to Sleman to Piyungan, in each place giving instructions to local commanders. At the end of the march Suharto and his troops climb an unidentified hill and sleep on the bank of a river in Plered. Given that all these places are within about a 15-kilometre radius of Jogja, the week-long march is somewhat unconvincing! There seems to be very little reason for it except to create a competing myth to match the Siliwangi's celebrated Long March.

The period between 19 December (Dutch occupation) and 1 March (*Serangan Umum*) is the history of interaction between the brave Indonesian army (that is, Suharto's Brigade X), the Dutch occupation forces, drunk with alcohol and hubris, and the *rakyat* (the ordinary people), helpless victims of Dutch brutality, needing the Indonesian army's protection (see illustration 7). The only positive contribution that the *rakyat* (men and women alike) make to the struggle is to provide food for the army and in one scene some women smuggle arms for the soldiers. Although early in the film both Suharto and Sudirman express confidence in the 'people's strength' that will defeat the Dutch, for the rest of the film Suharto is deeply concerned to 'protect the people'.

The diegetic *rakyat* themselves confirm the army's assessment of their need for protection, rather than their potential for resisting the Dutch. Noticeably, no member of Suharto's army is ever captured by the Dutch. Apart from the first surprise attack on the airport, only two soldiers fall in battle scenes that constitute about a third of the film, while masses of ordinary people are tortured and killed throughout the film, especially in the early scenes of Dutch occupation of Jogja.

In one scene Suharto says: 'How they [*rakyat*] provide us with food ... . Because they still believe that we will remain their protector and defender ... . But if we become cowards, cannot protect their interests, they won't even give us water out of the well if we ask for it.' He sighs, pats his distinctive Owen gun and adds, 'We must act.' This action is *for the people's* protection, but it is *by the army*.

When planning the March 1 attack Suharto expresses concern about the effect of a daylight attack on the 'people', particularly Dutch retaliation against non-combatants. Lieutenant Sugiono stresses: 'We [the army] must demonstrate to the Dutch that the people have no part in this.' The *rakyat* see themselves in the same way. In one characteristic scene of Dutch torture, an elderly man is dragged out pleading '*Kulo rakyat biasa*' (I am only one of the ordinary masses) and shot dead. Other captured men sit trembling in fear. The *rakyat*–army relations are thus grounded in two assumptions: first, that the army is completely distinct from the people and, second, the people need the army to protect them against injustice and suffering.

The women, similar to the *rakyat* in their dependence on the army, have another role. Rather extraordinarily for a film which is mainly focused on war, there are two pregnant women. Suharto provides vitamins from the army supply for one of them and, more importantly, Suharto's own wife is in an advanced stage of pregnancy from the moment she is introduced into the film. Suharto sees his first-born child immediately after the climactic assault on Jogja. In their first dialogue in the film, the concerned wife asks about his war, the concerned husband asks about her pregnancy. Suharto's and Sudirman's wives each fulfil the duty of suffering quietly to allow their soldier husbands to attend to theirs. Notably, the wives are without names apart from 'Bu Harto' and 'Bu Dirman'.

The narrative culminates in the General Attack of 1 March 1949. The attack turns into a celebration while the Brigade X is in the city. Dutch reinforcements arrive and the Indonesians retreat. Then follows a series of short episodes, not a coherently connected story but linked visually.

As the guerrillas retreat, the Dutch Commander charges the Sultan with helping them, but is unable to take over the palace in the face of the Sultan's resolute personal opposition. Cut to:[29] a brief union between Suharto and his wife. They part with Suharto saying he is waiting for the news of deliberations between the Dutch and Indonesian authorities at the United Nations. Cut to: the UN building and a voice over: 'The eyes of the world have opened to the young Republic.'[30] Dissolve to: the Sultan and the Dutch signing an agreement for Dutch withdrawal. Dissolve to: Withdrawing Dutch forces and advancing Indonesian army. The movement from the General Attack to the Dutch-Indonesian agreement to Dutch withdrawal establishes a visual continuity between historical incidents, where a narrative connection cannot be established.

Most press reports and reviews reconstructed the film in this way: After Jogja was captured by the Dutch, guerrilla actions by the Indonesian army continued with great success under the leadership of Suharto, who finally took the decision to carry out a daytime attack on Jogja to prove the ability of the armed forces. In the March 1 attack, Suharto's troops held Jogja from morning till noon. The show of force resulted in international recognition of the young republic and caused the Dutch to withdraw.[31] The movie-Suharto's conclusion about the result of Indonesian military action was that 'the Dutch left Jogja because they lost the war'. In an interview published in *Tempo* four years after the making of the film, the President said that the daytime attack on 1 March 'had a political purpose', and that although it lasted only six hours 'it was extremely significant'.[32]

*Janur Kuning* drew enormous press attention and official support during its making and distribution. The first special screening, on 1 March 1980, was attended by the then governor of Jakarta, Cokropranolo, and Vice-President Adam Malik. The film opened for the public on 11 March, another symbolic day of the New Order calendar, as part of the celebration of Super Semar, which brought Suharto to power in 1966.[33] Although involvement of the first family in any aspect of the film was loudly denied, the state secretariat was known to be coordinating the distribution of the film. Papers reported rumours and official denials that public servants in some provinces were being forced to watch the film, but there were 'government as well as private concerns' which were making arrangements 'so that their employees could see the film.'[34] The secretary general of the Department of Internal Affairs, on behalf of the minister, instructed the governors to facilitate the distribution of the film. In order to get the film distributed quickly, particularly in provincial towns and rural areas, KONI Pusat (National Sports Co-ordinating Body) was given the responsibility of pushing through exhibition of the film, as it was supposed to have good organisational networks down to the village level. *Janur Kuning* was entered in the ASEAN Film Festival held in Manila in 1981. Colonel Marsudi was the only private producer whose fares were paid from the ASEAN Cultural Fund. At the same time, the film failed to win any awards at the Annual Indonesian Film Festival. The New Order art establishment, so committed to depoliticised art, rejected its unabashed and unrelenting propaganda. It failed in the bid to become the 'great historical epic' that its makers had intended.

Even before *Janur Kuning* started to be distributed, plans were being made for the second Suharto film. Brigadier General G. Dwipayana, who headed the government's film production company PFN, felt that matters related to the person of the president were the concern of the state and that a private body, no matter how strong its links with the important members and institutions of the government, should not be allowed to make films about him. Brigadier General Dwipayana had long been a member of the president's personal staff, especially responsible for palace publicity. His two jobs came together when PFN decided to make *Serangan Fajar* (The Dawn Attack), which was to be even more expensive and epic than the first Suharto film. Arifin C. Nur, a prominent playwright and film director, was engaged to direct the film, in a bid to make not just a propaganda film, but a 'good and artistic' film. The attempt was successful – the film won six awards at the 1982 Indonesian Film Festival, including Best Film and Best Director.

Set in central Java in 1945, after the defeat of the Japanese and before the return of the Dutch to Indonesia, *Serangan Fajar* has three interlinked stories: the story of the aristocratic family, the story of the poor family and the story of the 'War of Independence'. The last of these moves around four confrontations between the Japanese and the Indonesian army divisions led by Suharto. These are not presented as chronological developments but rather as fragments of the nationalist movement, which is the context in which the two fictional stories unfold.

The first to be introduced is the story of an aristocratic family, headed by Handoyodiningrat. He, his wife (without name and referred to as *ibu*, mother) and their three adult children, the eldest son Danur and the two daughters Darun and Sito, are all caught up in the revolution and the war. Danur and Sito are members of youth brigades. Darun and her mother remain aloof from the political revolution raging outside the high walls around their residence. Handoyodiningrat's own commitment to nationalism is clear, but the nature of his involvement is not known. We know more about his attitude to the social revolution which he dreams will obliterate social hierarchies.

The idea that the revolution is breaking down differences between classes is worked out mainly through the romantic involvement of Sito with Ragil, a servant in the Handoyodiningrat household, and a comrade-in-arms of Danur. Despite the revolutionary comradeship between Danur and Ragil, the latter continues to call Danur *Ndoro* (master). It is Danur who in his generous egalitarianism asks to be called by his name. The social revolution is not one where the traditionally lower status people demand and win equality, but one where equality is handed to them as a gift. (It is interesting to think about the difference between this New Order interpretation of 'revolution' and that of some of Bachtiar Siagian's films discussed in chapter 2.) In the more problematic relationship between Sito and Ragil, the aristocratic mother opposes their union strongly, but her husband is determined to bless the liaison. During this conversation between them we discover

that Ibu Handoyodiningrat is of very humble origins herself, and that
her husband married her in the face of his family's opposition. The
true aristocrat, therefore, retains an egalitarian, socially revolutionary
image, while the opposition to the social revolution comes from a social-
climber out of the lower classes. The exploration of the consequence of
this inter-class relationship between the aristocrat's family and that of
his servant is avoided since Ragil is killed in the war.

Parallel to the aspiration of the controlled-from-above social revolution runs the aspiration of nationalism. Once again the verbal expression
of national unity comes from the aristocrat-nationalist. At two different
points in the film Handoyodiningrat talks about the unity of Indonesia.
In the opening sequence, at a meeting of the extended family, he is
taken to task by a younger member for not really talking about affairs
of the family. To this Handoyodiningrat asks: 'What extended family?'
and answers himself: 'We are all entering a new chapter in history. Our
extended family now is the one called Indonesia.'

Later in the film, when Anonim, a Sulawesian soldier and Ragil's
friend, brings the news of his death, Handoyodiningrat reflects how the
declaration of Indonesian independence has obliterated the differences
between people from different islands. The dissolution of ethnic differences through the process of the nationalist struggle is played out in
the relationship that Anonim establishes with Ragil's relatives. He brings
the family the news of Ragil's death and ends up spending his leave
with them. There is a hint of romance between Anonim and the war-
widow Sibu (literally 'the mother', Ragil's sister). There is a surrogate
mother–son relationship established between him and the old woman,
Simboh (Sibu's mother-in-law), who has lost all her sons in the war.
And for Temon (Sibu's son), Anonim almost immediately replaces Ragil
as a caring uncle, playing the same games and having the same conversations. The common war against a common enemy thus brings
together the people of Java and Sulawesi. Neither Temon nor the
women consciously have much appreciation of what the struggle for
independence is about, but they are drawn into the vortex of the unity
that the nationalist movement is establishing throughout Indonesia.

The resolution of regional differences, however, is on the basis of the
centrality of Java in the new set of relationships being established by
the revolution. Not only is the story set in Java but all the characters,
apart from Anonim, are Javanese. Anonim describes himself as an
orphan, a child of the oceans, who has never known any family or
relative. The war of independence brings him to Java, where he finds
a surrogate family – a child without a father, a wife without a husband,
a mother without a son. Anonim's identity crisis (for he is 'anonymous',
without a name) is resolved only by his achievement of an Indonesian
identity, which also binds him with Java.

While the unification of classes and regions is explained in terms of the nationalist movement, and the newness of this unity is emphasised in the statements of the intellectual aristocrat, nationalism itself is seen to be rooted deep in the past. Simboh, the old village woman, thinking of all the men of the family who have died in war, says:

> In this old house the long history of human beings is now in progress. People are born, people die. People come and people go. All this is homage to this earth. Since the days of Sultan Agung, since Prince Diponegoro, to this day and into the future people of this house will be used as sacrifice (*tumbal*) to keep away evil.[35]

The choice of the names of the early Javanese enemies of the Dutch Empire makes the sacrifice of life going on in the narrative's present part of a long historic tradition, which Suharto inherits, since he is the one now leading the sacrifice.

Suharto is introduced into the aristocratic storyline through Danur who takes part in battles where Suharto is in command. Danur is a member of a youth militia made up of impetuous, adventurous young men liable to err. Suharto, as member of the official army, relates to this group as one responsible for guiding, controlling and protecting them. He relates to the poor villager storyline in the same manner since Ragil is involved in the youth militia activities. But he also has a more complex and subtle connection with the poor villagers through Temon with whom he comes together in a single vital shot.

Temon is the central character in the story of the poor village family. The name is a pun on the Javanese version of *temuan* which means meeting or finding. Throughout the film this young boy (five or six years old) is seen waiting and searching for a father he has lost and adopting other fathers when he cannot find his own. To the director, Temon was 'the spirit of the revolution. A metaphor about searching for a father.'[36] When a youth brigade attacks the Japanese headquarters in Jogjakarta, Temon finds his way to the Japanese officers and demands his father. Every time a train passes through his village, Temon runs to the railway lines and waits for his father. In the last scene of his waiting, the frustrated child throws a stone at the fast-moving train and the camera holds the image of a very small and lonely figure against the background of the wilderness and the railway tracks passing through it. A link is established between Temon's fatherlessness and his helplessness. In the following scene, a despondent Temon comes through the trees just as Suharto and a group of his men are passing by in an open truck. As Temon had often called out after trains, he calls out after the truck *bapak* (father), and Suharto turns around for a split second before the truck passes out of sight. This is the very last scene where Temon will call out aloud for his father. In that single shot Suharto is established as the ultimate father to the poor boy in the village. Temon, the spirit of the revolution, finds a *bapak*, a leader and protector.

The character Temon finally adopts as father is an aeroplane mechanic in the Meguwo airport which Suharto has taken from the Japanese and is handing over to the Indonesian Republican Air Force. His name is Bagong. He and his friend Petruk provide the light relief in the middle of battle scenes. The names are important, since Petruk and Bagong in the Javanese version of the epic *Mahabarata* are sons of Semar. In the traditional theatrical form, *wayang*, Bagong, Petruk and their brother Gareng, along with Semar, are the clowns of the show and servants of the mythical Pendawas, the family of good and brave kings. Known as the *punakawan*, their task is not just to serve the kings but also to advise them. In a way they mediate between the masses and their venerable protectors, the *satria* princes.

The film uses *wayang* tropes quite consciously.[37] *Serangan Fajar* opens with the vision of a rumbling mountain covering the expanse of the cinemascope screen evoking a *wayang* opening, with the *gunungan*, the mountain-shaped symbol of the universe, casting its trembling shadow across the white screen on which the story or *lakon* is to be played out by the leather puppets. The symbols would not be lost on a Javanese audience and would reproduce in the film some of the structured relationships of the *wayang* world, putting the Indonesian freedom fighters at par with the *satrias*, and Suharto, as the bravest and calmest of the soldiers, at par with the best of them, Arjuna. The relationship between Bagong and Temon can be seen as the *punakawan*'s intermediary position between the commoner and the *satria*. The narrative connections between Temon, Bagong and the *satria* Suharto bind them into a continuum of father–child, protector–protected relationship that goes back to the very mythical roots of the Javanese society.

Though perhaps less deliberate, mystical allusions also underlie the earlier film *Janur Kuning*. The title, meaning yellow coconut-palm leaf, was chosen partly because coconut-palm leaves are used for ceremonial decorations. Brigade X wore palm leaves on their arms as a mark of identity during their guerrilla resistance in Jogjakarta. The original title suggested by Marsudi, *Janur Kuning Sakti* (Yellow Coconut Leaf of Supernatural Power) was rejected by the rest of the film team as too dramatic. A symbolic connection is made in the film between the ritual/spiritual use of dry coconut leaves and the identification mark of the Brigade X. As Suharto instructs his officers to use *janur kuning* as a mark of identity, the music changes to *gamelan*. This is followed by a moment's silence and the shot of a woman making ceremonial decorations with dried palm leaves. When the camera returns to the military headquarters, the officers are uttering 'Janur Kuning', one after the other, like a *mantra* (religious/spiritual chant).

Both the Suharto stories are structured, like a *wayang*, around a sequence of confrontations between the heroes and their enemies, ending in a climactic battle in which the *satria* triumphs over the demons and other trials placed in his way. *Janur Kuning* contains three such battles, exactly like the conventional *wayang* performance; *Serangan Fajar* has four. In *Janur Kuning*, Suharto's calm and controlled aggression is contrasted not only with the crudeness of the Dutch commanders but also with the over-enthusiasm of some of his lieutenants. Like the *wayang* heroes, Suharto also has his special weapon, the Owen gun. The greatest *wayang* warrior, Arjuna, is identified with his invincible arrow, before which no mortal can survive. In *Janur Kuning*, the scenario constantly refers to how Suharto points or holds or pats his 'Owen gun'. The camera draws attention to the special weapon in Suharto's hand in many a battle scene.

Though *Serangan Fajar* runs along three separate narratives and incorporates layers of meanings at the junctures of the different strands, both the Suharto films build into a remarkably unified set of meanings. Suharto appears as the central revolutionary figure, owing his protective leadership relation to the people, not merely to his immediate revolutionary activity, but (particularly in *Serangan Fajar*) by some inexplicable genealogy through which he inherits the historic and mythical mantle of royal heroes of the past. Suharto is moulded into the shape of the ideal ruler with a brave and loyal army, a generous and supportive aristocracy, and a unified population. He simultaneously inherits the nation and also makes it.

### The nation for an ageing New Order

There is little in the New Order historical films about Sukarno or Hatta or even about the youth militias. During the publicity campaigns for *Janur Kuning* there was much talk of Metro 77's (the producers of the first Suharto film) plans, which never materialised, to make a film about Sukarno and Hatta. It is difficult to know if they seriously planned such a film or were simply publicising it in order to be able to say that they were a group of committed nationalists keen to recount the contributions of the nation's leaders, rather than just Suharto propagandists. But history of Indonesian independence in New Order cinema is largely the history of the TNI, the Indonesian Armed Forces, particularly the army.[38] Even when films are about a time preceding the TNI, they are overwhelmingly about martial heroes in protective relationship to the 'people'.

But why is it that overt propaganda for Suharto in films appeared nearly 15 years after the regime established itself? The answer probably lies in both opportunities and perceived needs of the Suharto regime.

In 1978–79, flush with oil revenue, the government had the chance to put funds into comparatively less significant areas such as film production. The state-owned PFN (as noted in Chapter 3) had a substantial facelift in 1978–79. Metro 77 was also formed with oil money from Pertamina. Also in 1978 PFN came under the control, for the first time, of a member of Suharto's personal staff. However, the importance of this availability of funds should not be exaggerated. After all, in the context of state and corporate spending, films don't cost that much money.

Perhaps the important reason for the Suharto propaganda films was that the regime felt that new efforts were needed to justify Suharto's long and repressive control over the country. According to Abbas Wiranatakusumah (producer of *Janur Kuning*), by the end of the 1970s the time had come to remind the people, especially the younger generation which did not know the nationalist movement and did not remember 1965, that 'Pak Harto' had served the country well in the past. Brigadier General Dwipayana similarly insisted that the PFN film was a timely lesson in history, particularly for the younger generation.[39]

One needs to ask why in the late 1970s was there this urgency to 'educate' the community, particularly the younger generation? Why did this project of rekindling 'the spirit of national unity' involve the centrality of Suharto in a way that put him apart from and above military officers of the 1945 generation as a whole? Part of the answer may lie in the way in which, in the late 1970s, first serious student criticism of the President himself coincided with the fairly widespread criticism of the Suharto government from amongst prominent members within the military itself.

Student criticism of the Suharto government had surfaced periodically since 1970. David Jenkins suggests that in 1970 the student movement was primarily concerned with corruption. By 1974 'the area of student concern had expanded to include economic nationalism and the activities of Suharto's personal assistants'. By the end of 1976 'it was Suharto himself who was under direct attack.'[40] In 1977 student leaders in Jakarta nominated their own candidate for the presidency – Ali Sadikin, the dynamic ex-governor of Jakarta, and one of the retired generals who were increasingly critical of the Suharto government.

Jenkins also describes the way in which 'concerns about the political directions of the Suharto government' were expressed more and more frequently by groups of retired officers in 1977.[41] By the late 1970s, he shows that the various grievances of retired generals 'came together in one major current of dissent … . By 1980, there was a broad and somewhat unique alliance between a number of retired senior officers and "retired politicians" with linkages to the student movement.'[42]

The propaganda films are not, of course, a direct response to this alliance of dissenting forces in the way that imprisonments or buying off critics are. They are, however, part of the wider effort to broaden the appeal of Suharto, as someone unique and not comparable with even the other ABRI men of the '45 generation. That Nasution and Siliwangi are chosen as a target of implied criticism in *Janur Kuning* may well have to do with the fact that the retired military critics of Suharto 'included a disproportionate number of former Siliwangi officers, and that Nasution exercised a continuing influence over them.'[43]

*Serangan Fajar* had built into it an appeal to the young with its little boy Temon, its teenage lovers Sito and Ragil and its advertising emphasis on the *pemuda* (young revolutionary) Suharto. PFN was also particularly concerned to make a highly sophisticated film, employing a director whose artistic credentials were well-established among the students and intellectuals, particularly in Jakarta, in order to be able to reach these educated sections of the community. The publicity for the film emphasised not just its historical validity but also that it was a piece of good art. The director, in the forefront of the publicity for the film, constantly described it as poetry or music, influenced by values of humanism, patriotism and art books![44] The film was recognised for its artistic achievement and awarded every important prize at the FFI 1982.[45] There was a serious effort, too, to get *Serangan Fajar* accepted at the Berlin Film Festival since international recognition would boost the film's persuasive powers with Indonesia's urban students and intellectuals. The pursuit of international recognition was unsuccessful.

One further point needs to be made about the Suharto films, and the historical films of the New Order in general. In a speech in early 1980 the President listed the possible threats to 'our national ideology' as 'Marxism, Leninism, communism, socialism, Marhaenism, nationalism or religion'.[46] To the usual list of the New Order's banned philosophies Suharto had added nationalism, religion and Marhaenism.[47] By the late 1970s opposition to the Suharto leadership did indeed draw on at least three variants of nationalism: a revival of Sukarnoism, an anti-dependency cultural and economic nationalism, and the Islamic variant of the latter. One can see the Suharto propaganda films as an answer to these nationalisms, with the New Order's own brand of it. It is, however, an unusual kind of nationalism, where the nation is not imaged in a strident opposition to the West or any other outsider. It is difficult to imagine a 'war of independence' without the conflict with the colonial Dutch. But in *Serangan Fajar* the Dutch are absent and the Japanese are marginal.

Benedict Anderson has suggested (as mentioned in the introduction to this book), that at one level the coming of the New Order was a victory of the state over the society and the 'representational' and 'participatory' interests of the nation. The historical films of the New

Order (despite what their sales pitches say) cannot be read as nationalist texts *per se*, because anti-foreign nationalism itself is a threat to the New Order, which was created in opposition to the radical nationalism of Sukarno and has continued to be challenged by its anti-Japanese and anti-American nationalist critics. The Suharto propaganda films particularly are best understood as privileging a discourse of corporate hierarchy (represented in the films by the hierarchy within the diegetic families, households and the military) which suits the bureaucratic needs of the state, over the voices of contending social forces such as ethnicities, classes or generations.

# 5

# Telling Tales of a Class Society

Almost every new film that is produced shows an excessively luxurious lifestyle: the actors' clothes, in the latest fashion, are never crumpled throughout the film, the decor of houses is like that found amongst oil kings, and the night-life is that of those people who have too much money.

... Our question: when will dilapidated shacks with their cow-sheds find a place in national cinema? When will shabby little alleyways enter films? Not cars, but bicycles and old out-dated motorbikes enter films? Not the insides of mansions but houses of petty civil servants?[1]

So commented a senior journalist in 1974. As the disenchantment with the socio-economic and cultural developments associated with the New Order became increasingly widespread in the early 1970s, so did such criticism of films like *Jakarta-Hongkong-Macao* (1968) or *Honey, Money and Jakarta Fair* (original title in English), whose very titles bear witness to their fascination with glamorous lifestyles and international milieu.

For a while after 1966, the struggling film industry was exclusively preoccupied with the new fantasies of new-found access to foreign consumer goods denied to almost everyone during the economic down-turn, and political rejection of the West in the last years of Guided Democracy. But through the 1970s the concern with continuing poverty asserted itself in opposition politics and in film aesthetics. Successive FFI juries have highlighted their concern for a 'realist' depiction of society's ills by producing statistics on the social content of films. Gunawan Mohamad analysing cinema in 1973–74 noted the sharp rise in the number of films which contained some description of the conflict and contrast between the rich and poor as a response to critical opinion of the time.[2]

In the same period (as noted in Chapter 3) the censorship regulations both in codification and implementation became increasingly explicit about the exclusion of discussions of social conflict. Caught between censorship on the one hand and the realist aesthetics of the intelligentsia on the other, the industry developed a formula for dealing with poverty which might engage the socially conscientious without enraging the censors.

## Social mobility tear-jerkers

Typically the titles indicate the terms of the first wave of exploration of poverty in New Order films: *Yatim* (The Orphan), *Sebatang Kara* (All Alone) from 1974, *Jangan Biarkan Mereka Lapar* (Don't Let Them Go Hungry), *Ratapan Si Miskin* (Cry of the Poor) from 1975, *Nasib Si Miskin* (Fate of a Poor Boy) from 1977. In these films young orphaned protagonists go from poverty to destitution until their fortunes change and they are either discovered by kind friends or relatives, or they make good on their merit and the help of kind people. Unsurprising as the stories are, the strategy by which poverty, dispossession and corruption – the targets of student protests against the government – are resolved into easy moral solutions, is interesting.

*Nasib Si Miskin* was a cheap production directed at the bottom end of the film market. The film opens with an accidental outbreak of fire in a *kampung* on the outskirts of Jakarta. When the young protagonist, Iwan, returns from school he finds his house burnt down and his mother in hospital, critically injured. In a flashback, we find out that Iwan's mother was making a living and putting her son through school by working herself to the very limits as a washerwoman. Iwan is a perfect child – obedient, polite, and helpful to his mother. He feels sorry for his hardworking mother and says to her one day, 'If father was still around, we would not be in such a state, would we?' That provides the cue for a further flashback in which we learn that his father worked in the accounting section of a factory. He was wrongly charged with corruption, lost his job, and died of a broken heart soon after. One of the key elements in the student criticism against the government – bureaucratic corruption – is mentioned only to be dispensed of as somehow unjust.

At his mother's deathbed in the hospital, Iwan protests against his fate: 'This is unfair! Why should we poor people be inflicted with such disasters. Why not the rich?' His mother calms him by pointing out that protesting against God's will is a sin. She dies. The hero slips from poverty to destitution. The film now has the opportunity to depict the life of the Jakarta destitutes and at the same time set up the ideals of behaviour for these people.

In the following sequence, the young, helpless boy walking the streets in search of a job, encounters a group of young men singing cheerfully.

> In my song
> I'll tell the tale

Of how bitter is
The fate of the poor.

Fortune and sorrow
Follow each other
Like a wheel
On the ground.

All these
Are just the trials
That is the story
Of the poor man's life.

The first stanza, which promises to tell the story of the 'bitter' life of the poor, is sung only once. The rest of the three-minute song is made up of repeating the message about non-permanence of sorrow, antici-pated happiness and the idea that miseries are only trials and tribula-tions of life, soon to come to an end – anticipating the film's ending.

The ease with which Iwan finds his first job as helper to bricklayers gives credibility to the song. He is a good and cheerful worker, but loses his job when one day he is found reminiscing about his mother, instead of working. However, he soon finds another job as assistant to a roadside car washer. Here the big rude bully, Irman, who tries to monopolise the cars, ends up with less customers than the skinny, sickly and very polite Yus, who takes Iwan on as his helper. In one scene, Yus accepts Rp.500, instead of his normal rate of Rp.750, from a couple of school-girls who demand a 'student discount'. But the next customer leaves a Rp.250 tip, which compensates him for the earlier loss. The behaviour of the rich kids who drive around in cars and don't pay the legitimate amount is not seen as unfair, while the extra the next customer pays can only be seen as a reward for Yus' good grace in accepting less than his due earlier.

In the early days of their partnership, the happy worker Iwan polishes cars and sings about the pleasure of working hard for money, as long as the money is justly gained (*halal*). Soon, however, Yus contracts tuberculosis. And when Iwan is out looking for medicines, the police raze the unauthorised shacks and take away all the residents they can find, including Yus. The rest of the *kampung* dwellers, including Iwan when he returns, huddle under the bushes at the edge of the screen and watch the carnage.

The image of the shacks burning in the night reproduces the ex-perience of many thousands of poor Jakartans (and the apprehensions of many others), who have been evicted with no explanation or com-pensation and very little warning under the government's 'Master Plan' for the city of Jakarta. As one historian writes:

> The Master Plan specified areas which were never to be built on (land set aside for roads, parks and so on) or which were to be cleared for special construction purposes such as industrial estates. Housing in this area could be destroyed when the land was thus required. A catch here was that ... the details of the plan were never made public.[3]

As a result the slum dwellers were never sure if or when they might be affected.

> From time to time, the Governor ordered people in specified areas to leave, on the pain of forcible removal. ... Land clearances were conducted like military operations.[4]

Like the protagonist, the spectators see the horrors of the demolition. But an alternative interpretation is introduced in the assurance of a *kampung* elder to the dejected Iwan:

> Be patient Iwan. Yus will be okay. He has just been affected by the clean-up (*kena pembersihan*) along with other friends ... . Usually in the shelter the sick are taken care of. You don't need to worry, Iwan. Though they may not have freedom there, their good health is guaranteed.

The official euphemism 'clean-up' is used here for eviction, instead of the more popular term *digusur* meaning 'dragged' or 'hauled'. As the narrative develops, the 'official' view, rather than what the spectators, the protagonist and other slum-dwellers actually *see*, turns out to be correct. For when we next see Yus he has indeed been looked after at a government hostel. The primacy given to statements contradicting the visual representation in the eviction scene raises questions about the validity of what the audiences *see* not just in the film, but by extension the way they see real *kampung* demolitions. The 'truth' thus rests in the official discourse – in what we are *told*, rather than in what we see.

After the eviction, Iwan starts selling newspapers along with another orphan whom he has dissuaded from begging by preaching to him that it is wrong to beg when you are able-bodied. Through an adventure involving police and pickpockets, Iwan comes in contact with a kind man who turns out to be his uncle. Not only does the uncle take in Iwan but he also agrees to look after Yus and to make a huge donation to the hostel where Yus was placed after the police raid. Both Iwan and Yus are rewarded for having accepted their poverty – which is, of course, in the film's logic, by definition temporary – in good grace and without protest.

The film starts with an explanation of poverty: it lies in the misfortune of the individual. The reasons for the hero's poverty are strictly personal – death and accident in the family. Because Iwan takes the socially and morally correct path, he always finds jobs. Of the few beggars and thieves thrown into the film as a gesture towards a realist depiction of the urban under-class, we learn nothing except that they are either dissuaded from their evil ways or punished. It appears therefore that those who do turn to begging and theft do so only because they are immoral. The central issue of the film becomes proper behaviour contrasted with impropriety. The meek and kind Yus is the foil to the rude and aggressive Irman, hard-working Iwan to the lazy orphan who takes to begging. In the end the problem of poverty is resolved by the generosity and sense of responsibility of a well-off individual (see illustration 9).

The society, as portrayed in this film (and many similar ones), permits such total social mobility that any notion of class difference is inapplicable. The hero moves with total ease and grace from being an underpaid worker to the household of the successful doctor. Analysing similar films produced in earlier years, Gunawan Mohamad comments, 'indeed almost all of these films are not social protests. ... Conflicts in contemporary films are fundamentally moral conflicts.'[5]

### Texts of New Order radicalism

There have, however, been rare films at moments of political upsurge in New Order politics, which both the state and its critics have seen as partisan to the radical cause. These films not only reveal the limits of 'social protest' in cinema, but beyond that they can raise questions about how opposition politics in the New Order constructs social classes and their relations.

Among the flood of films in 1973–74 which dealt with the poor and the dispossessed, *Si Mamad*, written and directed by Syumanjaya, has acquired the status of a classic in Indonesian cinema. It is the story of a middle-aged clerk, Muhammad, called Pak Mamad, who works in the archives section of the Ministry of Internal Affairs. He lives in slum quarters on the edge of Jakarta. The *kampung* comes alive as we follow the day-to-day life of Mamad, his wife and their five children. Neighbouring couples scream and fight in the streets, women sit picking lice out of each other's hair in the afternoon. The camera looking in provides few glimpses of the dark and dingy houses. People spend most of their time on the narrow, winding lanes, where young men dance to the simple notes and rhythm of the modern, urban, popular music, *dangdut*.[6]

The film opens on the morning of an average day in the life of Mamad's family and neighbourhood. Mamad's wife Sriti brings him some weak coffee. It is almost the end of the month and there is no money to buy coffee until the next pay day. As on every other day of his life, Mamad puts on the white suit and hat of the Dutch colonial clerk and rides his bicycle to work. People set their watches by him. He leaves home exactly at six in the morning and gets back home at three in the afternoon.

The cleaner, Juki, is the only one around when Mamad arrives at his office at 6.30. The cars on the streets and the clothes on every other person apart from the hero (or anti-hero), set the story in the 1970s. The time-frame is directly identified when we are shown the masthead of the newspaper Mamad reads, *Indonesia Raya*, which was published from late 1968 to January 1974.[7]

At precisely 7 o'clock, Mamad puts on a pair of old black sleeve-covers (another piece of out-moded colonial costume) to start work. An hour later his co-workers drift in. They are of a different generation: a young woman in a mini-skirt, and half a dozen young men in contemporary, fashionable, Jakarta attire. The head of the section, Sukma, is a graduate and a relative of the director, Pak Samblun. Both factors have contributed to his rise in the department, as we learn from a dialogue between Mamad and Juki. Mamad, who has come up to the position of a clerk from having been an office boy, greatly respects graduates and does not resent young people with education who rise to positions of power. Nor does he question that the graduate who is the director's relative should do better than others with the same academic qualifications. When Juki demands a categorical statement about nepotism, he says merely 'Don't you go looking for trouble so early in the morning!' (*Pagi-pagi kok cari gara-gara!*) Juki, who has been a menial worker all his life, serves and tolerates but does not respect or admire those who have wealth and power. He can see through the pretensions and corruption and where there is no fear of retribution, he says what he thinks. He has an empathy with Mamad because of their common bond of poverty. But Mamad's position is ambivalent – he aspires to respectability and status, and because respectability is related to wealth and success, he cannot but be in awe of the powerful and the wealthy. At the height of his personal crisis, his sense of moral outrage against himself is matched only by his fear that he will lose his hard-earned and precarious white-collar respectability: 'I'll become an office attendant (*opas*) again, Sriti ... ordered around by everyone "go buy cigarettes", "get coffee"!'

Mamad, who can barely feed and clothe his large family, becomes desperate when his wife gets pregnant with their sixth child. The scene where he learns of his wife's pregnancy is poignant and contradictory. Sriti and Mamad talk about their sense of deprivation – they cannot afford foods they once used to be able to buy. Conversation leads to her craving for durian and to the fearful acknowledgement that she might be pregnant. Her husband turns away moaning: 'Sriti, Sriti, how could you go breeding again!' (*Pakai bunting segala!*) The conversation between husband and wife about the added burden of another child is cut across with shots of young men singing a love song. The lyric is about love as an inevitable and universal human phenomenon, which individuals cannot control. There is a contradiction between Mamad's reality and the strongly held beliefs of the society, voiced in the song. The romantic social ideal is to see the birth of a child as the fulfilment of a couple's love and as a gift from God. In the context of Mamad's life, childbirth is indeed beyond his own control, but it is a curse.

Forced to find extra funds for the medical expenses of the childbirth, Mamad starts to steal stationery from the office. Close to the time of birth, Mamad takes the stationery to a shop in one of Jakarta's major shopping complexes. As he is taking the money from the shopkeeper, his boss Samblun comes in. Though Samblun pays no attention to the matter, Mamad is terror-stricken, especially when he finds out that Samblun owns the shop. Mamad runs out after Samblun, trying to explain the situation. Samblun drives off saying, 'I understand'. What is petty misconduct to Samblun, is an awful moral crisis for Mamad.

The rest of the film is a tussle between a frightened, guilt-stricken Mamad, attempting to explain his crime to his superior, and Samblun trying to avoid him. Samblun is the director of a government department and a company he owns supplies the departmental stationery. He is also a pragmatic man and a not ungenerous boss. But Mamad obsessively pursues him and blurts out his confession in the most public and unsuitable circumstances. Samblun's embarrassment is compounded by the fact that any discussion of Mamad's minor offence involves too an acknowledgement of Samblun's own, much larger, corrupt financial ventures.

The conflict, and the consequent contact between Mamad and his boss, allows the film to explore the contrast between two lifestyles, that of Mamad's *kampung* and that of the wealthy. On his first visit, Mamad finds himself in a large home surrounded by gardens and brick walls insulating it from the road outside. When he picks up enough courage to knock on the door, Samblun's children take him for a beggar and throw him out.

After various other attempts to get Samblun to hear him out, Mamad seeks the help of Budiman who, as a university student, lived in Mamad's neighbourhood and now runs a psychiatric clinic. Sriti persuades Mamad that he should have someone 'respectable' (*terhormat*) to speak to Samblun on his behalf. Budiman, a successful doctor, fits the bill. As Mamad waits for Budiman in the reception area, he seems almost like one of the patients. His frantic obsession with his petty theft is similar to disorders that have led other patients to seek psychiatric help. Budiman first tries to dissuade Mamad from pursuing Samblun any more. Failing, he agrees to go along with Mamad's plan much as he panders to the obsession of a patient who wants everyone to kiss his pillow 'wife'. They get to Samblun's house and find that he has gone to a business meeting at Kartika Plaza, one of the big hotels. Budiman seems to succeed in persuading Mamad to delegate to him the responsibility of talking to Samblun. But as soon as Budiman's car turns the corner, Mamad turns his pushbike in the direction of the hotel. Mamad's behaviour in the hotel appears totally ludicrous. His colonial whites are mistaken by the hotel's guests as the waiters' uniform. He gets lost, ends up in the wrong room and is then accused of theft. He is only saved by the timely and fortunate intervention of Budiman.

Exhausted by his efforts and tormented by guilt and inadequacy, Mamad falls ill. When he revives slightly he decides to go to Samblun's house immediately, to make him hear the confessions and take whatever punishment is due. A pitiful figure in his ragged white coat on his old bicycle, he arrives in the middle of a banquet. He seems insane as he breaks down in the face of Samblun's fury, much to the bewilderment of the guests, and is dragged out by Samblun's servants.

This time his ailment is fatal. He dies dreaming of rising into the sky in his official white clothes, a proud smile on his face. At the burial site, Budiman, paying his last tribute to the dead man, says:

> People called him Pak Mamad. But he preferred Muhammad. Muhammad has left us. And the world has lost a person whom I knew as the most human of human beings ... . Muhammad who was honest and Muhammad who was truthful. Unfortunately, he died because of his honesty. I trust that God will receive him unto Himself.

What makes Mamad a misfit is that he actually tries to live by the moral principles to which the society pays lip service. Quite literally, he is honest to a fault because honesty is a weakness in the society in which he lives. The good psychiatrist tries in vain to save him from his own obsessive honesty. But Mamad is totally out of touch with the social realities around him.

Some reviews presented the film as the story of a man who had been 'left behind by the passage of time' (*ketinggalan zaman*). But associating Mamad with the past, as Gunawan Mohamad points out, also suggests that 'all that is good belongs to the past'.[8]

## Whose film?

The film earned Syumanjaya the Best Director's award from the 1974 Film Festival jury, made up of journalists, academics and artists. But the lower-class city dwellers, whose life is represented in the central character of the film and who are supposedly the main audience of Indonesian cinema, stayed away in droves. Syuman himself, and others who admired the film, have suggested that the film failed commercially because it was 'too sophisticated' for the average Indonesian film-goer. That may well be true, but we then need to ask what constitutes this 'sophistication' which speaks of the poor and the powerless in a way that excludes those very people from participating in that discourse.

The text provides little space from which the poor, represented by the hero, can either see or speak. Mamad is given no subjective shots in the film, except in one sequence of his impossible dream for his family to acquire the lifestyle enjoyed by his boss's family. Apart from that the camera's eye rarely coincides with that of the film's central character. The camera either stands apart, giving the spectator an autonomous perspective on Mamad and his world, or it looks at Mamad from the subjective positions, mostly of the upper classes, represented by Samblun, Budiman, Mamad's young colleagues, the occupants of the expensive hotel. The sequence of his final (indeed terminal) confrontation with Samblun starts with the camera looking at Mamad side-on as he rides through the night traffic of Jakarta. When he enters Samblun's house, the camera moves between the subjective shots of several surprised guests and the outraged host, to show a diminutive creature collapsed on the floor, literally blinded by tears and confusion.

Mamad cannot speak for himself (as his failed attempts to speak to Samblun show). Budiman, the well-intentioned professional, has to speak for him with Samblun. Nor can Mamad be spoken to (as Budiman's wise attempts to dissuade him from pursuing Samblun shows). He can only be spoken *about*. Mamad is the most objectified of heros. He is the object of derision, of pity, of admiration, the object, above all, of the liberal intellectuals' (socially the New Order intelligentsia, diegetically Budiman) concern with poverty and honesty. It is Budiman too, not a member of Mamad's own class, who provides the final interpretation of Mamad's social value, at the burial speech.

Robison has interpreted the turmoil of 1973–74 as a result of contradictions between fractions of the capitalist class. The opposition came, he suggests from the 'bulk of the middle-class intelligentsia', and 'leaders of the weaker elements of the indigenous business community'. Their rhetoric of egalitarianism notwithstanding, these critics 'proved unable and perhaps unwilling to establish political alliances with workers and peasants'.[9] As in the overall radical politics of 1973–74, so in the favourite radical intellectual film of the time, the lower classes did not speak, they were 'spoken' (represented/interpreted) by members of other social strata. Mamad and those he represents are not partners in New Order's discourse of political opposition, they are only the objects of that discourse. The poor are not only represented as socially powerless, they are textually rendered voiceless.

David Morley's work on British television audiences demonstrates how the same programme can be differently interpreted by different classes and ethnic groups. Following Mattelart, he argues that the way in which subaltern groups in society make sense of media messages –

or indeed refuse to consume some of it – can itself be seen as a form of popular resistance to dominant cultures.[10] It seems reasonable to ask whether the mass audience's reaction to *Si Mamad* was in effect a rejection of the image of itself (as members of lower classes) as helpless victims, not only in the film, but in 'middle-class' and 'intellectual' radicalism of the early 1970s as a whole.

Robison describes 1974 as 'the beginning of the end' for 'the liberal intellectuals'. He goes on to say:

> Since that time the New Order has successfully devoted its energies to controlling the bases of liberal influence: the universities, the press and the civil service. By the 1980s the apparatus of control and co-option has reached a level of efficiency and effectiveness far beyond that of the 1970s.[11]

As discussed in Chapter 3, the BSF underwent a similar process of increasing government controls through the 1970s.

When in 1977–78 there was a new upsurge of radical criticism against the developmentalist myth of the New Order,[12] film-makers faced a system of censorship which was much more rigid than the one that had allowed *Si Mamad* to be released without any problems.[13] More Indonesian films were banned, cut or revised, for reasons other than explicit sex, by different sections of the censorship machinery in 1977–78, than in any previous year.

### Another critics' choice

One of the most controversial films of 1978 was *Perawan Desa* (The Village Virgin). It was held by the BSF for a year and substantially changed from its original version before it could be released. At the 1980 film festival, the film got the three most coveted awards – Best Director, Best Scenario and Best Film. Never before (nor I think since) has any film which had so much difficulty getting through the censorship process been so enthusiastically received by the festival jury and film critics at large. A close look at the case of *Perawan Desa* not only produces an understanding of the nature of the political difference between the government and its 'middle class' critics, it also raises questions about how censorship affects the production of meaning in film texts.

*Perawan Desa* was based on a criminal lawsuit of 1970. Sumariyam, 17 years old, from the village of Jetak near Jogjakarta, was gang-raped by sons of senior civil servants in September 1970. But the police produced false evidence in preliminary hearings, so that the culprits were never brought to court. Even their names were never made public although there were hints about their identity in the press reports.[14]

The film closely followed popular knowledge and popular perceptions about the rape incident. Sumira, a schoolgirl from a poor family in

Bantul village, sells eggs in the city of Jogjakarta. There are rumours in her village and in the city market-place that there have been several rapes in town, all committed by the same group of four young men, who are protected by the high offices of their fathers.

Early scenes establish audience identification with the villagers' perspective. The opening scene introduces Sumira's village, with children returning from school, women working, talking to each other and singing. The soundtrack contains the polite Islamic greeting, *assalam alaikum*, neighbourly conversation, traditional Javanese songs, and then, as the evening sets in, the Islamic call to prayer. Most of the shots are set in the street and court-yards, the communal space of the people. Even when characters move in and out of houses, the houses are open, no closed doors cutting off the villagers from each other.

By contrast the scene introducing the wealthy would-be villains begins outside the closed doors of a large mansion. Aswab Mahasin has suggested that Indonesians perceive class difference in terms of the distinction between *orang gedongan* (mansion people), and *orang kampung* (*kampung* people).[15] The film visualises this particular mode of class distinction. The *gedung* is distinguished by its high fences and gate, which separates and hides the residence and its occupants from the surrounding community. The *gedung* is the personalised space of the wealthy. By contrast the *kampung* shifts the emphasis to a communal belonging rather than individual space.

When the camera moves into the mansion, we see a crowd of young people, through a haze of cigarette smoke and red lights switching on and off. None of the characters ever looks at the camera. Their voices are indistinct, muffled by the foreign disco music, laughter and the tinkling of glasses. The spectator thus looks on from the outside, as if through a hole in the wall that separates the people inside from the wider community outside. The behaviour of those inside, like the English lyric on the soundtrack, remains unfamiliar, their drinking, smoking and dancing condemnable in terms of Islam, which the earlier village scenes established as integral to the communal life of the village.

The loud noises emanating from the house late into the night draw protests from the neighbouring community. A group of men gathers in front of the house. The spokesman for this group, and several others in it, wear a *peci*, a small hat generally associated with Islamic dress, but also part of the Indonesian national costume for men.[16] The young people inside the house are in Western attire. Their clothes could have been an ambiguous code signifying youth, modernity and/or wealth. But in this instance the clothes, among other codes, overdetermine the status of these people as 'outsiders'. The four actors who play the rapists (and who are the hosts of this party) are unusually tall compared to the average Javanese, who form the crowds in this and later scenes of the

film. When the hosts of the party emerge to face the *kampung* group
they stand on the balcony, a low angle shot emphasising their largeness
compared to the figures in the group below.

The *kampung* people are in the foreground of the shot, some side-on
but mostly with their backs to the camera. The audience thus sees the
house, and later some of its occupants, over the heads of the *kampung*
people on screen. Spectators become, as it were, the back rows of the
crowd. Both morally and visually, the film positions its audience on the
side of the *kampung* people.

A brief scene reveals the ostentatious lifestyle of the parents of the
four young criminals. Once again it is a party, where the bureaucrats'
wives exchange news of how 'business' is going for them. The scene,
irrelevant to the narrative development, reinforces the film's partisan
position within the wider political debates of 1977–78.

The rape scene is extraordinary in the context of Indonesian films in
that there is a disjuncture between the perspective of the audience and
that of the rapists. In every other rape scene I have seen in Indonesian
cinema, the woman's sexual appeal is emphasised before the rape takes
place. Whether audience sympathy is with the woman or the rapist, the
audience shares with the rapist the vision of the woman as sexually
desirable. In *Perawan Desa*, Sumira is known to the audience (prior to the
rape) as a friendly, helpful, rural, high-school student who helps her
mother sell eggs in the city and enjoys singing. The rapists see her only
as poverty-stricken and young. They don't *know* Sumira the way the
audience does. Not once does the camera position Sumira from the
perspective of the rapists. The rape scene itself is seen entirely through
Sumira's eyes, in her frightened flashbacks and her final evidence in
court (see illustration 10). The scene where one of the would-be rapists
first sees Sumira starts with the man staring out of the window with a
look of bored frustration. The close-up of this face cuts to a long shot
which positions Sumira in the foreground and the rapist at a window in
the background, looking down. As in the crowd scene earlier, the
audience is visually (and figuratively) on Sumira's side, at approximately
the same line of vision of the rapist. There is no suggestion whatsoever
that Sumira is sexually desirable to any of the rapists. The rape thus
becomes not so much a sexual act as an exercise of arbitrary power.

Sumira's parents, shocked and ashamed by their daughter's plight
and embarrassed by the publicity surrounding it, are more inclined to
cover up the incident. But sympathetic students, journalists and lawyers
come to her aid and rally public opinion against the criminals. Meanwhile, the rapists use their contacts in the highest quarters of the police
force to get protection from publicity and prosecution. The Jogja Police
Commissioner, Murtono, obliges by arresting students and journalists
investigating Sumira's case. Failing to stem the tide of public sympathy

for Sumira, Murtono takes her into custody, claiming that this is for her own security. Isolated from her friends and supporters and under police pressure, Sumira not only withdraws the rape allegation but admits to having concocted the rape story because she wanted publicity. Sumira now stands trial on the charge of misleading the public. A leading woman lawyer, Sudarsini, takes up Sumira's defence, despite subtle threats from the police.

In the court, the police produce witnesses from among the petty market traders, who are highly susceptible to official bribes and threats. These witnesses, patently false, collapse in the face of the defence lawyer's cross-examination. Finally, the terrified defendant is put on the stand. She stands mesmerised as the prosecution attorney tries to persuade her to confess to the police story. Her mind moves between memories of the rape and those of Police Commissioner Murtono's threatening gestures. She finally breaks down sobbing: 'I was raped by long-haired boys. But I was forced to say things that were not true.' The case against Sumira is dismissed for lack of evidence. She leaves the court supported by her parents and her lawyer. The final shot holds a fainting Sumira against a hazy background of faces of the sympathetic, critical and curious public, and pages of newspapers, carrying her story, scattered across the screen.

That is how *Perawan Desa* originally ended: an indictment of the law-enforcing authorities and, by extension, of the state which favours the rich and powerful. The poor and powerless majority have no protection against the powerful minority. The middle-class professionals, with the best of intentions, can do little to rectify the injustice.

The film came into BSF in 1978. The three-member board, which initially viewed the film, rejected it. The film fell foul of at least two provisions of the 1977 *Censorship Guidelines*, which prohibited films (1) that could 'encourage social tensions'; and (2) were in conflict with government policies.[17] It went to the full membership of the board. An addition to the film's ending was devised that would substantially change what the censors saw as the film's unacceptable conclusion.

The added sequence takes only about seven minutes. After Sumira's trial, three of the criminals are irate as they listen to the news of the trial on the radio. The fourth member of the gang, who has been out pushing cocaine (for the first time in the film!), rushes in, announcing that he has been spotted by the police. All four then jump into a car and try to make a getaway with the police in hot pursuit. The chase ends with a car crash that severely injures the four criminals. As the screaming ambulance draws up in front of the hospital, Sumira emerges in a nurse's uniform. She is telling an old friend how wonderful everybody has been to her and how new opportunities have opened up before her because of people's sympathy. She sees the blood-drenched and groaning accident victims being brought in and recognises them (see illustration 11). Asked at this point whether she is still bitter about those who caused her to suffer so much, she says, looking at the men on the stretchers: 'They have already received the punishment they deserve.'

Sumira, and through her the audience, has the satisfaction of knowing that the criminals did suffer, that justice was done in the end. The new ending carried a reassurance about the maintenance of natural and social justice even when institutions have failed. It ensured that Sumira saw and accepted that her tormentors had received their punishment. The rape became almost a blessing in disguise, because it had, in the victim's own eyes, brought her in contact with people and possibilities (the job in the hospital) which she would otherwise never have had. Though the rape went unpunished, the police were, in the end, instrumental in the ultimate retribution for the criminals. This, combined with earlier indications that Police Commissioner Murtono had been transferred, shifted the criticism to individual, rather than institutionalised, corruption.

Some members of the film community suggest that the reason why the film was released despite criticism against the upper echelons of the bureaucracy, and the fact that it reminded people of a case that had been embarrassing to the government, was that it had been produced by Safari Sinar Sakti, a film company closely connected to Golkar. Although the film was commercially successful in Jakarta and other cities and later represented Indonesia in a number of international forums, *Perawan Desa* remained banned in Jogjakarta, the seat of the crime and of the fiction.

During the 1950s and early 1960s films which had undergone extensive revisions at the hands of the censors or local authorities were often advertised as such.[18] Extensive censoring suggested radical content whether of the right- or left-wing variety. At a time when open ideological debates marked Indonesian politics, conflict between radical filmmakers and the government helped make films attractive to audiences. In the New Order, deliberate publicity of a film's censorship would be regarded as an intolerable affront. But while institutions of censorship can cut or revise films, they cannot guarantee how an audience will understand a film. British film theorist Annette Kuhn has suggested that the very knowledge that censorship exists may trigger off readings of a film text, which go against the conscious purpose of censorship.[19]

The seven-member jury for the 1980 Film Festival, which included very prominent writers and journalists (Mochtar Lubis, Tuti Heraty and D.A. Peransi), commended the film in these terms:

> The film *Perawan Desa* is a film of very high social relevance, extremely relevant in the efforts of the Indonesian people to search for and establish truth

and justice and [it] depicts clearly the fate of the little people (*rakyat kecil*) who suffer, trampled by injustice. The film also shows the courage of the citizens, both men and women, including journalists and youth, who become involved, individually and socially, in the defence of someone who becomes the victim of arbitrary authority.[20]

The jury's reading of the film ignores its revised conclusion. There is no reference to the work of the police, or ultimate punishment to the criminals.

It is interesting, too, that the jury saw in *Perawan Desa* 'the courage' of journalists and youth and only 'the fate' of the 'little people'. Then BSF chairperson, Sumarmo, saw *Perawan Desa* as demonstrating the efforts of professionals to bring about justice and the effort of the court to be even-handed. It is possible, too, to see the making of *Perawan Desa* by Safari Sinar Sakti, as part of the effort of some elements within Golkar to distance itself from the military elite in an effort to identify with the wider middle class.[21]

Except in a single scene where the *kampung* people confront the hosts of the noisy party, initiative lies always with lawyers, journalists, doctors and university students – all *gedongan* people, who live in walled houses and work in offices. These are the people who defend and support Sumira. The lower classes – in terms of the film's images, people who live in *kampung*s and work on the streets or markets – are victims simultaneously of other people's power and their own ignorance and conservatism. Unfounded fears of Sumira's parents literally silence them. The lies in court by the petty traders are almost as wrong from the point of view of lawyers and university students, as are the criminal acts of the corrupt rich and powerful. Both the rich and the poor are for different reasons silent or lying through the major part of the film. The truth rests in the opinions of the professional middle class – journalists, lawyers and students. Close to the ending of the original version of the film, a journalist sums up the universal importance of the Sumira case. It has, he says, received international attention because it is a case of 'law being manipulated by those who are responsible for upholding it'. The issue then is not social equality, but only equality before law.

Howard Dick has argued that the urban middle class demand for equality does not imply its own foregoing 'all but adequate subsistence until such time as all other Indonesians are well off'. It implies rather a criticism of extravagance such as owning large numbers of cars and houses and making frequent trips abroad. He has suggested that 'in terms of the middle-class values, the lavish conspicuous consumption of high civil and military officials, far from being legitimised ... by proximity to the source of political power, is regarded as an abuse.' Equality has been redefined to mean not redistribution of wealth and income but rather equality of opportunity, the 'quintessentially middle class' ideal of upward social mobility on the basis of individual merit and experience.[22] *Si Mamad* and *Perawan Desa* can be seen as part of the middle-class demands and criticisms, voiced by characters whom the informed spectator would recognise as middle-class.

It is, of course, impossible to establish how the popular audiences read *Perawan Desa*. The film was reasonably popular at the lower end of the market. Unlike in *Si Mamad*, the lower-class protagonist of *Perawan Desa* is allowed her own perspective to some extent. The film opens with Sumira's eyes looking straight back from the screen. It is Sumira's subjective shots that consistently reveal the 'truth' about the rape and the identity of the rapists. Perhaps this allowed the audience at the lower end of the market some possibility of identification with the victim (in a way that *Si Mamad* did not), and some possibility of understanding the film in a different way from the jury's (and by extension the intelligentsia's) reading of it from within a privileged middle-class discourse.

### The modernisers

The diegetic professional middle-class of Indonesian films not only interprets the society, it also reforms and 'modernises' the masses, especially the rural masses. Much of cinema's representation of this aspect of class relations coincides with the New Order government's vision of the process of modernisation and development as one where 'the elite set tasks for the masses and control the style of mass participation'.[23] Ali Murtopo, once Information Minister and one of the most powerful generals of the New Order, defined modernisation as 'changing norms which no longer function in society, as well as norms that hinder development'.[24] He described 'the people generally, especially in villages' as living in 'a climate of thought which is not sufficiently rational'.[25] It is perhaps no coincidence that during Murtopo's period as Minister of Information (1978–83), Dewan Film, which was very much his creature, exhorted films to portray 'the struggle by scientists, technocrats and others to improve the prestige (*martabat*) of the nation'.[26] At this time, too, there was a spate of films that pitted the 'rational–modern–professional' reformers against the 'rural–archaic–superstitious' masses.

Generic difference notwithstanding, the relationship between the urban professional and the rural population remains the same. Whether in a fantasy adventure such as *Primitif* (Primitive, 1978) about young anthropologists amongst stone-age tribes, or in the more serious realist film such as *Perempuan Dalam Pasungan* (Woman in Chains, 1980) about the investigative journalist, the discourse turns quickly from one of 'learning about' to one of teaching/transforming. This is not surprising of course, as 'the urban elite of any period of twentieth-century Indonesian history has tended to regard the "people" as *bodoh* (uneducated, unenlightened, stupid) and as therefore potentially dangerous and to be led rather than consulted.'[27] What is interesting is the rather obsessive focus of Indonesian cinema on the dangerous aspect of this mass 'stupidity'.

Usmar Ismail's classic 1957 comedy *Tamu Agung* (mentioned in Chapter 2) drew its laughs from the ease with which a small rural community was misled by a phoney salesman. While mass politics was condemned, in a not-too-veiled reference to Sukarnoist populism, the return to sanity in the village did not require the intervention of any superior urban character, but a critical reassessment of their actions by the villagers. Indeed the dupe who led the villagers to ridiculous and frenzied mass action was the urban outsider. And this is by no means an exceptional treatment of the rural population in pre-1965 cinema. In the 1970s, apart from a small number of films set in colonial Indonesia, mass action is always seen as misguided, related to outdated mystical beliefs, usually causing enormous harm to innocent individuals.

Horror films about ghosts, witches and cycles of revenge provide the most frequent image of the village society. In these films, resolution of the issues (that initially led to the mass action) and the demobilisation of the masses comes in the person of an Islamic teacher from outside the village. In the serious films dealing with social issues (popular and censorship discussions recognise *sosial*, that is social, as a thematic/generic category) the solution to rural anarchy comes from outsiders who are professionals.

The visualisation of these mass actions is almost identical in every film. The action always takes place in the darkness of the night, with a mob of men (always men) in dark clothes carrying lit torches. Minimal lighting is used in these scenes – at times only diegetic lighting – showing only dark shapes of faceless masses carrying fire. The mob marches from the background to the foreground of the screen, that is, towards the spectators, thus including the audience as a target of its threatening actions. Most frequently these scenes are followed by those of death and destruction. Repeated over many horror films, the image has come to represent threat associated with anarchy on the one hand and evil mysticism on the other. The meaning of this image is so well-established that a film can mobilise the dangerous implications of mass action whether or not the narrative reveals its threatening consequences. Films about the modernising professionals in villages – a popular theme with the festival juries in the early 1980s – used these images of evil magic and anarchy to construct the rural.

Made in 1978, *Dr Siti Pertiwi Kembali Ke Desa* (Dr Siti Pertiwi Returns to the Village, henceforth *Dr Siti Pertiwi*) was the first feature film with extensive propaganda for specific government developmental projects. It was produced by the Golkar-connected Safari Sinar Sakti, and two

Golkar youth organisations, KNPI (Komite Nasional Pemuda Indonesia, National Committee of Indonesian Youth) and AMPI (Angkatan Muda Pembangunan Indonesia, Younger Generation For the Development Of Indonesia). *Suara Karya*, the Golkar daily, promoted the film in its columns extensively.

Directed by a well-regarded film maker, Ami Priyono, the film narrates the adventures of Siti Pertiwi, a woman medical graduate from Jakarta, who is sent to a transmigration area in Lampung for her year of compulsory rural service. She comes up against the prejudices of the Javanese transmigrants in her charge and the *dukun* (traditional medicine man and mystic) Atuk Raja and his villainous disciple Daying Madani. With the help of Adam Rangkuti, who has lived in the village for two years as a teacher in the BUTSI (Board of Volunteer Workers) programme, she manages to win the trust of the villagers and help them with many problems of health, hygiene and superstition. At the end of her year she leaves the village, having convinced the villagers of the value of modern medicine and the goodwill of the urban reformers. The film was propaganda for the government's rural health scheme, its education programme through urban volunteer workers as set out in the Second Five Year Plan, and the transmigration programme. However, the way this propaganda is placed within the overall social construction of the film is not determined exclusively by concerns of the government as such.

One of the heads of AMPI Central Leadership Committee, a co-producer of the film, claimed that the film had a special objective of showing 'how young people, who originate from villages, want to reinterpret rural life, after they have been successful in the field of education.'[28] Yet the film emphasises the urban background of the two principal modernisers, Siti and Adam. Siti's father is a successful Jakarta doctor, and her fiancé, Bagus, a successful businessman. Her social background is reflected in her appearance. The scenario describes her as 'not beautiful nor fair skinned'. But 'her skin is smooth indicating that she comes from a prosperous family … . She wears a pair of not-too-new jeans with a long-sleeved shirt … . Her shoes are rubber, but made in Europe.' She has few attributes of feminine beauty but all the attributes of class.

Adam's background is not spelled out in any detail. The only information we have on Adam is that he is a Batak who studied in the highly respected teacher's college, IKIP Gajah Mada, in the Javanese cultural capital Jogjakarta. There are two crucial elements in the characterisation of Adam Rangkuti: firstly, the incorporation of a non-Javanese, to emphasise the all-Indonesia nature of the modernisation project but, secondly, the Javanese socialisation of the Sumatran before he can truly fulfil his role as a broker for modern Indonesian culture.

Haji Faisol, the Islamic teacher, quietly spoken, and with influence over the local population, supports Siti and Adam. He joins Siti in her first meeting with the village community leaders and quotes the Qur'an in support of the health programme. Always in white clothes associated with Muslim preachers, he is visually coded as the good spiritual power, reminiscent of many horror films, where the Islamic teacher in white defeats the black-clad evil magician.

Ranged against the doctor, the educationalist and the Islamic teacher are the practitioners of a mystical cult. Their leader is the ageing Atuk Raja. He is first introduced sitting in his prayer room surrounded by his disciples. The room is almost completely dark, and smoky with the burning incense. 'A magical atmosphere possessed all those who were present' (scenario). Predictably, Atuk and his disciples are in black clothes. Later in the film, when Adam is attacked by Atuk's follower, Daying, and his gang, Faisol appears in his white clothes, starkly clear against the darkness of the night and frightens away Daying and his men by his very presence. As they make their getaway, Faisol throws out a challenge: 'Tell your teacher to come here. Even Atuk Raja could not defeat me.' This scene again is coded alongside the horror films about the good (white) spirit locked in a cycle of conflicts with the evil (black) one played out initially by the disciples of each. The twist here is that the 'white' spirit sides with modernity and science. Islam thus gives spiritual validity to the modernisation plan, and 'black magic' becomes identified with the rural belief system.

The inevitable scene of men with torches appears about three-quarters of the way through the film with Daying and his followers moving ominously towards Siti's house. It turns out, however, that they have come only with the somewhat misguided intention of marrying Daying to Siti! Nonetheless the visual codes reinforce Daying's criminal intent and the collusion of misled villagers in this. Although not organised for a violent purpose, the nocturnal march triggers off tragic consequences.

Frustrated and insulted by Siti's rejection of his proposal, Daying retaliates by stealing the entire medical supply of the PUSKESMAS (Community Health Centre) and poisoning the village wells. Next morning, as the cases of poisoning start to come in, Siti is caught without any medicine. However, under the influence of Haji Faisol and Adam, the whole village rises to the occasion and helps Siti's tireless effort at holding off deaths until fresh supplies of medicine arrive from the city. When she collapses from exhaustion, the villagers, not knowing where to turn, take her to Atuk Raja, who by now has distanced himself from the criminal Daying. Just as Siti has been revived (possibly through the chants of the mystic, though that goes against the logic of the rest of the film), Daying comes into the room and attacks Atuk, for having taken Siti's side against him. The commotion draws in the villagers. Daying escapes, but Atuk dies. Mysticism, defined as the core of traditional practices, dead or criminalised, Siti and Adam win the village for modern science.

While the direct propaganda of this film failed to please the festival jury, other films that pit 'science' against 'rural beliefs' have done well at the festivals. But more striking was the jury's response to one film that failed to castigate the rural society as inert and put the initiative for change firmly in the hands of traditional culture itself.

## An alternative approach

*Rembulan dan Matahari* (The Moon and the Sun, 1979) is set in a village in central Java. The developmental theme in the film is the problem of getting transport for the people of an isolated rural community. The film catapulted its director, Slamet Raharjo, from a film actor to the position of the most controversial Indonesian film director. It received an award for art direction at the 1980 film festival, but the jury panel was extremely critical of the film's legitimation of Javanese mysticism.

*Rembulan dan Matahari* is a criss-cross of different plots (some of which are explored further in chapter 6) coalescing around the central figure of its male protagonist, Wong Bagus (literally 'splendid man'). My main concern here is the story of the struggle between the villagers and the villain over transport.

The film opens with a brief scene in the squalid slums of Jakarta, where Bagus has been living with a prostitute since his expulsion from the village by his spiritual teacher for contravening the rule of celibacy. In the following sequence Bagus returns home to his isolated village after seven years. Sengkuni, the local agent for a fleet of mini-buses, which are the only means of transport in and out of the village, has raised the fares in league with other bus operators.

The day after his return to the village, Bagus discovers that his teacher Wirodongso has died. The discovery is of enormous importance for Bagus. Wirodongso's death signals to him the need to truly return to take up his position in the life of the village, which is both his right and his duty. He announces into the darkness of the night, 'Tell every one … ! I am amongst them again.' The next morning, Parjio, Bagus' spiritual brother and village madman, sings down the street:

> This is Prince Gatotkacha
> Gatotkacha has arrived from Jakarta …
> Listen, chief
> Look up to the sky
> Virtue will win over vice
> Friends, don't be afraid
> and don't lose hope
> Even if Sengkuni's car does not come.[29]

The conflict in the village translates into the righteous mythological war between the Pandavas and Kauravas. Bagus is the brave prince Gatotkacha, son of the Pandava hero Arjuna. Sengkuni, like his namesake in the epic Mahabharata, is a scheming crook.

The next few scenes spell out Bagus' past and present mystical experiences: scenes of Bagus and Parjio being trained by their teacher in martial and spiritual dances, and Bagus' communication with the spirit of his dead teacher. Finally, Bagus sits in prayer which ends in what seems to be a key *mantra* (spiritual or magical chant) of his cult, or perhaps of his final coming of age: 'Tell the Moon, Tell the Sun, I have arrived.' During his communion with his dead teacher, and from then on till the end of the film, Bagus is in the same black clothes in which in *Dr Siti Pertiwi* and many horror films the evil mystics are adorned.

The village elders now appoint Bagus as the *Jogoboyo*, the protector of the village, to lead the villagers in their conflict with Sengkuni. The same night, a band of men in dark clothes with torches attack Sengkuni's house. As a gesture of threat, Bagus cuts off Sengkuni's moustache. The implications of this much-repeated image of men in mob action is redefined, as their action, for once, seems entirely justified and is led by the hero.

Mass action does have unintended negative impact. Sengkuni and his men beat up the innocent village shopkeeper in retaliation and withdraw all transport from the village so that the village runs out of its supply of essentials like kerosene and sugar. The villain is not ultimately beaten until the hero takes the punishment entirely into his own hands. Bagus confronts Sengkuni, devastates him in a fight. But his final warning serves again to justify the mass action of the earlier scene: 'What more do you want ...? You want to rob again ...? They are silent! They are poor ... .They have got nothing left! Rob them one more time, and they will express their wrath! They will turn your stomach inside out!'

Sengkuni takes the warning to heart and his buses reappear on the main street of the village. Villagers rush to fill them with produce that they have not been able to get to the markets over the past days. Grateful villagers praise and bless both Bagus and Sengkuni. The main problem of the village is now solved. The rest of the film (about 20 minutes) is given over to the resolution of the heterosexual love story and the ritual re-establishment of natural and social harmony.

The film asserts the benefits of modern transport to village life. This faith in science is also reinforced in the characterisation of Dr Simbolon, the Batak physician (interestingly non-Javanised as he needs an interpreter to communicate with Javanese-speaking villagers), who not only serves the village well medically but also takes an active role in other village problems. His efforts are supported by all the 'good' characters in the film, including Bagus and Parjio, and especially the village head's son, Darsono, who is studying medicine at the university. As in *Dr Siti Pertiwi*, the value of science and technology is accepted without qualification. But science does not appear here as an alternative way of life, a new culture to be imposed on the village in place of the traditional unscientific one, but rather as an instrument with specific use in specific aspects of the life of villagers. In fact, Darsono suggests the possibility of a villager who is scientific, a contradiction in terms of most other representations of the rural. The problem associated with technology here is not that the rural culture does not accept it but rather that its controllers misuse it, for personal aggrandisement rather than common good. The main problem of 'developing' village life then arises not from the internal structures or belief systems of the rural society, but rather from its links to the outside world, which Sengkuni and the transport system represent.

The characterisation of Wong Bagus turns on its head any notion of the improving influences of urban education on rural youth. Bagus does indeed go to Jakarta. He does not come under the improving influence of dominant class culture or institutions, but fits into the lowest end of the society, with thieves and prostitutes. When he returns to the village and becomes involved in its problems, he has to rediscover his old self, and the skills he learnt in the village from his old spiritual instructor. It is the learning he acquired from his old teacher, which he uses against the enemies of village welfare. The need to return, culturally and spiritually, to his roots before he can play a beneficial role in the life of the village is emphasised by the elaborate scenes of re-establishing his spiritual connection with his teacher, the fount of all the power and knowledge he needs. In his final reintegration with the rural social structure, he is appointed to the position of the village guard, *Jogoboyo*. It is in this capacity, as a part of traditional social structure, that he takes on Sengkuni.

Nor are the village people simply pawns in the struggle between good and bad (read 'technology' and 'mysticism' in the case of other 'developmentalist' films). The saviour is not sent to the village by some legitimate institution outside, such as the government in *Siti Pertiwi* or the newspaper editor in *Perempuan Dalam Pasungan*, but appointed through local initiative. The villagers follow Bagus in his first attack on Sengkuni. When Bagus threatens Sengkuni with dire consequences, he does so in the name of the wrath of the people.

The FFI jury had a long critique of *Rembulan dan Matahari*'s approach to mysticism:

> Fortunately in the 1980 FFI there were no entries of superstitious films like *Tuyul* (about a little pet ghost who helped his master get rich!) and its kind

which were prominent in 1979, although there is in *Rembulan dan Matahari* the story of how a figure from a village received physical and spiritual power (*kekuatan dan kesaktian*) from Javanese mysticism and succeeded in destroying a gang which had been exploiting the rural population for some time ... .

Remembering how much the challenges that face us today, and even more those of the future, demand a still sharper rationality from the Indonesian nation, if our nation wants to move safely towards the future, it is beneficial to remind all producers, scenario writers and directors to be extremely careful in the use in films of themes of mysticism, which has such enormous influence on our people, whether in the general population, or amongst the leaders and authority figures of the state. This does not mean that the depiction of mysticism must be banned, since the existence of mysticism is a reality in the community today. However, one should not give mysticism credibility by implying that with some physical and spiritual power believed to be the consequence of mysticism, Indonesian people will be able to overcome problems and challenges which they face. Should this happen, we will certainly have been diverted down the wrong path.[30]

The sharpness of the jury's reaction against legitimisation of mysticism in *Rembulan dan Matahari* is interesting because the film does not invest mystical practices with any magical powers. While Bagus' charisma to the villagers lies in his relationship to a mystical cult, the hero confronts the villain physically and verbally not magically. The physical power of the hero and his martial skills are superior to those of the villain, as in the majority of Jakarta, Bombay, Hong Kong and Hollywood films. In the case of most film heroes there is little palpable explanation of physical strength, whereas Bagus' strength is associated with the physical and spiritual training of members of his religious cult. The single supernatural segment of the film consists of Bagus' brief encounter with the spirit of his dead teacher. That is an intensely personal experience for the hero, a hallucination even, and has nothing to do with overcoming social problems, except as an element in strengthening the resolve and confidence of the hero. Nor does Bagus hand out easy solutions to anything. Although compared to the flying prince, Gatotkaca, he does not defy the transport ban by flying supplies in and out of the village! As such, the film does not bestow mystical practices with supernatural ability to cure social ills; rather it acknowledges mysticism as a legitimate part of the human belief system.

In defending *Rembulan dan Matahari*'s depiction of mysticism as a 'social phenomenon', historian Ong Hok Ham talked about the universality of elements of mysticism in the legitimation of almost any belief system or power structure. He argued that all official religions, including Islam, contain elements of mysticism, though at the same time the official religions are often concerned about personal mystical experiences which can detract from orthodox views.[31]

The problem that *Rembulan dan Matahari* presented to the jury was not so much its heterodox religious view, but more its heterodox view of the process of development (what they held up against mysticism was 'rationality' not spirituality of any kind). The film justifies the culture and action of rural masses. It argues (very much against the dominant trend of Indonesian cinema) that what the jury call the nation's need to 'move safely into the future' can be charted from within the traditional (and evolving) rural culture. This unorthodox social commentary of *Rembulan dan Matahari* was largely rejected by the festival jury.

## On naming

There is a tension in this chapter in that it swings between naming and not naming the 'middle class'. In the New Order any mention of class relations is regarded as somewhat misguided, even subversive. In official language the term 'class contradictions', common in pre-1965 political discourse, has been displaced by expressions like 'social difference' (*kesenjangan sosial*). The word 'class', rarely used, is always excised from films by censors. In *Yang Muda Yang Bercinta* (Young and in Love), made in 1977, the hero's comment 'I'm not getting stuck into your Dad as an individual. I'm attacking a symptom. I'm attacking a class', was deleted by the censors. In 1985 comments about conflict between classes in *Matahari-Matahari* (Suns) again faced the censors' knives, even though these had been construed in the text as the mad ramblings of an over-zealous poet. But while words fail, images of difference and distance between rich and poor (or in terms of the verse also censored out of *Yang Muda Yang Bercinta*, 'Those who sit, [and] those sat upon/ Those who amass, [and] those who are drained'), are clearly visible, I would argue, to any spectator.

Films focusing on the mediating role of the middle class standing between the ostentatious and the destitute were remarkably successful with festival juries during the 1970s and much of the 1980s. Although over-represented in the award-winning films, only a small minority of the total number of productions, concerned overtly with social inequality, actually construct a three-tiered society with the middle class as central to the text. The average household drama or romance or comedy is about well-fed people in brick houses, with cars or motorbikes (that is, some form of individual transport), and servants. Until the series *Catatan Si Boy* (Boy's Journals) burst into unprecedented popularity in the history of Indonesian cinema in the mid-1980s, the upper class typically defined in films by conspicuous consumption on the one hand and corruption on the other (as in *Perawan Desa*) were marginal to films – both in the sense that they appeared in comparatively few films, and that they appeared in a very limited range of roles. The majority of films are seen by the industry and the critics as being about only one class – the middle class. Analysing films nominated for awards in 1977, Taufiq Ismail, well-known writer and member of the festival jury, suggested that all but two films were about the middle class.

Given the absence of the word 'class' from the verbal discourse of film texts we need to ask what allows the recognition of the subjects of these films as 'middle class'? Part of the answer is obvious: that the textually dominant characters behave in ways that appear to mimic those of the social middle class. That begs the question, however, what is seen socially as middle-class behaviour and by whom?

No one has as yet worked systematically on the semiotics of behaviour in Indonesia. But in a highly perceptive generalisation Howard Dick suggests that the middle class is not defined not by its lifestyle's quantitative difference from the rich (who have bigger houses, more cars and so on), but its qualitative difference from the other class, the masses (*rakyat*), the little people (*wong cilik/orang kecil*). Dick argues that the crucial difference is in the 'manner of consumption' of consumer durables. 'Among the *rakyat* consumer durables are shared … . Middle-class households, by contrast, confine the enjoyment of such goods to members of the household. Fences are raised, doors are locked, and windows are barred. In other words there is privatization of the means of consumption.' He suggests further that while 'in terms of consumption patterns and lifestyles there is a fairly clear distinction between the middle class and the *rakyat*, an upper class is much more difficult to identify.'[32]

Mimetic strategies reproduce these social patterns in film texts. (For instance I have shown earlier in this chapter how the poor are shown frequently in street settings, or in *kampung* houses with open doors.) But if we wrenched the film texts out of their social context which produces the recognition of the middle class in the texts, we would find that the formal characteristics of the films' representation produce two kinds of characters which we might broadly describe as follows. (1) One group who live and act as individuals (whether they are good like the lawyers and journalists in *Perawan Desa*, bad like the police commissioner in the same film, or indifferent), and are the subjects of the film's speech and action no matter what or who the overt subject matter of the film is. (2) The second group who are collective in their lifestyle, act only rarely and only as violent mobs, and are the largely silent objects of the film's discourse. In terms of these formal distinctions in the construction of social groups, we can start to read the film texts of the New Order (whatever their overt theme and whether the setting is rural or urban) as products of the tensions between voices/individualism/domination (textual and social) on the one hand and silences/collectivism/subordination on the other. *Si Boy* with its super-wealthy kids as heroes and heroines, does not constitute a shift of focus from a middle class to an upper class, but a revision of what the 'dominant' looks like. Instead of having one or two cars and one or two servants as in many films of the 1970s, the main characters in *Si Boy* have dozens of cars and English-speaking servants! The rare films with a 'social conscience' so liked by the intelligentsia, have tried to insert a mediating middle into the narratives. But in terms of the formal representation within film texts this 'middle class' remains firmly entrenched within a dominant, and is defined precisely by its social and textual opposition to the 'little people'.

A reading of films where the 'middle' class just about disappears goes against the mainstream Indonesian discussions of films as reflected in reviews in quality papers and other similarly 'serious' writings. My purpose in tentatively proposing an alternative reading of class relations in Indonesian films is to raise questions about the assumption of a three-tiered class structure that is implicit in seeing films as being about the middle (rather than the dominant) class. I am not claiming either that my reading is in any sense more correct than those of Indonesian journalists, critics or festival juries. Nor indeed can I claim that it corresponds to the reading of any particular real audience of Indonesian cinema. Nonetheless, given the evidence in recent research into audiences that class, gender, race and cultural divisions produce quite divergent readings of the same audio-visual text, there is no reason to assume that the perceptions of film audiences from a Jakarta *kampung* or a small town in Sumatra correspond to that of the festival jury, the film censors and the professional film critics who dominate the written discourse on cinema. My own research has had little access to what we might, for want of a better term, call the vernacular, unwritten appropriations of the film texts. But if an inventory of these readings can be taken we may have to revise seriously our reading of class relations in New Order cinema and society.

Howard Dick has suggested that in the midst of all the difference over class analysis of Indonesia, the agreement is that the middle-class 'has been discovered'.[33] It is possible, however, that the middle class is seen as such (that is *middle* and *in-between*) only in the stories that social scientists, film critics and other members of the intelligentsia see and tell. For many others, Indonesian cinema (and society) may be better represented as stories of the dominant and the subordinate, without an identifiable mediating middle class in between them.

# 6

# Women's Pictures in Men's Fictions

A film for women, by women, about women's problems.

That was the advertisement for *Halimun* made in 1982, based on a novelette by a woman, A.M. Amalia, and directed by W.D. Sofia, one of the three women directors since 1965.

*Halimun* (Mist) opens with the wedding ceremony between Inu and Awit, the central male and female characters, respectively, of the film. The camera pans a crowded room and comes to rest on the bride and the groom ceremonially feeding each other. Inu feeds Awit first but turns away as she goes to feed him, so that the rice is smeared across his cheek. This still is held as the credit title appears. The ceremonial feeding of each other by the bride and the groom is symbolic of the husband and wife committing themselves to each other's welfare. Awit goes through the motions of a ceremony many in the Indonesian audience would have seen brides go through. Inu's symbolic rejection of his bride cannot go unnoticed by an audience conscious of the ritual significance of the act. We see both the man and the woman, but even from the opening shot, it is the hero's actions that tell us what is going on.

After the credits the scene shifts to the bridal chamber. Inu sits in the corner of the room, the camera follows his eyes around the room until both zoom in on Awit sitting at the edge of the bed. He imagines his beloved, Mila, sitting in Awit's place. In the conversation that follows, almost all of it Inu's tirade against Awit's irresponsible behaviour, it becomes clear that Awit had become pregnant to some unknown person and that Inu was marrying her to save her family from disgrace. Inu's flashback provides more details of his family's debt of honour which he, as the son, was paying back by marrying Awit. The flashback ends with Inu saying: 'I am prepared to marry Awit. But ... this is only temporary.'

As Awit turns away from abuse from her groom, we see her again through his eyes, as they (and the camera) focus tenderly on the curve of her back. The scenario instructs (and the film follows it accurately):

'Inu stared at the young woman's back for a long while. He felt pity for her, he wanted to touch her back, and to caress her hair.' When he leaves the room, Awit turns around and with tearful eyes watches the door close. This is the first time that we see a fleeting hint of Awit's feelings – but these are never verbalised.

The narrative stays with Inu. His disturbed state of mind is evident to his colleagues at work and to the audience. Back in the house, he locks himself in his room and breaks into a long monologue addressed to his girlfriend's photograph:

> When this is all over, I will tell you all about this. Believe me, this wedding is only a farce. Tomorrow, or the day after I will talk to Awit's mother.

We then see Inu in his university. One of his friends has found out about his secret wedding. Inu decides to save Awit's honour by indicating to his friends that he is the father of her child. In all this time we have had only one brief sequence with Awit, a single panning shot of her lying in bed, staring at the ceiling.

Inu tries to discuss the possibility of an immediate divorce but is persuaded by Awit's mother to wait till the baby is born. He decides to return to his home-town, Garut. On the eve of his departure Awit asks Inu whether she or his girlfriend Mila is more beautiful. Inu does not reply but he perceives that 'Awit is definitely more beautiful and more attractive. But she has been *stained*, whereas Mila is *clean*.' (Scenario, my emphasis.) Awit's statement thus tells us nothing about herself, but rather adds to our knowledge of how Inu is dealing with *his* two women. Inevitably, the film follows Inu to Garut, to reveal his affectionate relationship to his mother, his sister and the woman who works as domestic help for his mother. We also see Mila for the first time.

The tension in his relationship to Mila is mainly because Inu suspects her of seeing another man. In response to Mila's charge that Inu does not trust her, he says: 'I trust you. But I am worried that our relationship is being disturbed by another man.' Like Awit, who had been 'made to get drunk and then seduced', Mila is not the agent of this 'disturbance'. Both of these significant narrative actions are the responsibility of men. But the women have to bear the burden of guilt. The story of Inu and Mila's relationship is also revealed to us in Inu's flashback, as he reminisces about the past. In a tender loving scene set at dusk, Inu asks Mila: 'Do you love me?' Mila responds: 'You must finish your studies first.' She promises to wait for him, as long as he wants her to, if only he will be true to her.

Soon after he gets back from Garut to his in-laws' home, Inu gets a letter from Mila saying that she has decided to marry another man because she has found out that Inu has married another woman without telling her. Inu goes into a furious rage against Mila, throwing things around and burning Mila's photograph and declaring his hurt to the audience. Mila is given no such opportunity to state her side of the story. Mila goes out of the film as soon as she goes out of Inu's life. Inu now goes around trying to soothe his wounded spirit with other women, but to no avail. Though he soon gets over Mila, his mind runs obsessively to the woman he has married. When Inu tries to seduce Awit, she asserts herself for the only time and refuses to be treated as a 'cheap woman'.

We are now three-quarters of the way through the film. While Inu has been shown in a whole range of different social and emotional relationships, Awit has not only had less screen time, but also she has related to a much more limited world. For much of this time she is silent, unquestioning and alone. She relates to nothing apart from her womb and her reticent husband, flanked by two clownish old women – her maids. After the birth of her child she becomes more vocal, mainly to allow the film to verbalise the definition of proper motherhood. In the very first scene with her child, we find her telling the baby that she will never leave it alone.

This criticism against the working woman becomes even more pointed when Awit runs away from home with her child and the two maids. Her mother then comes to realise that all of Awit's misery, including her unwanted pregnancy, had been caused by the fact that she was too involved in her life outside the home and did not pay enough attention to Awit.

Once she runs away, Awit is lost to the narrative until Inu tracks her down. With him we discover her new life, as the two maids tell the story to Inu. Awit is now working. When she comes home from the office, we see her again from Inu's perspective – he is disturbed because she has been driven home by a man. In the conversation that follows Inu remains critical of Awit's behaviour, reminding her again and again of her past follies. However, Inu declares his intention to look after the child who, after all 'is pure and not at fault'. At this point Awit explains that she is only working to support her fatherless child. The woman is forgiven for working because she is working under duress!

The last sequence building up to the final reconciliation between Inu and Awit starts with the child's illness. Awit has to go to work and cannot take the child to the doctor because she has no money. While she is at work, Inu arrives and takes the child to the hospital. When Awit returns, once more Inu sees her being dropped off by a man, and attacks her verbally for her neglect of the sick child while 'having fun with men'. Awit faints when she hears Inu's accusation. Her fainting makes Inu realise to some extent that Awit is concerned about her child and they go to the hospital together. The doctor tells them that the child has started to recover. As visitors start arriving from Awit's office to see her baby, Inu realises that the man who he had seen drop Awit off is 'only the office driver'. That night as they both stay up at the hospital sharing their common concern about the child, Inu and Awit acknowledge their love for each other and will presumably live happily ever after.

It is impossible here to avoid parallels with Mulvey's classic critique of Hollywood narrative cinema, where the camera acts as an extension of the male gaze.[1] Both visually and psychologically, the women here are constructed from the hero's perspective, judged from his point of view. What advertising touts as a woman's film sees with the man's eyes and speaks with a male voice.

## Men's reactions

Since publishing my first article on women in Indonesian cinema in 1981[2] I have had occasion a number of times to respond to men's reactions to my readings of these film texts. Referring to *Bukan Isteri Pilihannya* (Not the Wife of His Choice), made that same year, about a woman who makes a life for herself as a working woman, then asserts her right to choose between her husband and another man (although she does return to her repentant husband in the end), Misbach Yusa Biran, a member of the FFI jury for many years, suggested in an interview with me that my understanding of Indonesian women was based on unrealistic assumptions because I came from the country of Indira Gandhi. He pointed out that *Bukan Isteri Pilihannya*, a film I 'liked so much', did badly at the festival and in critical reception generally because of an unrealistic representation of a woman's superiority to men. Some years later I spoke to a group of Indonesian post-graduates – mostly men, quite by chance – in Paris. In addition to some Misbach-like reactions, the chorus of objection had to do with the visibility of women in so many Indonesian films. Dozens of films in which female presence dominated the screen were drawn to my attention. My point, however, is not that women are absent, but indeed that they are emphatically present*ed* to be seen, and so that the film is seen (sold). Some genres of Indonesian films are precisely about seeing the woman, but not about the woman seeing or speaking.

Most recently I have been taken to task by a non-Indonesian male anthropologist. Heider finds my arguments, (in that now dated 1981 piece referred to above) that women's images are used to sell films and that women are depicted as passive, not so much unconvincing as unsurprising. Such depiction he claims is so common to all (read Hollywood) cinema, that it would be 'surprising only if it were not true in Indonesia'.[3]

He then goes on to suggest that there are many 'stong images' of women in Indonesian films. The problem with not just Heider's analysis, but with a lot of cultural analyses of gender issues in Indonesia, is that it is caught between the universalist argument that 'women are so in the West as well', and the nationalist one that 'there are images of strong women in Indonesia'. But should we take entirely for granted the gendering codes of Hollywood cinema (or any other Western textual system) in Indonesian cultural production? On the other hand, we need to ask in what situation is the woman strong? The prime example of female strength that Heider offers is instructive, that of the film *Ibunda*, 'about a strong mother'.[4] Madelon Djajadiningrat-Nieuwenhuis talks of the hold in Indonesia of the 'ideology of Ibuism (Mother-ism)', 'which sanctions any action provided it is taken as a mother who is looking after her family, a group, a class, a company or the state, *without demanding power and prestige in return*' ... (my emphasis).[5] We need to ask, then, when the woman is represented as powerful or vocal, to what effect and in whose interest is this strength mobilised in the text?

Much the opposite argument is also mounted in the name of Indonesian cultural specifity, such as that of Misbach Yusa Biran cited above, which sees the weakness of the fictional female as a reflection of the real one. (The dead horse of realism is not worth beating yet again.) Films such as *Halimun* written and directed by Indonesian women add weight to such analysis, certainly in response to foreigners such as myself. It is worth noting, however, the extreme institutional marginalisation from which these women are working. As noted in Chapter 3, there are very few women in positions of control in the administrative or artistic spheres of the film industry. From 1965 to 1985, 1170 films were produced in Indonesia, only a dozen of them directed by women. In the powerful Board of Film Censorship the role of women has been strikingly diminished since 1965. In the Film Council even the representative of the Department of Women's Affairs has at times turned out to be an army man. It is not surprising, given the extent of male domination of the medium, that the women who do manage to enter (in any capacity other than as actors) can do little more than imitate the middle-of-the-road work of the men, in order to gain acceptance and survive.[6]

Also, many genres of Indonesian cinema, through long established production practice, place women in only subsidiary roles, so that women's images and actions make up a small and/or unimportant part of the total narrative. (By implication this is evident from the two preceding chapters since most of the films discussed there move around male protagonists.) Although there are notable exceptions, genres such as 'historical', 'martial arts', 'crime' and 'comedy' are on the whole about men and what the films define as men's desires and men's sphere of action. The two important genres where women have a substantial, even predominant, share of the diegesis are love stories or *film remaja* (teenage films), and 'drama'. In some years as many as half the films produced have been placed in these categories. The key characteristic of these genres is their focus on the relationship between men and women and the ties of family. *Film remaja*[7] are contained within the ideal nuclear family of a mother who stays at home, a father who goes to work and one or two children who go to school. The stories revolve around love affairs of the children of such families, and end in the union or prospective union of the young lovers. Dramas are about the relationship between older, often married, couples. The dramatic crisis is caused either by death or by some fault in one of the partners. The predominant construction of the woman thus takes place only in the context of romantic love and the family, leaving all other spheres of social (and fictional) action to male protagonists.

Rather than seeing the contemporary representations of women as the reflection of some essentially Indonesian condition, Carey and Houben's work suggests that some elements of these notions of femininity may be derived from Dutch colonial writings on Javanese women. '[T]here is little trace to be found of the simpering Raden Ayu (women of the aristocracy) or the passive sex object so beloved of nineteenth-century Dutch writers' in the 'archetypal images of womanhood' portrayed in Javanese mythology or pre-colonial history.[8]

Gatot Prakosa, Indonesia's leading short-film maker and animation artist goes further to suggest that the very division of humans into the male–female binary is a result of Western influence. His cartoon film *Koen Faya Koen* (Be, and it was, 1981)[9] starts with the hand of God (and artist) sketching a male and a female figure. The two find an apple and turn away from the audience. When the apple core is tossed away and the figures turn around, the secondary sexual characteristics have changed place – the figure with the penis now has the breasts and the one with the female genital has a beard.

According to the director this three-minute film was inspired by the mythology of creation of the island of Nias (off the West Coast of Sumatra), which acknowledges three kinds of human beings rather than two – the male, the female, and those in between. According to Gatot Prakosa, not just Nias, but many traditional cultures of Indonesia accept a whole range of combinations of masculine and feminine characteristics. 'Only today's metropolitian society, having been influenced by Western thinking, so that its [West's] ethic became generalised – uniform, changed [the traditional acceptance of] variety.'[10]

Cultural generalisations about gender construction in Indonesia are then at best matters of controversy. As such it may be most useful to think of women's images in cinema in relation to the generic and industrial constraints of film production in contemporary Indonesia, while acknowledging that these images are related to other cultural representations and the lived realities of Indonesian men and women in complex and contradictory ways. (The elision between artist and God in Prakosa's film is instructive!) Instead of speculating on the ideological heritage of images of women, the rest of this chapter attempts to work out the changing construction of women in Indonesian cinema and the implications of these for contemporary politics.

### Productive men, reproductive women

*Zaman Edan* (Crazy Times), a popular comedy made in 1978, is a particularly crude, but exemplary, construction of gender roles. Jalal (also the name of the film character), a well-known screen and television comedian whose clowning success derives partly from his extreme obesity, plays the house-bound husband. His attractive wife Sri earns a lot more than him. In the opening scene, as the couple set out for their respective places of work, Sri wants to drive the motorbike and make Jalal the pillion passenger much against his wishes. Sri has her way and the bike crashes into a roadside stall. This image of the dire consequences of 'role reversal' is held as the credits appear.

The narrative crisis begins when the couple lose the maid who looks after their baby daughter and Sri insists that Jalal look after the baby and run the house while she keeps her job. In the argument that follows Jalal protests that, as the father, he should do the earning while the mother looks after the child. In response Sri does not offer any arguments contrary to this assumption, but reminds him, instead, of his wedding vows where he promised to obey his wife.

Significantly, the maid has left their employment on the grounds that her four small children need her to be with them, emphasising that the mother's constant attention may be more important than the money she is earning. The maid's action negates Sri's only argument for continuing to work – that she earns more than her husband – and sharpens the criticism against her as a negligent mother and wife.

Jalal resigns from his school-teaching job. Sri gets a promotion and her salary is doubled. But this does not redress what the film defines as the absurdity of the domestic situation of this man and his wife. Terribly embarrassed and worried that he will be seen by the neighbours, Jalal takes on his domestic duties and makes a mess of them. The lyric in the background, 'this age is indeed the age of madness', suggests that the work he is doing is inappropriate, rather than that he is incompetent.[11]

In his eagerness to find a well-paid job, Jalal allows himself to be duped by an old friend and ends up in prison. When this confusion is cleared up, Jalal goes to the doctor for a fitness test. The doctor asks him to bring in his urine for examination. The results of the urine test indicate pregnancy! The change in Jalal's socially produced gender role thus transforms his biological sexual identity.

When Jalal tearfully reports his predicament to his wife, she explains that the urine he had tested was not his at all but hers – she is the one who is three months pregnant. As this conversation is taking place, a letter arrives for Jalal, which offers him the job of the school principal. Joyfully, he tells his wife that he has now got a 'good job with an adequate salary' so that she must now give up her job, while he takes up his new one. His concluding line, 'The end of the crazy times', appears across the screen in red against the background of the smiling faces of Jalal, his wife and their child in his arms.

The film ends with the restoration of the 'proper' social and 'natural' roles of man and woman. The man's castration is reversed and his sexual role restored only when his wife becomes pregnant and he is released from domesticity. Similarly, Sri's femininity is salvaged when she becomes pregnant and is restored to domesticity. Men produce in the paid public sphere, women reproduce in the unpaid domestic one.

Not only are social productive roles thus implicitly defined by natural reproductive ones, sexuality itself is legitimised mainly through reproduction. This is especially so when there is any overt reference to women's sexuality. In the critically acclaimed 1980 film, *Bukan Sandiwara* (Not Just a Play), which contains a number of scenes of husband and wife in bed, their sexual relationship is completely identified with their desire to have a child. The sexual unions are an endless cycle of expectation of pregnancy and disappointment. Ultimately, when the woman gives birth through artificial insemination, the child, which physically is only the woman's and not the man's, destroys their relationship, because there is no ideological space for a sexual relationship not legitimised by reproduction (see illustration 15).

Noticeably, the *banci*, the male transvestites and transsexuals, the most visible subversion of gender-based behaviour stereotype in urban Indonesia, are rarely anything other than figures of fun, and appear mainly in the films for the lower end of the market. Challenges to the binary gendering of the world are rare in all modern Indonesian art forms, and not just in popular cinema.[12]

### Producing women

'Female nature' in New Order cinema, ultimately sanctified in reproduction (motherhood), appears constantly in danger of being perverted. *Tangan-Tangan Mungil* (Little Hands), hailed by critics in 1981 as an exemplary children's educational film and awarded a special prize as such at the 1982 Indonesian Annual Film Festival, is about 'curing' female children who behave like boys. The problem at the centre of the film is Lala, who terrorises everyone at home and at the kindergarten. Her delinquency is referred to continuously by everyone around her as 'boyish behaviour', unsuitable in a female child. As 'proof' of her unnatural behaviour she wears only shorts and refuses to play with dolls. This worries her mother so much that she takes Lala to a psychologist. The psychologist, Seto, concludes that the root of Lala's problem is her father's frustrated desire for a son, as all three of his children were girls. The father had therefore treated his youngest daughter as a son. As evidence of the father's culpability in Lala's 'abnormality', we find him flying a kite and playing football with Lala and bringing her 'boyish toys' like guns and cars. He refuses to see Lala as an abnormal child or to cooperate with the psychologist.

The expert prescribes behavioural therapy. With the support of Lala's mother, the psychologist tries to show Lala how absurd one sex looks in the role of another. A childhood friend of Seto, a man whom Lala knows and likes, comes dressed up as a woman. Lala is first amused and then somewhat disconcerted. Her recognition of her own abnormality has started. The final stage of the cure is a puppet show organised by Seto with the help of Lala's sisters. The puppets are all animals of the jungle who come boasting that they are the great male animals. Finally there comes a hen with a false cock's comb on her head, claiming like the others to be a great male. The others do not believe her and as the sun comes out they ask her to prove that she is a rooster by crowing. When the hen crows everyone knows her 'real' identity; they attack her and take away her false comb. Then the sun intervenes and declares that 'Uncle Sun likes all creatures equally, whether they are girls or boys.'

Reading against the grain of the film's narrative, the puppet show could be seen as a parable of men's violence against women who try to participate in 'male spheres'. But that such a reading of the fable is suppressed by the film, could well suggest that violent repression of women can be culturally legitimised on the grounds that female nature has been perverted.[13] Lala, of course, understands the parable as the psychologist intended. Later at night she dreams she is in a flowing frilly dress and carrying a doll!

The casting of the psychologist, Seto, was important in the pedagogic intention of the film. The role was played by Seto Mulyadi, well known to Indonesian television viewers as Kak Seto in a children's programme. He is, reportedly, a child psychologist and educationist of some repute in the elite circles of Jakarta and particularly close to the children of the First Family.[14] Seto Mulyadi, playing himself, thus brings to bear on the film his own professional reputation and gives the educational message of the film more than usual credibility. The film is not just a story about one little girl who behaves like a little boy. It is an extension of the puppet-show in the film, expected to do for other abnormal little girls, and presumably their parents, what the psychologist did for Lala and her father. The film sets out to provide a model for socialisation that emphasises the difference between men and women. The social practice of girls playing with dolls and boys with guns is equated with the natural law of cocks having combs and hens not being able to crow.

In this film (as in other variations on this theme of salvaging the feminine essence of a female) men are the social agents of both the corruption of natural femininity and its restoration. Lala's father's dream of a son is at the root of her unnatural development. Those who retrieve feminine nature for Lala, the psychologist Seto, and Uncle Sun of the puppet parable, are both men.

Adult women's claim to autonomy from and equality with men is similarly defined as a personality defect. *Guruku Cantik Sekali* (My Teacher is Very Pretty), the first film by the woman director Ida Farida, was commercially so successful that the new director got funding for her next film almost immediately.

The central character in *Guruku Cantik Sekali* is Dina, a dedicated botanist and draconian school teacher. Most of the story unfolds in a nature camp to which Dina has taken some high-school girls. It is clear from the start that she hates men and will not allow the girls in her charge any contact with the group of boys camped nearby. Nor will she herself have anything to do with Danu, the ecologist who gets interested in her, first professionally and then personally.

Dina's hatred of men is depicted as something approaching madness. When she catches a schoolboy waiting for one of the girls, Dina breaks into a veritable tirade: 'Do you think you can play around at will with every woman? Do you think that women are mindless objects? That have no feeling? ... Don't you dare think women are inferior, because we too have self respect!' Later when she finds the girls cheering the boys on their motorbikes, she becomes hysterical and collapses from emotional stress as she runs into the woods.

In the flashback that follows, we discover the cause of Dina's attitude to men. She had an unpleasant encounter with the man she loved, Henry. Dina and Henry are in a car. She is attractively dressed, her hair down. This is very different from what we have seen so far of Dina – bespectacled, in dull clothes buttoned to the neck, and a scarf covering her hair. The car stops at a hotel. Dina is surprised: 'What do we want here?' Henry: 'Do I need to explain?' Dina: 'You are being driven by the devil, Henry!' Henry laughs. Finally Dina charges him with tarnishing the purity of their love and treating women as targets of sexual passion. When Henry declares that that indeed is 'one of the functions of women', Dina rushes from the car in desperation.

Thus we know that Dina was once 'normal', before this, presumably shocking, sexual attention. This episode from her past seeks to render her strident arguments about equality as expressions of a psychic disorder, resulting from past trauma.

From this point her slow recovery starts with the loving attention of Danu, until in the final scene Dina stands with the schoolgirls and boys, singing Christmas carols and glowing in a man's love. Needless to say, the glasses are off, as are the top buttons of the dress and her lovely hair loose! The claim to gender equality rather than being an issue to be intellectually understood and socially accommodated, becomes a derangement, to be psycho-therapeutically eradicated.

### Feminity as silence

In all the films discussed so far the final moment of restoration of femininity is represented by silent passivity in the woman. Even noisy little Lala is blissfully silent in the final shot. In *Guruku Cantik Sekali* and the many other films of its ilk, anger and speech are both taken from the women in the process of the restoration of their femininity. That femininity is silence and passivity is not just implied in a large number of popular films, but some of New Order's most critically acclaimed films have used the metaphor of silence to construct the ideal woman.

In 1970 Asrul Sani, one of Indonesia's best known literary and intellectual figures, made his award-winning film *Apa Yang Kau Cari, Palupi?* (What are You Searching for, Palupi?). It was hailed by the Indonesian critics as an art film, rejected by the audience as too arty, and shown around the world as a glowing example of Indonesia's film culture. It is a film about a woman who loses herself in search of an undefined 'something' – which she sees as happiness, and the film's dominant discourse shows as greed, immorality and the rejection of man's love.[15]

Palupi walks out on her author husband, is dissatisfied in her love affair with film-director Chalil, tries to become a movie star, goes from one man to another and ends up alone, a miserable failure. Palupi's folly and misery (mainly as seen by the protaganist, Chalil) is the subject-matter of the film. Her foil, Putri, who appears only once in the whole film, stands as a silent criticism of Palupi's revolt. In fact Putri is not even her name. Chalil calls her 'Putri', meaning 'princess'. We don't know what her name is. We know nothing about her apart from what Chalil tells us; Putri herself never speaks.

Putri is presented the very first time we see Palupi and Chalil together. They are at a little restaurant on the beach when Putri appears. She wears a fine silken veil, on her shoulder a bag that Chalil has given her, and a flower in her ear. 'Her face is beautiful and clean, without a blemish or fault' (Scenario).

Chalil (tenderly): Not tonight, Princess! Tonight I want to eat with this guest who comes from up above. You go play in the garden with your attendants, Princess.

The girl nods. As Chalil goes to light a cigarette, she picks up the matches and lights the cigarette for him.

Chalil: Good night, Princess.

The girl takes the flower from her hair, kisses it and give it to Chalil. Chalil kisses it and returns it to her. The girl walks away.

In reply to Palupi's curious questions about Putri, Chalil says:

Whenever I come here she eats with me. Eat is not the right word. Because she hardly eats. She is too busy watching over me with her loving eyes. If my tea-cup is empty, she fills it, if I want to smoke she lights the cigarette for me .... She just looks. There is joy in her if I come. But not a word from her lips.

Palupi: Why?

Chalil: She is a mute .... After eating we walk along the beach. I tell her all kinds of tales. She believes in all my fairy tales.

Putri appears again, not in person, but the idea of Putri, when Palupi comes to say farewell to Chalil. It is dusk; a pensive Chalil is looking into the distance as Palupi approaches. He does not notice her until she calls his name. Then he turns and looks at her and breaks into a long speech:

I thought you were a spirit come out of the past. I was trying to put myself into the role of a person who was assigned to guard this place hundreds of years ago. [And so on and on, until Palupi interrupts.]

Palupi: Chalil, I want to talk. [Chalil ignores her and continues.]

Chalil: Once we have seen a human face we are touched. [Another long romantic speech about the beauty of the past! Again Palupi interrupts.]

Palupi: I feel you only ever think about the past. What about today!

Chalil: Ah, today. Today is no more than a station at which to halt. It is the end of yesterday and the beginning of tomorrow. [And another long speech which turns from nostalgia about the past to bitterness about women!]

Palupi: That young girl, your beloved on the beach, she is a woman too.

Chalil: Putri? Putri is no woman. She is a character out of a fairy tale that I heard when I was a boy.

It is this fairy-tale character then, a figment of man's imagination, who listens, loves and serves, in total silence, who is held up as a model against a woman who questions, rebels and rejects what men have to give her.

Ten years later, Slamet Raharjo, a film director more than 20 years younger than Asrul Sani, made *Rembulan Dan Matahari* (The Moon and the Sun, some aspects of which are discussed in Chapter 5) which, within a very different narrative structure, sets up an ideal female type very similar to Putri in *Apa Yang Kau Cari, Palupi*. This film, too, was hailed by Indonesia critics as an art film and taken around the international circuit.

*Rembulan Dan Matahari* has two central female figures, both in love with the hero Wong Bagus. Ayu (literally 'beautiful woman') is his childhood sweetheart in the village, and Paitun is a prostitute from a city slum, with whom he lived during his banishment from the village. When Bagus leaves the city and returns to the village, Paitun manages to find out his whereabouts and follows him. Ayu, by contrast, had resigned herself to her fate when Bagus left the village, and married a much older man to give a name to Bagus's illegitimate child born to her.

The scenes of the meeting after a period of separation, between Ayu and Bagus, and Paitun and Bagus, construct the two women in their absolute difference (see illustrations 16 and 17). Ayu sees Bagus after seven years, the morning after he has returned to the village. The scenario (the film is completely true to it) describes her reactions thus: 'Ayu was surprised to see Bagus standing before her. Her body trembled, her hand covered her mouth restraining a scream ... . She grew confused. Restraining her tears, she went inside the house.'

The meeting brings back memories of the past. She takes out an old photograph from the times when she was with Bagus. She looks into the mirror and ties her hair in two braids as she used to in those days. The keynote here is restraint – non-expression and internalisation of emotions.

Paitun arrives in Bagus's village in the evening, at the place where men meet to drink and have fun. As soon as she realises that this is the right village, she takes out all the photographs of her and Bagus and talks loudly and cheerfully of their love. When Bagus arrives, she screams in delight and throws herself at him. Paitun's first days in the village make her not only a foil to Ayu's quiet resignation but also a misfit in the rural society. She is vocal; she is loud; she questions the norms of quietness and won't be bound by them; she is immensely energetic and demands attention from Bagus.

The conflict between Paitun and Bagus grows until, after a furious row, Paitun rushes out into the night crying loudly. She goes to Ayu's house. Ayu accepts this odd nocturnal guest as she has accepted everything else – with deep resignation. Ayu tells Paitun the story of her love for Bagus and concludes: 'Now you love him. Look after him. Be gentle for that's what he wants of you.' The conflicts (and the film) are about come to an end. When we next see Paitun, she is quiet; her whole personality has been altered. The make-up is off her face; she is dressed for the first time in rural Javanese clothes, sitting in the kitchen, stirring a pot! She is striving now towards the ideal of the speechless female. The film ends with the hope that she will now be accepted by Bagus and the society to which he belongs.

Ayu is director Slamet Raharjo's ideal of womanhood. He conceived of this character as natural perfection.[16] Nowhere in the film is Ayu held responsible for her actions. She is like nature itself, accepting man's actions towards her.

The metaphor of Ayu as nature is most clearly explored in the sequence preceding her death. The village festivities are interrupted suddenly by rumbling thunder. In the confused rush for shelter, Gombloh, Bagus' illegitimate son, automatically turns to his natural father for protection. A torrential downpour starts just as Bagus is united with his son. Ayu stumbles and her labour pains begin. Bagus runs to fetch the doctor. But it is too late. Simultaneously, we hear the dying breath of Ayu and the cry of the newborn child. The village river rushes out breaking the dam. Ayu leaves behind sons for both the man she married and the one she loved. Bagus explains her death to his son: 'Your mother has gone away gently. She was longing for the moon.' The woman becomes one with elements of nature.

## Incurable perversions

Ayu's silence is, in the end, not enough for a symbolic order that requires a woman's sexuality to be totally contained within monogamy. Once her sexual fidelity is thrown into turmoil by the return of Bagus, Ayu's perfection can only be preserved in death. Indeed a woman's own virtue has little impact on how the text deals with her. In one sense there are no good or bad women in Indonesian cinema. There are only models of femininity – in a state of natural perfection or vitiated usually by the actions of predatory male sexuality. Some processes of corruption of female nature, as we saw earlier, can be reversed. But when a woman's sexuality is aroused outside the sphere of monogamy, it signifies a crisis for the symbolic world.

One mode of dealing with this problem is through the witches and female ghosts in the horror films. The woman is raped or seduced and then left by a man. In revenge she turns to evil in the sphere of the supernatural, either as a ghost haunting men who had hurt her or as a witch torturing her previous tormentors with her magic until the right man, a religious figure, usually a devout Muslim,[17] exorcises the evil spirit and kills the woman.

The most frequent construction of the adult female protagonist outside the scope of monogamy and motherhood, however, is as a prostitute. The popular success in 1970 of Turino Junaedi's two films about prostitution, *Noda Tak Berampun* (Unforgivable Stain) and *Bernafas Dalam Lumpur* (Panting in the Mud)[18] started a trend in melodramatic films about prostitutes. The titles of the two films, most explicitly *Noda Tak Berampun*, encapsulate the notion of filth and contamination of the woman's sexualised body. Although she is not responsible for causing the blemish since, as with the heroine of *Halimun* (discussed at the beginning of this chapter) the women in these films are seen as 'made stained' ('dinodai', a passive or object-focus construction in Indonesian), they bear the guilt for their condition and become 'unforgivably stained'. While the fascination of the early 1970s with prostitution has passed, in most years there are some films dealing with the subject.

The early 1970s films about prostitution all followed a highly predictable pattern of a woman's betrayal by men, combined with lack of moral guidance leading to promiscuity and then prostitution. These films were set in the glamorous new Jakarta hotels and night-clubs, reflecting the mushrooming of expensive night-spots in the early years of the New Order. The popularity of prostitutes as subjects was understandable. It allowed films to use images of the female body in ways that would be difficult when films only had 'good' girls and wives in them. Many a screen prostitute died in the arms of the only man she truly loved, praying to God for forgiveness. The moralistic conclusion allowed these films to get past the Board of Censorship while the visions of expensive female flesh drew audiences from a sociey that was just emerging from a decade of restraint (sexual and economic) imposed materially by economic decline and ideologically by the dominant political discourse of Revolutionary Nationalism.

The 'prostitution' films, more than any other, directly use the female body to sell the product (the film) while at the same time condemning that body. Once the woman has been frustrated in her natural and innocent instinct to be wife or mother by a man's actions (rape or seduction in the case of unmarried women, desertion by husband in the case of married women), she transforms her body into a weapon against which men have no defence, until the woman herself is released from this perversion, ultimately through death. Like the witch, the prostitute demands sympathy because she is in the final analysis a victim of men's actions. But her death is inevitable in a moral order which cannot tolerate an unattached woman who is sexually active.[19]

Of all the films about prostitution, Arifin C. Nur's 1977 film *Suci Sang Primadona* (Suci the Divine Primadonna) is probably the most exceptional, in that the woman's discourse struggles for and ultimately achieves dominance.

Suci is the star actress and singer of a *srimulat* troupe,[20] made up of men and women who have come from villages to try to make a living in the city of Surabaya. They live and perform in a squalid *kampung* area. Suci, however, has a car, a driver and lives in a large luxurious house. The house and the car belong to a Chinese businessman, Mr Condro. Suci is also the mistress of two other men, Tuan Kapiten, an impotent ex-captain of a merchant ship, and Pak Daud, a corrupt parliamentarian. Suci easily keeps her three clients from knowing of each other's existence, because each wants to play out the fantasy of being her only and completely satisfying lover.

Into this enters Eros, 18 years old, from a prosperous family in Jakarta. He is spending his school holidays and taking out his frustrations with his parents by travelling across Java on his motorbike. Suci and Eros disrupt each other's normal life. The film is, on the one hand, Eros's investigation of Suci (purity) as his rite of passage into adulthood, and on the other, Suci's investigation of Eros, the erotic, which has never before been present in her life as a prostitute (see illustration 18). The most explicit scenes of physical love in the film are those of Suci with Eros. He fantasises about pure love outside society, living in the forest with Suci. She knows all the time that their enormous social differences will only allow a fleeting union between them. Her determination to resist their mutual fantasy of escaping from society with their passion leads to a conflict. Eros reminds her that though she has achieved wealth and security, her life is unfulfilled.

At that night's performance Suci sings the final song of the film, *Kupu-kupu Malam* ('Night Butterflies', a commonly used euphemism for prostitutes), in which she gives a touching description of the prostitute's work where 'she must stake her whole body and soul'. The song goes on to ask: 'Is what she does a sin? Are those who come to her pure?' The question at the heart of the film's representation of prostitution is answered in favour of the film's prostitute protagonist by the end of the film.

The following sequence shows Suci in open confrontation with her three clients, who have all come back-stage at the same time, brought together by the machinations of Suci's jealous colleagues. Once the men are confronted with the fact that none of them has had control over Suci, they completely reject her. Together they accuse Suci of immorality and deception. Suci, following the argument of her song, accuses the men of hypocrisy for their deception of their wives and for the way they have acquired wealth and power by deceiving society. In the perception of the men their relationship with their wives is quite distinct from their relationship with a prostitute. As Daud says: 'This is not a matter of wives. This is a matter for men. The wife is a matter of the household. This is outside the house.' Time and again throughout the confrontation the men say, 'Our manhood has been insulted'.

The businessman's suggestion that her relationship to him is a business matter (since he has invested in her) brings Suci's final explanation of herself and, by extension, of prostitution: 'That is precisely correct. This is a matter of business. Oh! I've only just realised that! So what did you buy? My flesh, or my heart ... or my soul, perhaps?' In finally taking stock of her life, she says that she has been most severely duped.

'Earlier, in my village, my life was peaceful ... way before men like you appeared advertising your luxuries. Now the further I get from my peace, the more I am dragged along behind your expensive cars.' For once the explanation of prostitution is found in wider social dynamics, rather than in a malfunction of feminine nature.

As in the scenes of their sexual overtures, so in their scene of confrontation, the men are ridiculous. Daud sniffs furiously to contain his asthmatic cough; Tuan Kapiten is in an incongruous red suit and frilly shirt like something out of an old adventure movie; Condro is fat and pompous. Suci is still in her dramatic red traditional Javanese costume in which she performed on stage and enchanted the audience (both the diegetic and the real) with her song. In a sense, in all her encounters with these men, and most emphatically in this last one, she remains the theatrical star performer in relation to the men who are really clowns (see illustration 19).

Like other films about prostitution, *Suci Sang Primadona* uses the woman's body to sell the film. But here the woman *performs* her sexuality, both as a singer on stage and as a lover to her clients. Even when her own desire is aroused by Eros, Suci remains emphatically autonomous. To Eros's insistence on marriage, she responds: 'I cannot marry you. I am a primadonna. I must remain virgin to fulfil the dreams of men.' The virgin-prostitute so frequently used to sell films is thus problematised as is the relationship between men's pleasure and their power over women.

The final sequences show Eros on his motorbike returning to his family and his friends. Suci, back in her village, tells her driver to return the car to its owner, since she will not be back to work for a while. In the closing scene, Suci is with her mother, who is calling out to Suci's two children. The scene is an anti-climax. Nothing has been resolved in the contradictions of the woman who *is* sexual and who must *perform* simultaneously as virgin, prostitute and mother.

## Roles and regulations

Some of the dominant representations of the woman-qua-woman in the foregoing discussion, especially the attack on women working outside the home, appear to be peculiar to post-1965 cinema.[21] The frequent representation and the near universality of the characterisation of prostitution as something akin to terminal illness could also be specific to the New Order. (*Kabut Desember* for example, a 1955 film dealing with prostitution, discussed in Chapter 2, provides a quite different interpretation.) This may be to some extent a function of the New Order state ideology which constructs women primarily as wives, men's dependants, and only secondarily as citizens.[22] However, contemporary Indonesian cinema's persistent reinforcement of the ideology of sexual division of labour and gender hierarchy is not maintained through any direct state intervention in the form of propaganda or censorship.

There are, nonetheless, film institutions which operate in ways that discourage attempts by individual directors to move away from the mainstream. One instance of this is the selection of films for FFI awards. While Joice Erna got the Best Actress award for her performance as Suci in *Suci Sang Primadona*, neither this film nor any others deviating from the standard presentation of gender divisions as I have described had, up until 1991, been awarded any major prizes, particularly the coveted Best Director or Best Film Award. By contrast, films with narratives of corruption and restoration of femininity have had a great deal of success with the festival juries.

A good example of the FFI Award reinforcement of mainstream gender construction was the jury's response to two films by the same director in successive years, 1980 and 1981. Edward Pesta Sirait's *Gadis Penakluk* (The Girl Conqueror) (1980), a film very similar to *Tangan-Tangan Mungil* (discussed earlier), was about the transformation of a tomboyish teenager into a true woman through the patient persuasion of a school teacher.[23] *Gadis Penakluk* won the Best Supporting Actress for Ita Mustafa playing the heroine's best friend and the feminine foil to the boyish heroine. Adi Kurdi, playing the reforming teacher, was voted Most Promising New Actor. The film also got the highly regarded Best Scenario prize, and a special award from the Psychology Foundation for its representation of the teacher in behavioural correction in young people.

The following year Pesta Sirait made another film about a woman. *Bukan Isteri Pilihannya* (Not the Wife of His Choice) (mentioned earlier), also starring Ita Mustafa and Adi Kurdi, was about a deserted wife who manages to make a life for herself as a working woman and preserve herself and her mother-in-law in reasonable dignity. The film was not all that different from the usual deserted wife story, since most of the sympathy for the female protagonist came from the fact that she had been a good wife who was deserted and remained faithful to her husband and his mother. But the film presented the image of an extraordinarily strong female character who, at the end of the film, forgives her husband and takes him back, rejecting another man with whom she has formed some attachment. Her explanation for taking back her husband is that he needs her more than the other man does. Quite clearly she is in a position of strength *vis-à-vis* the men, particularly the husband. The film received no awards. Its lack of critical success, as mentioned earlier, was due to what the critics, the FFI jury and other keepers of aesthetic laws, saw as the film's unrealistic representation of the woman's superiority over men.

Institutions affect the formation of film texts in contradictory ways. Ironically, film festivals, which ostensibly reward creative artistic work, in effect reinforce status quo, while the operation of state censorship (albeit unintentionally) appears to have opened up new modes of representing women in Indonesian cinema since at least the mid-1980s. Film censorship is generally understood as a negative process of eliminating particular signs, linguistic or visual, from films. But we can usefully think of film texts as being 'not merely marked' but 'positively structured, by operation of censorship'.[24]

Censorship regulations which are intended to encourage self-censorship in the film industry also identify for film-makers the spaces where there is no active state intervention. Given the concern the state has shown about depictions of many aspects of social conflict (discussed in the three foregoing chapters), the lack of interest amongst censors in gender as an area of dissident ideas opens the possibility for films to use female characters to express a certain amount of critical opinion, thus providing new contexts in which women are represented.[25]

It is possible to read a number of critically acclaimed films of the mid-1980s as moves towards using gender relations to allude to areas of conflict that films are not permitted to explore except in very circumscribed ways. In Teguh Karya's nationally acclaimed and internationally screened *Doea Tanda Mata* (Mementos) (1984) two female characters represent alternative modes of anti-Dutch activism in the 1930s, alternatives, that is, to male armed revolutionary modes.

*Doea Tanda Mata* tells three stories – that of Gunadi, his wife and of Miss Ining. Gunadi's wife is without a name of her own. The spectator identifies her only through the letters she receives from Gunadi, addressed to 'my beloved wife'. She is a teacher in a nationalist school in Central Java and plays a leading role in the promotion of nationalist awareness amongst the local population. She is finally imprisoned by the Dutch for singing the banned national anthem of Indonesia with her students. Her struggle for Indonesian independence, one that has a large number of women in it, is united, determined and draws its strength from the international revolutionary movements. This civilian movement concentrates on educating the community and building up its will for independence.

The wife's story, her revolutionary anti-Dutch activities, remain entirely unconnected with Gunadi's. They are tied in the narrative only through three letters which Gunadi writes, telling his wife about *his* revolution. The letters add in minor ways to the story of Gunadi (he is lying in the first two letters about his own development as an activist, and only in the last one does he admit to conflicts, contradictions and failure), and not at all to the wife's. Her prominent presence in the film is inexplicable, except in terms of the political position she represents

– an unarmed civilian, successful, united political movement, in contrast
to the underground, armed one with which the film is centrally concerned through the hero (or anti-hero) Gunadi.

From the opening scenes of the film, Gunadi's story is tied up to that
of the *stambul* performer Miss Ining. Ining's brother, who is also involved
in the underground movement, is shot by the Dutch army about five
minutes into the film, as he is driving Gunadi on the back of a motorbike. This incident is the beginning of Gunadi's personal crisis. He
holds himself responsible for the younger man's death, and commits
himself to avenging this death by assassinating the commander of the
Dutch battalion, de Kocke. This leads to conflicts with his revolutionary
colleagues who suspect his motives for putting his personal emotions
above collective needs. Gunadi is forced to leave the organisation and
works at Dutch nightclubs, hoping to find de Kocke. His revolutionary
friends regard him as a traitor. The very same night that Gunadi finally
assassinates de Kocke, his revolutionary colleagues misjudging his
actions, kill him.

Not only is Gunadi torn apart by his inner contradictions, but so is
the underground movement as a whole. In every sequence in which
they appear, these revolutionaries are engaged in angry debates and
suspicion of each other. By contrast, the civilian movement speaks, quite
literally, with one voice, through Gunadi's wife. That the underground
movement is shot largely in darkness, behind closed doors, operates at
one level as a historically realist representation of a secret society. But
the dark secrecy operates at the same time to connote a movement
isolated from the rest of society. Neither their goals nor their achievements are ever made clear. Their only act which does have a clear effect
is the misjudged shooting of the hero, just as he is about to return to
the revolutionary fold, having performed his most effective personal and
revolutionary action.

Gunadi's assassination of de Kocke is made possible only by the
intervention of Miss Ining, who disappears from Gunadi's life (and
indeed from the spectator's view) after her brother's death. She returns
to the story when Gunadi finds her performing in a Dutch nightclub
and living as de Kocke's mistress. Miss Ining, too, is planning her own
revenge. It is she who steals de Kocke's revolver for Gunadi and gets
him a job as de Kocke's driver. A woman, one whose position is dubious
at least in terms of conventional morality, is thus instrumental in the
only successful armed political action.

The film needs to be seen in the context of other New Order films
about the struggle for Indonesia's national independence. I argued in
Chapter 4 that these films consistently reproduce and legitimise the
military's interpretation of history, where independence is seen as having
been won in a war in which the Dutch were defeated. *Doea Tanda Mata*,

while not challenging the military interpretation directly, adds to the picture the civilian side of nationalism through the story of Gunadi's wife. More than that, by implication it raises questions about armed action whose valorisation is fundamental to the military's interpretation of history.

Ining's role as a woman who manipulates her position as a sex object to dangerous effect against the morally decrepit, ageing colonialist, represented by de Kocke is at one level a replay of the theme of woman's dangerous sexuality. De Kocke's vulnerability to this female sexuality is evidence of his moral weakness. But the hero Gunadi also seems affected by Ining to some extent. The guilt which drives him through the film, is a guilt he feels towards her, for her brother's death. And he is finally able to kill de Kocke only after ascertaining that Ining, who is living as the old man's mistress, is not in fact in love with him. It is possible then to see both deaths in the film as results of woman's sexual appeal.

The one power women seem to have in mainstream representation is the power to use men's own sexual appetites against them. In most Indonesian films only prostitutes have this power. But they become vulnerable once they themselves fall in love with a man. Interestingly, Ining's attraction for Gunadi, alluded to in the scene of their first meeting, is never acted upon. As the film closes, the two women – the wife who is asexual and the performer who evokes desire but has none of her own – seem to symbolise the strength of the emerging nation.

In an equally acclaimed film of the previous year (1983) which also moves around a rebellious woman, her sexual passion intrudes upon the story to lead to a quite different resolution. Ami Priyono's *Roro Mendut*, following the traditional legend, is set in the context of the expansion of the central Javanese kingdom of Mataram to the coastal areas of the island. The heroine of the legend, Roro Mendut, is captured as part of the loot and given by the king to the General Wiroguno. Mendut refuses to give in and uses her sex appeal to make the money to pay the taxes that the General imposes on her to force her to surrender. She sells half-smoked cigarettes from behind a screen, intoxicating men with the cigarettes and the silhouette of her pouting lips on the screen (see illustrations 20 and 21).

It is the story of a woman using her sexuality to resist a powerful man she does not want. But her resistance also signifies the regional struggle of Java's coastal periphery against the Central Javanese heartland. In comparing popular theatrical renderings of the legend with the film, Hatley argues that the film emphasises Mendut's cultural difference in a way that earlier renderings of the story do not.[26] Such exploration of regional cultural conflict between central and coastal Java was permissible, I think, because at some level the protagonist is seen as 'only a woman', and not, almost by definition, a 'real' rebel in the political sense.

At the height of her successful resistance to the ageing General Wiroguno, Mendut falls in love with the young, handsome Pronocitro. The young lovers attempt to escape and are captured. Wiroguno slays Pronocitro in a sword fight. Mendut kills herself with Pronocitro's dagger. Mendut's successful rebellion against her captor is doomed from the moment she allows her own desire to be aroused. It is Mendut who first sees Pronocitro and desires him. It is she who initiates their first meeting. But from this point on, both the 'look' of the camera and the diegetic action belong to the men. In the closing scene we see Mendut through the eyes of the ageing patriarch, as a young woman hopelessly in love driven to suicide. She is no longer the clever rebel outwitting the powerful general.

Wiroguno also defines the central conflict of the narrative in his final address before setting out to recapture Mendut. He says he must capture Pronocitro and Mendut, not because of his desire for a woman, but because their escape would represent an insult to the imperial authority of Mataram. The struggle of the woman to refuse her body to a man is thus subsumed under another political question. Mendut's death is also a denial in the symbolic order of the woman's right to have sexual desire – symbolically, she is destroyed for desiring Pronocitro.

### New roles, old images?

Do the new connotative uses of femininity imply new visual representations of women, new modes of address, new ways of inviting the spectator to look at women's images on the screen?

*7 Wanita Dalam Tugas Rahasia* (Seven Women on a Secret Mission) made in 1985 is about a group of women on a revolutionary anti-Dutch operation, carrying secret messages from one division of the nationalist army to another. Some of them are identified as lovers, wives or sisters of soldiers in battle although, with one exception, these men are not seen. As such the women are soldiers in their own right.

The film begins with a scene of their capture by a group of armed men. The women are taken to a camp, deep in the forest, which is under the control of a mystic addressed as 'Aba' (father) by his men. Aba turns out to be a frustrated former nationalist soldier, who mutinied because he felt he was superior to the leaders of the nationalist army. As the story unfolds, we also discover another reason for his passion for power. In a flashback it is revealed that he killed his wife after discovering that she had borne a child by a Japanese soldier. The Japanese also has magical powers. And Aba becomes locked in a long struggle with the Japanese. As the women escape from captivity and try to work their way out of the jungle, pursued by Aba and his men, the Japanese re-emerges, his young Indonesian son on his shoulder, and helps the women every time Aba's men get close to them. In a final battle he kills Aba, entrusts his son to the women and kills himself. In the film's final scene, which follows his suicide, the women are at a military ceremony being decorated, presumably for the successful completion of their mission.

As mentioned earlier, war films are generally about men fighting men. A film about a group of women setting out on a mission, without male guidance, creates roles for women that are quite out of the ordinary. Yet in terms of its visualisation of women, I would argue, it has much in common with the mode of address of soft-core pornography, a common and conventional genre in the visual representation of women.

Some of the elements of Anglo-American pornographic photographs that Annette Kuhn identifies are useful here. First, soft-core porn shows women without men, frequently a number of women together, engaging each other sexually. Secondly, because enjoyment of pornography involves voyeurism, the enjoyment of the woman's body depends on her being unaware of the viewer. This, argues Kuhn, is the reason for the frequent use of the woman in a 'caught unawares' pose. Thirdly, and most importantly, pornography is about discovering the sexual difference of women. Soft-core porn functions through the promise of revealing the ultimate difference of women – the female sex organs. The promise of revelation is as important as the revelation itself, because it is the promise that keeps the spectator looking, maintains the possibility that if he looks long enough and hard enough, he is going to gain knowledge of what the female 'really' is.[27]

With that in mind let me go over the way 7 *Wanita* develops visually. The women are introduced as a group, all in dresses around knee length, which are ripped as they are pushed and dragged by their captors. The process of tearing of clothes continues in every confrontation with the male captors through the first half of the film. After their escape, when the women are by themselves, their tiredness and tension leads them to physically abuse each other, resulting in more torn clothes. The dresses recede quite consistently, upward from the knee, down from the neck and just under the breasts (see illustration 22).

The women are not in control of how much they reveal. They are either unaware of being seen, or are attempting to hide themselves from the pursuing men. An early shot, immediately after their capture, shows the seven women lying on the ground, most probably asleep, in postures of total abandonment, with legs apart. They are lying in a circle, legs opening inwards into the circle, the camera shooting from above. The spectator knows that from another angle he might see more, but he is thwarted at this point. There is also a sado-masochistic edge to the film's revelation of the women's bodies, as much of this is achieved through physical abuse, both of men against women, and of women against each other.

Clearly, the audience would consist of men and women. But I use 'he' for the spectator, because the film text constructs the 'seeing' subjects as men, and the 'seen' as women. The women's task is 'secret', they are to get from one point to another unseen. But they are *seen by men* and captured. The camera sees them at precisely that same moment of being seen by Aba's men. In this sense, the rest of the film is a tussle between the women trying to be invisible and the men trying to find (that is, see) them. Of the two magical abilities that Aba demonstrates, one is the ability to see beyond the normal range of the human eye. It is this power that he deploys in his search for the women, after they escape from their initial captivity. The Japanese similarly keeps watch over the women, unbeknown to them. The spectator has the choice of identifying with either the protective male, 'looking after', or the predatory one, 'looking at'. But either way, seeing is an exclusively male power, which the spectator shares as he observes the women.

Ultimately, too, the film is about asserting the sexual difference between men and women. Although the women are seeking to take part in the war, they in fact do not kill any of the male villains. That is the function of their Japanese protector. There are a number of shots of the women carrying guns. But when finally, in the climactic confrontation with Aba, one woman shoots at him, the magical powers of Aba prevail – the bullets bounce off him. The gun, overdetermined as a symbol of manhood across so many genres of so many national cinemas, is ineffectual in the hands of a woman.

The film does not, however, have the essential ingredient of pornography – an overt concern with sex. On the other hand, this film has more exposed female bodies than most (post-censored) Indonesian films. How can we explain this soft-porn disguised as a war film? Of course pornographic films do often have a story that begins prior to, and as an excuse for, the sexual imagery. But pornography as understood in the West would ultimately reveal the female body. This film, however, plays on the power of seeing and the promise of showing but remains, by and large, outside the discourse of sexuality. Only one clownish male in the film ever expresses any overt desire for the women. Sexuality is referred to, rather obliquely, through the relationship of Aba's wife and the Japanese soldier. We don't see that sexual act but only its results: the birth of a child and the woman's death.

We need to return, I think, to the operations of censorship, both institutional and cultural, in contemporary Indonesia, to understand a film such as *7 Wanita*. At the institutional level the censorship regulations contain a number of restrictions on the representation of sex. No sexual act can be clearly or even indistinctly filmed, and neither humans nor animals can be shown in the act of sexual intercourse. There can be no close-up of kissing mouths, nor any use of obvious sexual symbols. An example of sexual symbolism cited in the *Censorship Codes* of 1980, is 'a mouth sucking on an ambon banana (*pisang ambon*) resembling the male genital'! A noticeable absence here is a clause about violence against women.

Usmar Ismail, regarded in the New Order as the father of Indonesian cinema, wrote in 1951 about the problem censorship posed for film-makers. The article starts with a report of the Censorship Board's decision to cut out a scene where the husband pinches his wife's ear to get her attention! Usmar Ismail goes on to claim that far greater acts of intimacy would have been permitted in a foreign film released in Indonesia.[28] There is, in fact, far more physical contact between men and women accepted on the Indonesian screen today. However, the complaint from Indonesian film-makers, that censors allow far greater latitude to sex scenes in foreign films than in local ones, persists.

The point of Usmar Ismail's statement is not precisely what can or rather cannot be shown, but more a cultural sense of the division between private and public, and the unwillingness of influential sections of the society, represented by the censors, to accept the translation of private acts of intimacy into the public domain of the film screen. This restriction does not appear to extend to European or American films, perhaps because the society in which these films are set is regarded as having different codes of sexual behaviour. Because foreigners are seen to be publicly sexual, the depiction of their sexuality in the public medium of cinema is much more acceptable. It seems to me that *7 Wanita*, in representing women's bodies in the context of a very public event – the nationalist war – manages to circumvent some of the cultural and institutional restrictions on sexual representation.

## In protest and in pleasure

In the 1980s political and economic considerations operating in the film industry created new diegetic spaces for women. For quite some years film producers had been aware of the ever-increasing competition with European and American videos. Internationally, video is probably the most popular medium of soft-core pornography today. It was clear from the Indonesian national conference on the video industry in 1980 that the film industry was troubled by what it saw as a losing battle with the legal and black market video imports. Some of the new representations of women's bodies are no doubt the film industry's attempt to compete with the black market foreign videos.

Politically, the breach between the government and sections of the dominant classes has been widening since the late 1970s.[29] Growing dissent has led to periodic tightening of restrictions on all forms of public speech by the state. But critical opinions have continued to find expression in new ways, through new media and new metaphors. Representations of women as civilian nationalists, as protesting workers (as in Syumanjaya's last completed film *Kerikil-kerikil Tajam*, 1984), as champions of regional autonomy, may not be due to any revolution of gender relations, but related rather to repression and resistance in the predominantly male sphere of political discourse in Indonesia.

In cinema, the oppositional positions voiced by women and new representations of women outside the conventional roles of wife, mother or prostitute, could perhaps be seen as new ways of colonising women's voices and women's bodies, whether for radical political causes or for pleasure.

# 7

# The New 'Ordered' Cinema

This book started with the implicit assumption that a study of cinema has something to offer in the understanding of the New Order. It assumed too that the state was important in conditioning the texts and context of Indonesian films. In that spirit the book documented the period from the late 1960s to the early 1980s – a time of increasing government policy declarations, legislative initiatives, executive intervention and expenditure on cinema. Ironically the book is being completed at a time when the industry in decline (only 20 films were produced by June in 1992) is screaming out for state protection without avail, and when the government's latest intervention into the film industry is being guided by the interests of other industry's access to the US market. In May 1992 when the US trade representative extracted concessions on the entry of more American films into Indonesia in return for an extension of Indonesian textile exports to the US, Indonesian officials were at pains to point out that the film concessions should not be seen as a defeat of the Indonesian negotiators, but rather as a fair exchange – American film imports in return for Indonesian textile exports. From the point of view of Indonesian films, things had moved backwards since the former Information Minister, General Ali Murtopo's, exhortation to make Indonesian cinema 'the master of its house' and a major export item. Market forces have never seemed to favour national cinema in Indonesia. Those engaged in the national cinema have always had to fight politically to move governments to secure a place for it in the market. In the 1990s that seems to be a losing battle, not only because the state is unable or unwilling to move against vested interests of capital, local and foreign, but also because national cinema is increasingly less important as a sphere of constructing a 'cultural order' for the New Order.

As one Indonesian political scientist has commented, the New Order government from the beginning aimed at creating 'a mechanism of "ordered politics" to guarantee a fast, effective and efficient process of policy-making and policy-implementation.'[1] The New Order represented precisely the political foil to the revolutionary excesses of the Old (dis)Order of Sukarno's government. Screaming voices of mass demonstration had to be ordered to silence, or at any rate to well-modulated civil speech. All of public life, including the media, was to be reordered.

The significance of cinema in what might be called the 'mediascape'[2] of post-1965 Indonesia lay on the one hand in the extent and diversity of its potential appeal and on the other in the ease of central bureaucratic control over it. Cinema is not restricted to an age group, as schooling, on the whole, is. Nor is it restricted to the literate, as are the print media. Unlike most of the traditional art forms, it is not restricted to particular regional and linguistic groups. It is not even necessarily restricted to those who can pay for a ticket (*layar tancep* shows are rarely paid for by the spectators themselves).

At the same time, for global technological as well as national historical reasons cinema was far more amenable to central control than the newer competing forms of audio-visual entertainment such as video cassettes and advanced television technology, which spread through the cities of Indonesia in the 1980s. Portability of videos meant that laws restricting their entry into and production and circulation in Indonesia were almost impossible to police. The parabola antennae mushroomed on the rooftops of Jakarta at such speed that viewers had access to dozens of foreign broadcasts before the government had had time to react to the phenomenon or attempt to restrict these breaches of the national boundary.

Socially established modes of audience reception of films also makes cinema more controllable than many of the performance arts, whether traditional theatre or rock music concerts. The control of the state over cinema is not, of course, perfect or seamless. As we have noted earlier, at the moment of decoding the state loses control over the individual spectator. Nevertheless this level of autonomy cannot be seen as significant when the contradictory meanings made in the privacy of individual receptions have no public resonances. By contrast, public readings by radical young poets or rock concerts of popular musicians provide occasions where communally felt pleasures, publicly expressed, can and do burst into disorderly, excessive, carnivalesque modes, breaching the 'order' that is the foundation myth of the New Order.

It is not impossible in any sense for films to be the focus of communal feelings. While on the whole Western film theory has constructed the pleasure of cinema as private and psychoanalytic, in India large audiences singing along with the heroine or collectively anticipating the popular hero–villain dialogues, evoke the image of a much more social and participatory event. The implication of cinema in the mass politics of 1964–65 may have opened up the possibility for Indonesian movies

to become the kind of mass cultural events that their Indian counterparts frequently are. But state control over cinema being historically
legitimised and technologically possible, and because the medium had
become so closely associated with left-wing politics, cinema was quickly
purged of its collective rebellious euphoria after 1965 and became,
perhaps second only to state television, the most 'ordered' space of the
New Order's mediascape. The state's attention to Indonesian cinema in
the 1970s and the early 1980s – both in terms of policy initiative and
financial input – can be seen as efforts to maintain cinema as an
'ordered' space and to expand that space in the mediascape overall.

The archetypal text of this 'ordered' medium is about order. Every
film (with one exception) discussed in this book – and I would argue
almost every film produced in New Order Indonesia – has a narrative
structure that moves from order through disorder to a restoration of the
order. This formal characteristic is not altered by differences in themes,
genres or other aesthetic attributes. The ordered beginning and end of
the film narrative are signified in various ways. In a children's tear-
jerker such as *Nasib Seorang Miskin* (discussed in Chapter 5) the presumed
order of a family household is broken by accidents and deaths. While
the story is played out in the disorder of the street, it concludes back
in the walled space of another family home. In the generically and
thematically very different 'serious' historical film *Nopember 1828* (discussed in Chapter 4), the order of the walled space of the village is
similarly breached by the arrival of the Dutch. Many battles and deaths
later, the narrative closes in the same walled space, restored to pre-
Dutch order. Even in the thematically, artistically and ideologically off-
beat film, *Rembulan dan Matahari* (discussed in Chapters 5 and 6), the
return of order in the village is the paramount narrative concern –
disrupted transport is *restored*, the prodigal son of the village *returns* to
his rightful place, the sexually problematic women are *repositioned* within
monogamy or moved out of society, whose order they threaten, into
nature (Ayu is reunited with the moon in the hero's closing line).

This interpretation of New Order films' formal characteristic, while
not emphasised in each reading, is implicitly present through the last
three chapters. In the 200 or so post-1965 films I have seen and another
similar number of which I have a reasonable understanding from scenarios or shooting-scripts, I can think of only two exceptions to what we
might call the 'new ordered' film form – *Si Mamad* (discussed in Chapter
5) and *Petualang-Petualang* (The Adventurers). The latter is not discussed
here since it had extremely limited exhibition and was so transformed
by the operations of censorship that, according to the director, the film
that was released in 1985 (and which I have not seen) bore no resemb-
lance whatsoever to the film that was submitted to the censors in 1978
(which I have seen in a restricted screening).

In *Si Mamad*, the ordered world in which Mamad lives has already been destroyed before the diegesis begins. The new world of 'disorder' is represented as much by the changing fashions, unruly traffic and erratic work practices of Mamad's colleagues as by the uncertain morality and uncontrolled avarice of most other characters. Mamat's own practices on the other hand are perfectly regular, predictable and orderly. He always wears an uniform, is perfectly punctual, believes in social hierarchy. Mamad represents an archaic order, which is in complete contradiction to the new disorder. Mamad's death at the end of the film is the final passing of that old order. In one sense the 'problem' is resolved, the narrative is closed – the old order is dead. On the other hand, as the diegisis ends in the death of the old order, the narrative opens up to the continuations of the new disorder outside and beyond this particular text. In associating the *old* (and closed) with *order* and the *new* (and open) with *disorder*, *Si Mamad* not only provides a break from the New Order archetype in cinema, it turns on its head the very idea of the New Order.

Even while calling into question the idea of the *new order*, however, *Si Mamad* maintains the ideal of order itself. Indeed it mourns the loss of order in life. It could be tempting to explain the centrality of order in the form and content of contemporary Indonesian cinema in terms of the ordered hierarchical structures of the wayang repertoire, representing some fundamental cultural characteristic of Indonesia – a Javanised Indonesia at any rate. Yet, historically, Indonesian cinema in terms of both its audience and its performers has had closer links to the 'implicitly anti-order, anti-hierarchy' and anti-establishment urban performance arts such as *Ketoprak* and *Ludruk*,[3] born earlier this century at approximately the same time as the first Indonesian films were being made. Nor was Indonesian cinema always quite so single-mindedly committed to the message of order (as some of the films discussed in Chapter 2 show). Nor is all of contemporary Indonesian media imbued with the orderliness of cinema. To take the example of the music industry – another commercial, technological sphere of the media – the most popular of its rock performers have sung and performed about disorder, and in an anti-order style. Examples of this abound. In the late 1970s Ahmad Albar roared on to the stage on a motorbike screaming '*frustrasi*' (frustration). In the early 1980s Leo Kristi's song about entrapment in the 'clowns' ring' ended with the noise of a shotgun. The late 1980s' most popular performer, Iwan Falls, constantly and explicitly calls for disorderly and disruptive behaviour – singing about the private emotions of the father of a starving child, he calls on the child to be not controlled, to scream loudly; singing about public issues such as wealth he drives his audience to a frenzy with the call to 'destroy' (*bongkar*).

Post-1965 cinema's commitment to order – in form and content –

cannot then be explained in terms of some fundamental 'Indonesian-ness'. Nor can it be seen as simply another instance of a totalitarian state's total control of the media. It needs to be understood with reference to the particular history of this medium, and the characterisitics attributed to it by the New Order establishment (and government policies resulting from that).

I said at the beginning of this chapter that the government seems less interested in national cinema in the 1990s than it did in the two preceding decades. In terms of policy initiative, the contrast with the television industry is glaring. Since 1989, while active initiatives of the government have revolutionised Indonesian television through the introduction of private stations for the first time in the country's history, policies in the film industry have been largely *reactive* and of minor importance. The 1992 expansion of American film imports was the first substantive policy change in the film industry since the appointment of the current minister of information in 1982 – a striking contrast to the preceding ten years.

Part of the explanation for the shift may lie in the changing nature of the film technology which has made it increasingly difficult to control centrally, at all stages, production, distribution and circulation. By the mid-1980s just about every director seemed to have video copies of their films. I do not know whether or not most of these copies are the censored versions of the films, and whether or not they do in fact circulate in any significant way. The point is that video technology makes possible both surreptitious circulation of films and communal enjoyment of these outside the gaze of the state. It thus becomes possible, technologically at least, for cinema to some extent to resist being entirely restricted to the New Order's ordered space. By contrast, though our choice of what we see on national television is private, the total offering can always be policed. The expansion of national television by the introduction of private channels can be seen in part as a move to bring larger parts of televiewing audiences away from foreign broadcasts, into the domain of the policed sector of the mediascape.[4] As it becomes more difficult and less important (because national television, the fastest expanding medium, can engage much the same people at much the same times as cinema) to keep national cinema under state order, the products of the Indonesian film industry may become more diversified. Parts of the industry might even learn the language of radical disorder, that aligns rock music to youth culture on the one hand and radical opposition on the other.

# Notes

## Introduction

1. There are only two other English-language books on the subject. These are Karl Heider, *Indonesian Cinema: National Culture on Screen*, University of Hawaii Press, Honolulu, 1991; and Salim Said, *Shadows on the Silver Screen: A Social History of Indonesian Film*, Lontar Foundation, Jakarta, 1991. The latter is a translation of an earlier Indonesian publication, *Profil Dunia Film Indonesia*, Grafitipers, Jakarta, 1982.

2. Teshome H. Gabriel, 'Towards a Critical Theory of Third World Films', *Third World Affairs*, 1985, pp. 355–69.

3. Teshome Gabriel, *Third Cinema in the Third World*, UMI Research Press, Ann Arbor, 1982, pp. 1–5.

4. Julianne Burton, 'Marginal Cinemas and Mainstream Critical Theory' in *Screen*, Vol. 26, No. 34, May–Aug., 1985.

5. Robert Kolker, *The Altering Eye: Contemporary International Cinema*, Oxford University Press, 1983, p. 5, cited in Burton, 1985, p. 19.

6. Roy Armes, *Third World Film Making and the West*, University of California Press, Berkeley, 1987, p. 8.

7. Andrew Robinson, *Satyajit Ray: The Inner Eye*, University of California Press, Berkeley, 1989, p. 91.

8. Richie, cited in Yuejin Wang, 'Mixing Memory and Desire: *Red Sorghum*, A Chinese Version of Masculinity and Femininity', *Public Culture*, Vol. 2, No.1, Fall 1989, p. 31.

9. See, for example, Esther Yau 'Yellow Earth: Western Analysis and a Non-Western Text', *Film Quarterly*, Vol. 41, No. 2, 1987–88, pp. 22–33; or Jenny Kwok Wah Lau, 'Towards a Cultural Understanding of Cinema: A comparison of Contemporary Films from PRC and Hong Kong', *Wide Angle*, Vol. 11, No. 3, 1988, pp. 42–9.

10. Vijay Mishra, 'Filmic Narrative: Text and Transformation in Bombay Cinema', *Continuum*, Vol. 2, No. 1, 1988/89, p. 15.

11. Trinh T. Minh-ha, *Woman, Native, Other: Writing Postcoloniality and Feminism*, Indiana University Press, Bloomington, 1989, p. 88.

12. Philip Schlesinger, 'Media, the Political Order and National Identity', in *Media, Culture and Society*, Vol. 13, No. 3, July 1991, p. 299.

13. Joseph Straaubhar, 'Beyond Media Imperialism: Asymmetrical Interdependence and Cultural Proximity', in *Critical Studies in Mass Communication*, Vol. 8, No. 1, March 1991, p. 43.

14. Armand Mattelart, *Mass Media, Ideologies and the Revolutionary Movement*, The Harvester Press, Brighton, 1980, p. 26, published earlier in French.

15. 'Cultural Imperialism, Mass Media and Class Struggle: An Interview with Armand Mattelart', in *The Insurgent Sociologist*, No. 4, 1980.

16. There have been some moves away from the symbolic world of the individual psyche, for instance in Lovell's notion of 'collective social pleasures' in place of individual psychological ones (*Pictures of Reality: Aesthetics, Politics and Pleasure*, BFI, London, 1980) or Jameson's theorising of the 'political unconscious' (*The Political Unconscious: Narrative as a Socially Symbolic Act*, Methuen, London, 1981).

17. See Keith Foulcher, *Social Commitment in Literature and the Arts: The Indonesian 'Institute of People's Culture' 1950–1965*, Centre of Southeast Asian Studies, Monash University, Clayton, 1986, pp. 1–12.

18. Benedict Anderson, *Language and Power: Exploring Political Cultures in Indonesia*, Cornell University Press, Ithaca, 1990, Ch.3.

19. *Ibid.*, p. 109.

20. Richard Robison, *Indonesia: The Rise of Capital*, ASAA and Allen & Unwin, Sydney, 1986, pp. 119–20.

21. Dipesh Chakrabarty, 'Robison Reviewed' in *Inside Indonesia*, No. 9, December 1986, pp. 4–5.

22. Burhan Magenda, 'Ethnicity and State Building in Indonesia: The Cultural Bases of the New Order', unpublished paper presented to the Colloquium on Ethnicity and Nations: Process of Inter-Ethnic Relations in Latin America, Southeast Asia and the Pacific, Houston, Texas, October 1983.

23. *Ibid.*, p. 6.

24. See, for example, Kathy Robinson, 'Women and Work in an Indonesian Mining Town' in L. Manderson (ed.), *Women's Work and Women's Roles: Economics and Everyday Life in Indonesia, Malaysia and Singapore*, Australian National University, Canberra, 1983. And Barbara Martin Schiller, 'Weeding Out Women? Changing Agricultural Practices and Adaptive Work Patterns in Rural Java', *Kabar Sebrang*, Vol. 13, 1984.

25. See Saskia Wieringa *et al.*, 'Indonesian Women's Organisations Since 1950', in Saskia Wieringa (ed.), *Women's Organisations in Historical Perspective*, Institute of Social Studies, The Hague, n.d., and Umi Wiryani, 'The Second Sex in Indonesia', *Inside Indonesia*, 2:1, January–March 1985.

26. See, for example, Valery Hull, *Women in Java's Rural Middle Class: Progress or Regress?* Population Institute, Gajah Mada University Working Paper Series No. 3, Jogjakarta, 1976, and Norma Sullivan, 'Gender and Politics in Indonesia', in Maila Stivens (ed.), *Why Gender Matters in Southeast Asian Politics*, Monash Papers on Southeast Asia No. 23, Clayton, 1991.

27. GERWANI was the largest Indonesian women's organisation before 1965. It was connected to the Indonesian Communist Party.

## 1. The Beginning: Early 1900s to 1956

1. More detailed accounts of the early history of Indonesian cinema are: (1) Armijn Pane, 'Produksi Film Cerita Di Indonesia: Perkembangan Sebagai Alat Masyarakat', in *Indonesia: Majalah Kebudayaan*, Vol. IV, No. 1–2, Jan.–Feb. 1953, pp. 5–112; (2) Bachtiar Siagian, *Ichtisar Sejarah Perfilman di Indonesia*, Komite Nasional Indonesia FFAA3, Jakarta, 1964; (3) Misbach Yusa Biran, *Sepintas Kilas Sejarah Film Indonesia*, Badan Pelaksana FFI, Jakarta, 1982. Misbach Yusa Biran has also written several longer works on the early history of Indonesian cinema which are unpublished; (4) Salim Said, *Profil Dunia Film Indonesia*, Grafitipers, Jakarta, 1982.

2. For this and other information on the theatres early this century I am grateful to Susan Abeyesekere of Monash University, Melbourne.

3. 'Films in the Orient: Interesting Interview With F.M.S. Censors', *Inter-Ocean*, Vol. 7, No. 11, November 1925, pp. 750–2.

4. 'The Cinema in the East', in *The Times*, 18/9/1926. Reproduced in *Review of Indonesian and Malaysian Affairs*, Vol. 15, No. 1, 1981, pp. 151–5.

5. *Panorama*, 27 August, 1927. Cited in Salim Said, 1982, *op. cit.*, p. 16.

6. See Jay Leyda, *Dianying Electric Shadows: An Account of Films and the Film Audience in China*, Massachusetts Institute of Technology, Massachusetts, 1972, pp. 15–59.

7. Misbach Yusa Biran, 1982, *op. cit.*, p. 6.

8. An account of the first published versions of the story in Pramudya Ananta Tur, *Tempo Doeloe*, Hasta Mitra, Jakarta, 1982, pp. 26–9.

9. Kwei Tek Hwei, 'Film Si Conat', in *Panorama*, 20/5/1930, cited in Said, 1982, *op. cit.*, p. 18.

10. For details of film production under the Japanese, see Aiko Kurasawa, 'Propaganda Media on Java under the Japanese 1942–45', in *Indonesia*, No. 44, October 1987.

11. Usmar Ismail, 'Sari Soal Film-film Indonesia', *Star News*, No. 5–6, September 1954.

12. Siagian, 1964, *op. cit.*, p. 7.

13. In the years following independence, Indonesians distinguished between the 'co', the collaborators, who worked with the Dutch, and the 'non', non-collaborators, who did not.

14. Usmar Ismail, 'Film Saya Yang Pertama', in *Majalah Intisari*, 17 August 1963. Included in Usmar Ismail, *Usmar Ismail Mengupas Film*, Penerbit Sinar Harapan, Jakarta, 1983, p. 164.

15. *Harta Karun* was based on the French comedy *L'Avare* by Molière.

16. Usmar Ismail, 1954, *op. cit.*

17. *Ibid.*

18. Misbach Yusa Biran, 1982, *op. cit.*, p. 21.

19. Mannus Franken, 'Film Cerita Di Indonesia', *Cinemagia*, Vol. 1, No. 1, February 1950. Translated into Indonesian by M.D. Aliff, copy at Sinematek, p. 5.

20. A. Teeuw, *Modern Indonesian Literature*, Martinus Nijhoff, The Hague, 1967, p. 143.

21. Charles A. Coppel, *Indonesian Chinese in Crisis*, ASAA and Oxford University Press, Singapore, 1983, p. 3.

22. Robison, 1986, *op. cit.*, p. 42.

23. Armed rebellion led by the Communist Party. For details see M.C. Ricklefs, *A History of Modern Indonesia: c. 1300 to the Present*, Macmillan, 1981, pp. 216–17.

24. Islamic separatist movement in West Java, 1948–62. *ibid.*, pp.215–16

25. Pane, 'Produksi Film Cerita di Indonesia: Perkembangan sebagai Alat Masyarakat', in *Indonesia: Majalah Kebudayaan*, Vol. 4, No. 1–2, 1953, p. 94.

26. *Ibid.*, pp. 92–3.

27. Usmar Ismail, 1954, *op. cit.*

28. *Ibid.*

29. *Indonesia: Majalah Kebudayaan*, special issue on the Second Cultural Congress at Bandung, January–March, 1952, p. 261.

30. *Ibid.*, p. 278.

31. *Ibid.*, p. 279.

32. Siagian, 1964, op. cit., pp. 8–9.

33.  See Gerlof D. Homan, 'American Business Interests in the Indonesian Republic, 1946–49', *Indonesia*, No. 35, April, 1983.

## 2.  Political Polarisation and Cinema: 1956–66

1.  Herbert Feith, *The Decline of Constitutional Democracy in Indonesia*, Cornell University Press, Ithaca, 1962, p. 330.

2.  Herbert Feith, 'Dynamics of Guided Democracy', in Ruth T. McVey (ed.), *Indonesia*, Yale University and HRAF Press, New Haven, 1963, p. 325.

3.  Rex Mortimer, *Indonesian Communism Under Sukarno: Ideology and Politics, 1959–1965*, Cornell University Press, Ithaca, 1974, p. 79

4.  *Ibid.*, p. 159.

5.  *Ibid.*, p. 171.

6.  Daniel S. Lev, *The Transition to Guided Democracy: Indonesian Politics 1957–59*, Cornell University Modern Indonesia Project, Ithaca, 1966, p. 10.

7.  See Harold Crouch, *The Army and Politics in Indonesia*, Cornell University Press, Ithaca, 1978, pp. 55–62.

8.  Mortimer, 1974, pp. 243–4.

9.  Iskandar Tejasukmana includes SARBUFIS in his list of 19 'most important' unions out of the '39 national and more than 800 local unions affiliated with SOBSI in 1957', although the declared membership of SARBUFIS at this time was only 5,320, which made it one of the smallest unions listed by Tejasukmana. *The Political Character of the Indonesian Trade Union Movement*, Monograph Series, Cornell University Modern Indonesia Project, Ithaca, 1958, pp. 31–3.

10.  *Apa Siapa Orang Film Indonesia 1926–1978*, compiled by Sinematek Indonesia, published by Sinematek and Yayasan Artis Film, Jakarta, 1979, pp. 455–6.

11.  See Julie Southwood and Patrick Flanagan, *Indonesia: Law, Propaganda and Terror*, Zed Press, London, 1983, pp. 65–79.

12.  Usmar Ismail (under pseudonym S.M. Ameh), 'Sejarah Hitam Perfilman Nasional', *Sinar Harapan*, 6 October 1970.

13.  Sumarjono, 'A Glance at the Socio-Cultural Aspect of the Development of the Indonesian Film Industry', in Muhammad Johan Casmadi and Chaidir Rahman (eds.), *Indonesian Film Festival Information*, Indonesian Film Festival Executive Body, Jakarta, 1983.

14.  Keith Foulcher, 1986, *op. cit*, p. 19n.

15.  Herbert Feith, 1962, *op. cit.*, p. 554.

16.  See my discussion of the LEKRA critique of Asrul Sani's *Pagar Kawat Berduri* in 'Hidden from History: Aspects of Indonesian Cinema 1955–65', in *Review of Indonesian and Malaysian Affairs*, Vol. 19, No. 2, 1985, pp. 1–55.

17.  Foulcher, 1986, *op. cit.*, pp. 24–5.

18.  *Ibid.*, pp. 27–58.

19.  See Sen, 1985, *op. cit.*

20.  MULO – Extension of Elementary Education, AMS – General Secondary School.

21.  Abu Hanifah, *Tales of a Revolution*, Angus and Robertson, Sydney, 1972, pp. 136–7.

22.  Usmar Ismail, 'Lahirnya Kafedo' in *Pedoman*, No. 22, December 1953. See also 'Inilah Hollywood' in *Harian Pedoman*, 1/10/1953. Both included in Usmar Ismail, 1983, *op. cit.*

23.  Usmar Ismail, 1954, *op. cit.*

24. Sitor Situmorang, 'Juri Festival Pecah', in *Star News*, No. 14, 1955.

25. *Ibid.*

26. See Mohammad Hatta, 'A Revolution Should Not Last Too Long', in Feith and Castles, *Indonesian Political Thinking: 1945–65*, Cornell University Press, Ithaca, 1970, pp. 94–7.

27. *Harian Rakyat*, 24/5/58.

28. For the political position of Gintings and his role in the suppression of the regionalist movement in North and Central Sumatra, see Feith, 1962, *op. cit.*, pp. 525, 528–30.

29. For a discussion of the development projects in this area and resistance to them, see Susan Abeyasekere, *Jakarta: A History*, Oxford University Press, Kuala Lumpur, 1987, pp. 210–12 and 262–4.

30. Detailed discussion in Sen, 1985, *op. cit.*

31. Mortimer, 1974, *op. cit.*, pp. 278–95.

32. For an account of the social and cultural work TURBA required, see Helmi, *Di Tengah Pergolakan*, Yayasan Langer, Limburg, 1981.

33. *Bintang Timur*, 5/5/1963.

34. Sen, 1985, *op. cit.*

35. Gabriel, 1985, *op. cit.*

36. Daniel Lev has written that the main threat to the elite's position 'would appear to be the growth of forceful egalitarianism. In fact, however, the elite escaped this threat partly by adopting egalitarian ideological symbols', but it remained in fact 'decidedly conservative'. (Lev, 1966, *op. cit.*, p. 10.)

37. M.C. Ricklefs, *A History of Modern Indonesia*, Macmillan, London, 1981, p. 247.

38. See Crouch, 1978, *op. cit.*, pp. 101–34.

39. *Ibid.*, p. 197.

40. Robison, 1986, *op. cit.*, p. 97.

# 3. Institutions of New Order Cinema

1. These women are Ratna Asmara, wife of writer and film director Anjar Asmara; Citra Dewi, wife of film producer L.J.N Hoffman; Ida Farida, younger sister of screenplay writer and film director Misbach Yusa Biran; and Sofia W.D. who is an exception to some extent since she is more prominent within the film community than her two successive actor husbands, Waldy and W.D. Mochtar.

2. Ministerial Decree No. 34/SK/M/1968.

3. Misbach Yusa Biran, 'Pengaruh Festival Film', paper presented to the Jakarta Press Club, 29/4/82. The speaker documented the cases of award-winning films setting certain trends in Indonesian film-making.

4. I use the term cameramen self-consciously as there had never been a camerawoman until the late 1980s. And even now the women are mainly involved in still photography in cinema

5. Interview, 9/5/81.

6. Sumarjono, 'Perjalanan dan Tujuan: Sekapursirih Ketua KFT' in *KFT Buku Anggota 1964–74*, Jakarta, 1974, pp. 5–12.

7. Ministerial Decree No. 114A/Kep/Menpen/1976.

8. For a general account of changes in the government's economic policies in response to the rise of economic nationalism, see Robison, 1986, *op. cit.*, Chapter 5.

9. *Ibid.*, p. 151.

10. Robison listed Suptan among the biggest Chinese business interests in the mid-1980s. *Ibid.*, p. 287.

11. Richard Robison, 'Authoritarian States, Capital-Owning Classes and the Politics of Newly Industrialising Countries: The Case of Indonesia', in *World Politics*, Vol. 41, No. 1, pp. 52–74.

12. *Ibid.*, pp. 72–3.

13. *Far Eastern Economic Review*, 28/3/91.

14. See Sen, 'Si Boy Looked at Johnny: The Indonesian Screen at the Turn of the Decade', in *Continuum*, 5:1, January 1991.

15. J.E. Siahaan and Tony Ryanto (eds), *Berkala BSF*, August 1971, n.p., Jakarta.

16. Arief Budiman, 'Sepatah Kata', in *Ibid.*, 1971, p. 5.

17. I was unable to obtain access to these tapes despite persistent efforts. Virtually everyone I talked to had predicted that this would be a futile chase.

18. Secretariat BSF, *Kriterium Penyensoran Film – Ordonanntie Film 1940 Dan Pengumuman Lain-lainnya*, Department of Information, Jakarta, 1978.

19. *Kode Etik*, 1981, pp. 170–4.

20. David Jenkins includes Sutopo Juwono among the comparatively liberal stream in the Indonesian military intelligence group. David Jenkins, *Suharto and His Generals: Indonesian Military Politics 1975–83*, Cornell University Modern Indonesian Project, Ithaca, 1984, p. 121.

21. This restriction has been popularly dubbed Miss SARA, the letters standing for Suku-Ethnicity, Agama-Religion, Ras-Race, Antar Golongan-group identity.

22. Ang has demonstrated this idea convincingly in relation to European television audiences. See Ien Ang, *Desperately Seeking the Audience*, Routledge, London, 1991.

23. Wilbur Schramm, 1964, p. 10, cited in Eduard J.J.M. Kimman, *Indonesian Publishing: Economic Organization in a Langganan Society*, Hollandia, Baarn, 1981, p. 15.

24. See BPS, *Statistical Yearbook of Indonesia 1990*, Jakarta 1991, p. 70.

25. See BPS, *Statistik Bioskop Indonesia*, Republic of Indonesia, Jakarta, 1979 and 1984.

26. In the context of Jakarta and other big cities, *kampung* implies slums or lower class residential quarters.

27. *Audience Research Film*, Department of Information, n.d. [1972?] p. 3.

28. Kimman, 1981, *op. cit.*, pp. 23–7.

29. Award-winning directors like Slamet Raharjo, Teguh Karya and Ami Priyono frequently attend and speak at seminars and screenings at universities in various parts of Indonesia, including the elite University of Indonesia and Bandung Institute of Technology.

## 4. Narrating the Nation for a Military State

1. From a report (on the scenerio of *Perang Padri*) written by Sutrisno Kutoyo, an official in the Department of Education and Culture.

2. For an explanation of the term Padri and a brief account of the history of the Padri War, see Ricklefs 1981, *op. cit.*, pp. 133–5.

3. Scenario for *Perang Padri*, pp. 52–3.

4. Benedict Anderson, *Imagined Communities: Reflections on the Origin and Spread of Nationalism*, Verso, London, 1983, p. 19.

5. Foulcher reads the nation in the discourse of the Javanese aristocracy in a contemporary romantic film. See Keith Foulcher, 'The Construction of an Indonesian National Culture: Patterns of Hegemony and Resistance', in Arief Budiman

(ed.), *State and Civil Society in Indonesia*, Centre of Southeast Asian Studies, Monash University, Clayton, 1990.

6. Benedict Anderson, 'Narrating the Nation', *Times Literary Supplement*, 13/6/86, p. 659.

7. 'Mengapa Belum Ada Film Cerita G30S/PKI?', *Indonesia Raya*, 30/9/73.

8. There are some questions regarding the terminology used to describe the 1945–49 period of the Indonesian struggle for freedom. Clearly the momentum of the nationalist movement was radically altered by the outbreak of the Second World War. Indonesian nationalists have called the final years of resistance against the Dutch attempt to re-establish her hold over the colony after the fall of Japan, 'revolution'. Major English language histories of the period have accepted that term. See Anthony Reid in his *Indonesian National Revolution 1945–50*, Longman Australia, Hawthorn, 1974, p. 179. However, Benedict Anderson's *Java in a Time of Revolution*, Cornell University Press, Ithaca, 1972, questions the extent to which the revolutionary potential of the period was fulfilled. Indonesian historians after the military coup of 1965 have tended to call the crucial years of 1945–49 the 'War of Independence'. In this chapter, wherever I have used either of these labels I have put them in quotation marks because it seems to me that both terms are politically motivated in that they constitute the historical understanding of particular political interest groups of the Indonesian society.

9. James Schiller, 'Development Ideology in the New Order Indonesia', unpublished Masters thesis, Ohio University, 1978, p. 84.

10. Ben Anderson partly anticipates (though in quite different terms) this difference in the construction of Indonesia before and after 1965 in his analysis of cartoons as political communication, when he analyses the absence of foreigners in the work of the popular cartoonist Hidayat in the 1970s. 'At the bottom the foreigners make no difference. Including them in the world of cartoons would not change its character ... . Sibarani (pre-1965) drew his Americans because their presence and actions were major contributing elements to the conflict he saw working itself out in his generation in his society.' 'Cartoons and Monuments: The Evolutions of Political Communication Under the New Order', in Karl Jackson and Lucien Pye (eds.), *Political Power and Communication in Indonesia*, University of California Press, Berkeley, 1978, p. 320.

11. For a brief account of the Java War 1925-30, see Ricklefs, 1981, *op. cit.*, pp. 111–13.

12. *Ibid.*, p. 113.

13. J.D. Legge, *Sukarno: A Political Biography*, Penguin Books, Middlesex, 1972, p. 35.

14. Teguh Karya, 'In Search of Ways and Means for Making the Film an Instrument of Expression', in Krishna Sen (ed.), *Histories and Stories: Cinema in New Order Indonesia*, Centre of Southeast Asian Studies, Monash University, Clayton, 1988, p. 7.

15. Again there are resonances with parts of Ben Anderson's analysis of early New Order cartoons cited earlier: 'In Hidayat's work, Johnson, Nixon, Kissinger, or better, in keeping with his Jakarta style, local American diplomats and businessmen can be counterposed to nothing: they would merely be a further ramification of an indefinitely extended family' (Anderson, 1978, *op. cit.*, p. 320).

16. *Tempo*, 19/5/79.

17. For a semi-official history of Indonesia's independence movement, see Nugroho Notosusanto (ed.), *Pejuang dan Prajurit*, Penerbit Sinar Harapan, Jakarta, 1984, pp. 33–59.

18. For information on the author and the original publication in Dutch, see Roy Edwards, English translation, *Max Havelaar: or the Coffee Auctions of the Dutch Trading Company*, University of Massachusetts Press, Amherst, 1982.

19. 'Penjajahan Baru Lewat Seluloid', *Tempo*, 23/7/77, p. 13.

20. Mohammad Said, quoted in 'Saidja, Tidak Untuk Kita', *Tempo*, 23/7/77, p. 12.

21. The novel *Max Havelaar* had been praised by Indonesians of very different ideological persuasions. The left-wing intellectuals before 1965 regarded Multatuli as a revolutionary who spoke out against social injustice both of imperialism and feudalism. See Nyoto, 'Multatuli: Sastrawan-Pejuang dan Pejuang-Sastrawan', in *Harian Rakyat*, 24/2/62, p. 1. Two other prominent left-wing literary figures who admired Multatuli greatly were Pramudya Ananta Tur and Bakri Siregar. See Teeuw, 1967, p. 137 and 180. On the other hand, H.B. Jassin, who translated the novel into Indonesian, was not a leftist by any means. He is the doyen of New Order literati, and his translation of *Max Havelaar*, first published (by Penerbit Jembatan) in 1972, was popular enough to go into a second printing within a year.

22. 'Penjajahan Baru Lewat Seluloid', *op. cit.*, p. 13.

23. *Ibid.*

24. *Tempo*, 10/9/1977, p. 16.

25. He was a G-30 S category B detainee 1968–78.

26. Scenario, p. 3.

27. See Atmakusumah (ed.), *Tahta Untuk Rakyat: Celah-celah Kehidupan Sultan Hamengkubuwono IX*, Gramedia, Jakarta, 1982, p. ix. Hamish McDonald's short but highly favourable (to Suharto) account of the 'General Attack' suggests that the idea of the attack came not from the young army colonel but from higher authorities and was conveyed to him through Sultan Hamengkubuwono. *Suharto's Indonesia*, Fontana/Collins, Blackburn, 1980, pp. 19–20.

28. Since the production of the film, the discussion of where the initiative for the attack came from has been taken up in the media again and again. For claims and counter-claims, see 'Pak Harto Tentang 1 Maret', *Tempo*, 9/11/85, p. 15. Most of the article consists of long quotations from an interview with Suharto by his image manager, Brigadier General G. Dwipayana, where Suharto asserts that the initiative came exclusively from himself.

29. 'Cut' and 'dissolve' are amongst the commonest means by which individual shots are put together during editing to form what we perceive as integrally related segments. 'Fades, dissolves and wipes are perceived as gradually interrupting one shot and replacing it with another. Cuts are perceived as instantaneous changes from one shot to another.' See David Bordwell and Kristin Thompson, *Film Art: An Introduction*, Addison-Wesley Publishing House, Massachusetts, 1979, p. 152.

30. The film does not make clear to which particular United Nations resolution this is a reference. The crucial Security Council Resolution regarding the 'restoration of Republican leaders to their state functions in Jogjakarta' and 'eventual transfer of full sovereignty not later than 1 July 1950' had been accepted on 28 January, four weeks before the General Attack. See Anthony Reid, *Indonesian National Revoluton 1945–60*, Longman, Hawthorn, 1974, pp. 158–60.

31. See reviews in *Berita Buana*, 6/6/79, *Merdeka*, 4/5/79 and *Terbit*, 1/3/80.

32. See 'Pak Harto tentang 1 Maret', *Tempo*, 9/11/85.

33. Super Semar is the acronym for 'Surat Perintah Sebelas Maret' (11 March Instruction) by which Suharto received, for all practical purposes, the mandate to rule the country in 1966. For a discussion of the political and symbolic significance of the day, see Crouch, 1978, *op. cit.*, Chapter 7.

34. See *Yudha Minggu*, 5/10/80.

35. The use of the Javanese word *tumbal* here is interesting since it has the implication of preventative medicine. The men of the poor rural family have been sacrificed as *tumbal* presumably against the Dutch by the princes and leaders such as those mentioned by the old woman. Being thus sacrificed is sacred and natural law. But the common people are the objects rather than the agents of the sacrifice.

36. 'Ini Propaganda Patriotisme', *Kompas*, 17/1/82.

37. The director has said so in several interviews.

38. This echoes the semi-official analysis as incorporated in *Pejuang Dan Prajurit* edited by Nugroho Notosusanto, who was then Minister of Education and Culture and head of the Centre of Military History. See especially pp. 33–59, for comparison with military-historical films.

39. See, for example, 'Arifin dan Nyanyian Fajar' in *Tempo*, 22/8/82.

40. Jenkins, 1984, *op. cit.*, pp. 74–5.

41. *Ibid.*, pp. 66–70; pp. 234–48.

42. *Ibid.*, p. 248.

43. *Ibid.*, pp. 255–6.

44. See 'Arifin Dan Nyanyian Fajar', in *Tempo*, 22/8/82; 'Ini Propaganda patriotisme', *Kompas*, 17/1/82; 'Temon, Merangkai Episode', *Topik*, No. 7, 22/2/82.

45. The cynical response in some circles to the film's critical success, that the FFI jury was acting under official pressure, is unlikely to be correct, since only a year previously the first Suharto film had failed to get any awards at that forum.

46. President Suharto's speech at Pekanbaru, cited in Jenkins, 1984, *op. cit.*, p. 157. For a discussion of reactions to the speech, see pp. 157–64.

47. Marhaenism was Sukarno's adaptation of Marxism for the Indonesian context. 'Marhaen' was the term he used for the archetypal member of the poor masses in Indonesia. See Legge, 1972, *op. cit.*, pp. 72–4.

## 5. Telling Tales of a Class Society

1. Jakob Sumarjo, 'Image Indonesia dalam Film Nasional Kita', *Kompas*, 16/4/74, reprinted in Misbach Yusa Biran (ed.), *Tentang Perfilman Nasional*, Yayasan Artis Film, Jakarta, 1983, pp. 17–18.

2. Gunawan Mohamad, 'Sebuah Pengantar Untuk Film Indonesia Mutakhir – Catatan Tahun 1974' in *Prisma*, No. 3, June 1974, pp. 54–5.

3. Abeyasekere, 1987, *op. cit.*, p. 227.

4. *Ibid.*

5. Mohamad, 1974, *op. cit.*, p. 56.

6. For a discussion of *dangdut* music, see Frederick, 1982, pp. 103–7.

7. *Indonesia Raya* had been banned in 1958. It was re-established in October 1968 and was banned again in 1974 in the aftermath of the Malari affair.

8. Gunawan Mohanad, 1974, *op. cit.*, p. 56.

9. Robison, 1986, *op. cit.*, pp. 159–65.

10. David Morley, 'Cultural Transformations: The Politics of Resistance', in Howard Davis and Paul Walton (eds), *Language, Image, Media*, Basil Blackwell, Oxford, 1983, p. 104.

11. *Ibid.*, p. 165.

12. For a brief account of the issues and incidents surrounding student radicalism in 1977–78, see van Rees, 1981, and also Bandung Institute of Technology Student Council, 1978.

13. According to one source, when the producers of the film sought to get a second release in 1982, it was disallowed by the BSF.

14. See Kamajaya, *et al, Sum Kuning, Korban Penculikan Pemerkosaan,* UP, Jakarta, 1972.

15. Aswab Mahasin, 'The Santri Middle Class: An Insider's View', in Richard Tanter and Kenneth Young (eds), *The Politics of Middle Class Indonesia,* Centre of Southeast Asian Studies, Monash University, Clayton, 1990, p. 141. *Gedongan* is derived from the word *gedung* meaning a brick house, usually surrounded by a high fence.

16. Sukarno was particularly responsible for associating the *peci* with national dress. In 1978, in the context of revival of Sukarnoism, a group of men protesting in nationalist attire may well have had connotations of mass actions that were part of Sukarnoist politics, but more or less banned under the New Order.

17. Ministerial Decree, 1977.

18. For example, advertisements for *Daerah Hilang* (1958) mentioned in Chapter 2.

19. Kuhn, *The Power of the Image, Essays in Representation and Sexuality,* Routledge and Kegan Paul, London, 1985, pp. 122–6.

20. *Bulletin KFT,* 1980, p. 29.

21. For a discussion of military–Golkar relations in the context of democratisation in Indonesia, see David Reeve, 'The Corporatist State: The Case of Golkar', in Arief Budiman (ed), *op. cit.,* pp. 151–76.

22. Howard Dick, 'The Rise of a Middle Class and the Changing Concept of Equity in Indonesia: An Interpretation', in *Indonesia,* No. 39, April 1985, p. 90.

23. Schiller, 1978, *op. cit.,* p. 38.

24. Ali Murtopo, *Akselerasi Modernisasi Pembangunan 25 Tahun,* Centre for Strategic and International Studies, Jakarta, 1972. Cited in *ibid.,* p. 39.

25. *Ibid.,* p. 38.

26. *Kode Etik,* 1981, *op. cit.,* p. 177.

27. David Reeve, *Golkar of Indonesia: An Alternative to the Party System,* Oxford University Press, Singapore, 1985, p. 357.

28. 'Dr Siti Pertiwi Disambut Meriah', in *Suara Karya Minggu,* 30/11/80.

29. Translations in the film subtitles.

30. 'Pertanggungan Jawab Penilaian Oleh Dewan Juri F.F.I. 1980 Semarang', in a special edition of *Bulletin KFT,* No. 3, Vol. VIII, pp. 28–9.

31. Ong Hok Ham (interview), 'Mistik Dalam Film', in *Sinema Indonesia,* No. 2, Year 1, pp. 10–13.

32. Howard Dick, 'Further Reflections on the Middle Class', in Tanter and Young (eds.), 1990, *op. cit.,* pp. 64–5.

33. *Ibid.,* p. 63.

# 6. Women's Pictures in Men's Fiction

1. Laura Mulvey, 'Visual Pleasure and Narrative Cinema', in Tony Bennet, *et al* (eds), *Popular Television and Film,* British Film Institute and Open University Press, London, 1981.

2. 'Wajah Wanita Dalam Film Indonesia: Beberapa Catatan', *Prisma,* July 1981. English translation, English edition of the journal, March 1982.

3. Karl G. Heider, *Indonesian Cinema: National Culture on Screen,* University of Hawaii Press, Honolulu, 1991, pp. 116–19.

4. *Ibid.,* p. 119.

5. Madelon Djajadiningrat-Nieuwenhuis, 'Ibuism and Priyayization: Path to

Power', in Elsbeth Loches-Scholten and Anke Neihof (eds), *Indonesian Women in Focus*, Foris Publication, Dordredch, 1987, p. 44.

6. This is not to argue that women writers or directors are closet feminists. But, given that they have to struggle to be part of a male-dominated art form, it is particularly difficult for them to take a radical position, particularly on women's issues. Elaine Showalter in her analysis of Anglo-America women writers says, 'one might suppose that the 19th century woman writer would have supported the feminists, since both were struggling against the same destructive stereotypes and discriminatory policies ... . Yet the relationship between women writers and feminists has been generally strained.' Elaine Showalter (ed.), *Women's Liberation and Literature*, Harcourt Brace Jovanovich, New York, 1971, p. 4.

7. For a discussion of the characteristic features of this genre, see Sen, 'Film Remaja: The Construction of Parental Power', in *Asian Studies Association of Australia Review*, November 1986.

8. Peter Carey and Vincent Houben, 'Spirited Srikandhis and Sly Sumbadras: The Social Political and Economic Role of Women in Central Javanese Coaurts in the 18th and Early 19th Centuries', in Elsbeth Loches-Scholten and Anke Neihof (eds), 1987, *op. cit.*, p. 13.

9. 'Koen Faya Koen' is a Quranic phrase which translates as 'Be and it was'. It refers to the creation of life by God and also refers specifically to the creation of the first man.

10. Personal correspondence from the director, 2/6/83.

11. The song describes the terrible things that happen to him 'because my wife goes out to work/ While I stay in the kitchen'.

12. The only feature film addressing the issue of transsexuals seriously, and sympathetically, *Mereka Memang Ada* (They Really Exist), was made in 1983. I have not seen the film, but from reviews and synopses it appears to be about the research by a journalist, Arifin, into the lives of transsexuals in both lower and upper class Jakarta, and ends with both the rich and poor families accepting their transsexual sons for what they are.

13. Violence against women, at least at the symbolic level, did indeed mark the beginning of the New Order when GERWANI's (*Gerakan Wanita Indonesia*, Indonesian Women's Movement) left-wing politics was represented as perversion. See Southwood and Flanagan, *Law, Propaganda and Terror*, Zed Press, London, 1983, pp. 69–71.

14. He was later appointed the Director of the *Proyek Istana Anak-Anak* (Children's Palace Project), at Taman Mini, the amusement park built in 1972–73 at the initiative of Mrs Suharto. The new children's palace project had the blessing of the first couple. See *Kompas*, 17/4/86.

15. For a more detailed analysis of the film see Sen, 1981, *op. cit.*

16. Interview, Jakarta, 25/5/81.

17. A few exceptions, such as *Leak* (1981), set in the context of Balinese Hinduism, have non-Muslim mystics.

18. The titles in the English subtitled versions of the films are *Road of No Return* for *Noda Tak Berampun* and *The Longest Dark* for *Bernafas Dalam Lumpur*.

19. This intolerance of the sexual woman is not by any means peculiar to Indonesian cinema. Feminists have produced similar readings of many Hollywood films. See E. Ann Kaplan, *Women and Film: Both Sides of the Camera*, Methuen, New York, 1983, Chs. 2–5.

20. *Srimulat* is a traditional theatrical performance from East Java.

21. A number of older films I have seen contain successful professional women, where their success outside the home is not seen as contravening their femininity.

22. See Wieringa, *et al, op. cit.*; and Sullivan, 1991, *op.cit.*

23. See Sen, 'The Taming of the Shrew or Film in the Production of Femininity in Indonesia', second Women in the Asia Workshop Paper, Monash University, Clayton, 1983.

24. Kuhn, 1985, *op. cit.*, p. 79.

25. The failure to see women as a political force, symbolically and really, may be common to many military regimes of the Third World. Jaquette has argued, for example, that in many of the military dominated Latin American states women were able to organise politically more effectively than men because of the military regime's disregard of women as a political force. See Jane S. Jaquette (ed.), *Women's Movement in Latin America: Feminism and the Transition to Democracy*, Unwin Hyman, London, 1989. See 'Introduction'.

26. For a detailed discussion of the legend and the film, see Barbara Hatley, 'Texts and Contexts: The Roro Mendut Folk Legend on Stage and Screen' in Krishna Sen (ed.), 1988, *op. cit.*

27. Kuhn, 1985, *op. cit.*, pp. 19–47.

28. Usmar Ismail, 'Masalah Sensur di Indonesia', 1951, republished in Usmar Ismail, 1983, *op. cit.*, pp. 28–31.

29. David Jenkins has argued that by the late 1970s the opposition to the Suharto government had grown to a widespread alliance between students, intellectuals, Muslims and former army officers who had themselves once been key members of the New Order. See Jenkins, 1984, *op. cit.*, Chapter 11.

## 7. The New 'Ordered' Cinema

1. Mochtar Mas'oed, 'The State Reorganisation of Society under the New Order', in *Prisma*, No. 47, p. 4.

2. This term has been coined by Arjun Appadurai to 'refer both to the distribution of electronic capabilities to produce and disseminate information (newspapers, magazines, television stations, film production studios, etc.) which are now available to a growing number of public and private interests throughout the world; and to the image of the world created by these media.' In 'Disjuncture and Difference in the Global Cultural Economy', *Media, Culture and Society*, Vol. 7, No. 2–3, June 1990, pp. 298–9.

3. Ruth McVey, 'The Wayang Controversy in Indonesian Communism', in Mark Hobart and Robert Taylor (eds), *Context, Meaning and Power in Southeast Asia*, Southeast Asia Project, Cornell University, Ithaca, 1986, p. 33.

4. The idea that private television would wean sections of the Indonesian population from foreign television via satellite was widely discussed in the media during the late 1980s. For a discussion of this, see my 'Changing Horizons of Indonesian Television', *Southeast Asian Journal of Social Sciences*, special double issue, 1994.

# Bibliography

(n.p = no publisher; n.d. = no date)

## Books, Monographs, Theses, Articles and Unpublished Papers

Abercrombie, Nicholas, Stephen Hill and Bryan S. Turner, *The Dominant Ideology Thesis*, Allen and Unwin, London, 1980.

Abeyasekere, Susan, *Jakarta: A History*, Oxford University Press, Singapore, 1987.

Ameh, S.M., see Ismail, Usmar.

Anderson, Benedict, 'The Languages of Indonesian Politics', *Indonesia*, April 1966.

— 'American Values and Research on Indonesia', paper given at the Annual Conference of Association of Asian Studies, USA, 1971.

— 'The Idea of Power in Javanese Culture', in Holt, *et al.*, (eds), 1972.

— *Java in a Time of Revolution*, Cornell University Press, Ithaca, 1972.

— 'Notes on Contemporary Indonesian Political Communication', *Indonesia*, October 1973.

— 'Nationalism and the State in Modern Indonesia', paper presented to the Japanese Political Science Association Round Table Conference on National Interest and Political Leadership, Tokyo, 1982.

— and Audrey Kahin (eds), *Interpreting Indonesian Politics: Thirteen Contributions to the Debate*, Cornell University, Ithaca, 1982.

— *Imagined Communities: Reflections on the Origin and Spread of Nationalism*, Verso, London, 1983.

— 'Narrating the Nation', *Times Literary Supplement*, 13 June 1986.

— *Language and Power: Exploring Political Cultures in Indonesia*, Cornell University Press, Ithaca, 1990.

Andrew, J. Dudley, *The Major Film Theories: An Introduction*, Oxford University Press, London, 1976.

Ang, I, *Desperately Seeking the Audience*, Routledge, London, 1991.

Appadurai, A., 'Disjuncture and Difference in the Global Cultural Economy', *Media Culture and Society*, Vol. 7, No. 2–3, June 1990.

Ardan, S.M., 'Pertanggungan Jawab Dewan Juri Pada 1977 Paling Keras', *Indonesian Film Festival Information*, Yayasan FFI, Jakarta, 1983.

Armes, R., *Third World Film Making and the West*, University of California Press, Berkeley, 1987.

Atmakusumah (ed.), *Tahta Untuk Rakyat: Celah-celah Kehidupan Sultan Hamengkubuwono IX*, Gramedia, Jakarta, 1982.

Atmowiloto, Arswendo, 'Komik Silat: Menggambar Kue Menghilangkan Lapar', unpublished seminar paper presented at Taman Ismail Marzuki (TIM), Jakarta, 16 November 1981.

Aeusrivongse, Nidhi, 'Fiction as History: A Study of Indonesian Novels and Novelists', unpublished PhD thesis, Department of History, The University of Michigan, 1976.

Bandung Institute of Technology Student Council, 'White Book of the 1978 Student Struggle', *Indonesia*, No. 25, April 1978.

Barthes, Roland, *Image-music-text*, Fontana/Collins, Glasgow, 1977.

Bennett, T., S. Boyd-Bowman, C. Mercer and J. Woollacott (eds), *Popular Television and Film*, The British Film Institute and Open University Press, London, 1981.

Bigsby, C.W.E. (ed.), *Approaches to Popular Culture*, Edward Arnold, London, 1976.

Biran, Misbach Yusa, see Misbach Yusa Biran.

Bordwell, David and Kristin Thompson, *Film Art: An Introduction*, Addison-Wesley Publishing House, Massachusetts, 1979.

Bourchier, David, *Dynamics of Dissent in Indonesia: Sawito and the Phantom Coup*, Cornell Modern Indonesia Project, Cornell University, Ithaca, 1984.

Boyd-Barret, Oliver, 'Media Imperialism: Towards an International Framework for the Analysis of Media Systems', in Curran *et al.*, (eds), 1977.

Brewer, Anthony, *Marxist Theories of Imperialism: A Critical Survey*, Routledge and Kegan Paul, London, 1980.

Budiman, *Folklor Betawi*, Pustaka Jaya, Jakarta, 1979.

Budiman, A. (ed.), *State and Civil Society in Indonesia*, Centre of Southeast Asian Studies, Monash University, Clayton, 1990.

Burton, J, 'Marginal Cinemas and Mainstream Critical Theory', *Screen*, Vol. 26, No. 3–4, May–Aug 1985.

Chakrabarty, D., 'Robison Reviewed', *Inside Indonesia*, No. 9, December 1986.

Coppel, Charles A., *Indonesian Chinese in Crisis*, ASAA and Oxford University Press, Singapore, 1983.

Creed, Barbara, 'Feminist Film Theory: Reading the Text', *Lip*, No. 7, 1982–83.

Crouch, Harold, *The Army and Politics in Indonesia*, Cornell University Press, Ithaca, 1978.

Curran, James *et al.* (eds), *Mass Communication and Society*, The Open University Press, London, 1977.

Davis, Howard and Paul Walton (eds), *Language, Image, Media*, Basil Blackwell, Oxford, 1983.

Dick, H.W., 'The Rise of a Middle Class and the Changing Concept of Equity in Indonesia: An Interpretation', *Indonesia*, No. 39, April 1985.

— 'Further Reflection on the Middle Class', in Tanter and Young (eds), 1990.

Dyer, Richard, 'Stars as Signs', in Bennett *et al.* (eds), 1981.

Evans, P.B. *et al.*, *Bringing the State Back In*, Cambridge University Press, Cambridge, 1985.

Feith, Herbert, *The Decline of Constitutional Democracy in Indonesia*, Cornell University Press, Ithaca, 1962.

— 'Dynamics of Guided Democracy', in McVey (ed.), 1963.

— and Lance Castles (eds), *Indonesian Political Thinking 1945–65*, Cornell University Press, Ithaca, 1970.

— 'Legitimacy Questions and the Suharto Polity', in Fox *et al.* (eds), 1981.

Foulcher, Keith, *Social Commitment in Literature and the Arts: The Indonesian "Institute of People's Culture" 1950–1965*, Monash University CSEAS, Melbourne, 1986.

— 'The Construction of an Indonesian National Culture: Patterns of Hegemony and Resistance', in Budiman (ed.), 1990.

Foulkes, A.P., *Literature and Propaganda*, Methuen, London, 1983.

Fox, J.J., *et al.* (eds), *Indonesia: Australian Perspectives*, ANU Press, Canberra, 1981.

Frank, Andre Gunder, 'Development of Underdevelopment', in Wilber (ed.), 1973.

Franken, Mannus, 'Film Cerita Di Indonesia', *Cinemagia*, (translated into Indonesian by M.D. Aliff, copy at Sinematek), Vol. 1, No. 1, February 1950.

Frederick, William H., 'Rhoma Irama and the Dangdut Style: Aspects of Contemporary Indonesian Popular Culture', *Indonesia*, No. 34, October 1982.

Gabriel, T.H., *Third Cinema in the Third World*, UMI Research Press, Ann Arbor, 1982.

— 'Towards a Critical Theory of Third World Films', *Third World Affairs*, 1985.

Ganes T.H., *Tuan Tanah Kedaung*, n.p., n.d.

— *Si Buta*, n.p., n.d.

Guback, T.H., 'Film as International Business', *Journal of Communication*, Winter, 1974.

Hanifah, Abu, *Tales of a Revolution*, Angus and Robertson, Sydney, 1972.

Hatley, Barbara, 'Kethoprak-Performance and Social Meaning in a Javanese Popular Theatre Form', unpublished doctoral dissertation, University of Sydney, 1985.

— 'Texts and Contexts: The Roro Mendut Folk Legend on Stage and Screen', in Sen, K. (ed.), 1988.

Hatta, M., 'A Revolution Should Not Last Too Long', in Feith and Castles (eds), 1970.

Heath, Stephen, *Questions of Cinema*, Macmillan, London, 1981.

— 'Jaws, Ideology and Film Theory', in Bennett *et al.* (eds), 1981.

Heider, K., *Indonesian Cinema: National Culture on Screen*, University of Hawaii Press, Honolulu, 1991.

Helmi, *Di Tengah Pergolakan*, Yayasan Langer, Limburg, 1981.

Hill, David T., 'Romance And Coincidence – A Formula for Success: The Popular Novelists Marga T. and Ashadi Siregar', unpublished honours thesis, Department of Indonesian Languages and Literatures, ANU, Canberra, 1977.

Holt, Claire *et al.* (eds), *Culture and Politics in Indonesia*, Cornell University Press, Ithaca and London, 1972.

Homan, Gerlof D., 'American Business Interests in the Indonesian Republic, 1946–49', *Indonesia*, No. 35, April 1983.

Hull, V., *Women in Java's Rural Middle Class: Progress or Regress?*, Population Institute Gajah Mada University, Jogjakarta, 1976.

Ikranegara, K. Sen and D.T. Hill (trans.), *Indonesian Folk Tales*, Balai Pustaka, Jakarta, 1981.

*Indonesia: Majalah Kebudayaan*, special issue on the Second Cultural Congress at Bandung, January–March, 1952.

Ingleson, John, *In Search of Justice: Workers and Unions in Colonial Java, 1908–1926*, ASAA and Oxford University Press, Singapore, 1986.

*Inter-Ocean*, 'Films in the Orient: Interesting Interview with F.M.S. Censors'. Vol. 7, No. 11, November 1925.

Ismail, Taufiq, 'Cerita Angka, FFI 1977', *Tempo*, 12/3/1977, reprinted in Misbach Yusa Biran (ed.), 1983.

Ismail, Usmar, *Lakon-lakon Sedih Dan Gembira*, Balai Pustaka, Jakarta, 1948.

— 'Sari Soal Film-film Indonesia', *Star News*, September, 1954.

— (under pseudonym S.M. Ameh), 'Sejarah Hitam Perfilman Nasional', *Sinar Harapan*, 6 October 1970.

— *Usmar Ismail Mengupas Film*, Penerbit Sinar Harapan, Jakarta, 1983,

Jackson, Karl D., and Lucian Pye (eds), *Political Power and Communications in Indonesia*, University of California Press, Berkeley, 1978.

Jameson, F., *The Political Unconscious: Narrative as Socially Symbolic Act*, Methuen, London, 1981.

Jaquette, J.S. (ed.), *Women's Movement in Latin America: Feminism and the Transition to Democracy*, Unwin Hyman, London, 1989.

Jassin, H.B., *Max Havelaar*, Penerbit Jembatan, Jakarta, 1972.

Jayadiningrat-Nieuwenhuis, M., 'Ibuism and Priyiyization: Path to Power', in Loches-Scholten, E. and Neihof, A. (eds), 1987.

Jenkins, David, *Suharto and His Generals: Indonesian Military Politics 1975–1983*, Cornell Modern Indonesian Project, Ithaca, 1984.

Kamajaya, Slamet Jabarudi, *et al.*, *Sum Kuning, Korban Penculikan Pemerkosaan*, U.P. Indonesia, Jogjakarta, 1972.

Kaplan, E.A., *Women and Film: Both Sides of the Camera*, Methuen, New York, 1983.

Karya, T., 'In Search of Ways and Means for Making the Film an Instrument of Expression', in Sen, K. (ed.), 1988.

Kimman, Eduard J.J.M., *Indonesian Publishing: Economic Organization in a Langganan Society*, Hollandia, Baarn, 1981.

Kolker, R., *The Altering Eye: Contemporary International Cinema*, Oxford University Press, 1982.

Kress, G.R., 'Structuralism and Popular Culture', in Bigsby (ed.), 1976.

Kuhn, A., *The Power of the Image: Essays on Representation and Sexuality*, Routledge and Kegan Paul, London, 1985.

Kuraswa, K., 'Propaganda Media on Java under the Japanese 1942–1945', *Indonesia*, No. 44, October 1987.

Kwok, J.W.L., 'Towards a Cultural Understanding of Cinema: A Comparison of Contemporary Films from PRC and Hong Kong', *Wide Angle*, Vol. 11, No. 3, 1988.

Legge, J.D., *Sukarno: A Political Biography*, Penguin, Middlesex, 1972.

Lev, D.S., *The Transition to Guided Democracy: Indonesian Politics 1957–59*, Cornell University Modern Indonesia Project, Ithaca, 1966.

Leyda, Jay, *Electric Shadows: An Account of Films and the Film Audience in China*, Massachusetts Institute of Technology, Massachusetts, 1972.

Liddle, R. William (ed.), *Political Participation in Modern Indonesia*, Monograph Series No. 19, Yale University Southeast Asia Studies, New Haven, 1973.

Loches-Scholten, E. and A. Neihof (eds), *Indonesian Women in Focus*, Foris Publication, Dordredch, 1987.

Lovell, T., *Pictures of Reality: Aesthetics, Politics and Pleasure*, BFI, London, 1980.

MacCabe, Colin, 'Theory of Film: Principles of Realism and Pleasure', *Screen*, Vol. 17, No. 3, 1976.

— 'Realism and Cinema: Notes on Some Brechtian Theses', in Bennett *et al.* (eds), 1981.

Mackie, J.A.C., *Konfrontasi: The Indonesia-Malaysia Dispute 1963–1966*, Oxford University Press, Kuala Lumpur, 1974.

Magenda, Burhan. 'Ethnicity and State Building in Indonesia: The Cultural Bases of the New Order', unpublished paper presented to the Colloquium on Ethnicity and Nations: Process of Inter-Ethnic Relations in Latin America, Southeast Asia and the Pacific, Houston, October, 1983.

Mahasin, A., 'The Santri Middle Class: An Insider's View', in Tanter, R. and Young, K. (eds), 1990.

Malassa, M.A., and Imam Soepardi (eds), *Festival Film Indonesia 1980*, FFI, Semarang, 1980.

Manderson, L. (ed.), *Women's Work and Women's Roles: Economics and Everyday Life in Indonesia, Malaysia and Singapore*, Australian National University, Canberra, 1983.

Marga, T., *Karmila*, Gramedia, Jakarta, 1973.

Martin-Schiller, B., 'Weeding Out Women? Changing Agricultural Practices and Adaptive Work Patterns in Rural Java', *Kabar Sebrang*, Vol. 13, 1984.

Mattelart, A., *Mass Media, Ideologies and the Revolutionary Movement*, The Harvester Press, Brighton, 1980.

— 'Cultural Imperialism, Mass Media and Class Struggle: An Interview with Armand Mattelart', *The Insurgent Sociologist*, No. 4, 1980.

McDonald, Hamish, *Suharto's Indonesia*, Fontana/Collins, Blackburn, 1980.

McVey, Ruth T. (ed.), *Indonesia*, Yale University and HRAF Press, New Haven, 1963.

— 'The Wayang Controversy in Indonesian Communism', in Hobart, M. and Taylor, R. (eds), *Context, Meaning and Power in Southeast Asia*, Southeast Asia Project, Cornell University, Ithaca, 1986.

Misbach Yusa Biran, 'Pengaruh Festival Film', paper presented to the Jakarta Press Club, 29 April 1982.

— *Sepintas Kilas Sejarah Film Indonesia*, Badan Pelaksana FFI, Jakarta, 1982.

— (ed.), *Tentang Perfilman Nasional: Dari Penerbitan 1971–1983*, Yayasan Artis Film, Jakarta, 1983.

Mishra, V., 'Filmic Narrative: Text and Transformation in Bombay Cinema', *Continuum*, Vol. 2, No. 1, 1988/89.

Mohamad, Goenawan, 'Sebuah Pengantar Untuk Film Indonesia Mutakhir – Catatan Tahun 1974', *Prisma*, No. 3, June 1974.

Morfit, Michael, 'Pancasila: The Indonesian State Ideology According to the New Order Government', *Asian Survey*, Vol. XXI, No. 8, August 1981.

Morley, David, 'Cultural Transformations: The Politics of Resistance', in Davis and Walton (eds), 1983.

Mortimer, Rex (ed.), *Showcase State: The Illusion of Indonesia's 'Accelerated Modernisation'*, Angus and Robertson, Sydney, 1973.

— *Indonesian Communism Under Sukarno: Ideology and Politics 1959–1965*, Cornell University Press, Ithaca, 1974.

Multatuli, *Max Havelaar: or the Coffee Auctions of the Dutch Trading Company*, translated by Roy Edwards, The University of Massachusetts Press, Amherst, 1982.

Mulvey, Laura, 'Visual Pleasure and Narrative Cinema', in Bennett *et al.* (eds), 1981.

Notosusanto, Nugroho (ed.), *Pejuang Dan Prajurit*, Penerbit Sinar Harapan, Jakarta, 1984.

Oliven, Ruben George, 'The Production and Consumption of Culture in Brazil', *Latin American Perspectives*, Vol. 11, No. 1, Winter 1984.

Ong Hok Ham (interview with), 'Mistik Dalam Film', *Sinema Indonesia*, No. 2, 1981.

Pane, Armijn, 'Produksi Film Cerita Di Indonesia: Perkembangan Sebagai Alat Masyarakat', *Indonesia: Majalah Kebudayaan*, Vol. IV, No. 1–2, January–February 1953.

Pigeaud, Th., *Javaans-Nederlands Woordenboek*, Martinus Nijhoff, The Hague, 3rd printing, 1982.

Pramudya Ananta Tur, *Tempo Doeloe*, Hasta Mitra, Jakarta, 1982.

Pye, Lucian, *Communications and Political Development*, Princeton University Press, Princeton, New Jersey, 1963.

Reeve, D., *Golkar of Indonesia: An Alternative to the Party System*, Oxford University Press, Singapore, 1985.

— 'The Corporatist State: The Case of Golkar', in Budiman, A. (ed.), 1990.

Reid, Anthony, *The Indonesian National Revolution 1945–1950*, Longman Australia, Hawthorn, 1974.

Ricklefs, M.C., *A History of Modern Indonesia*, Macmillan, London, 1981.

Robinson, A., *Satyajit Ray: The Inner Eye*, University of California Press, Berkeley, 1989.

Robinson, K., *Women and Work in an Indonesian Mining Town*, in Manderson (ed.), 1983.

Robison, R. 'Politics and Economy in the Political History of the New Order', *Indonesia*, No. 31, April 1981.
— *Indonesia: The Rise of Capital*, Allen and Unwin, Sydney, 1986.
— 'Authoritarian States, Capital-Owning Classes and the Politics of the Newly Industrialising Countries: The Case of Indonesia', *World Politics*, Vol. 41, No. 1, 1988.
Rusli, Marah, *Sitti Nurbaya*, Balai Pustaka, Jakarta, 1922.
Said, Salim, *Profil Dunia Film Indonesia*, Grafitipers, Jakarta, 1982.
— *Shadows on the Silver Screen: A Social History of Indonesian Film*, Lontar Foundation, Jakarta, 1991. Translation of Said, S., 1982.
Schiller, James W., 'Development Ideology in New Order Indonesia: The Suharto Regime and its Critics', unpublished MA thesis, Ohio University, 1978.
Schiller, Herbert I., *Communications and American Empire*, Kelley, New York, 1969.
Schlesinger, P., 'Media, the Political Order and National Identity', *Media, Culture and Society*, Vol. 13, No. 3, July 1991.
Schramm, Wilbur, *Mass Media and National Development*, Stanford University Press, Stanford, 1964.
Sen, Krishna, 'Wajah Wanita Dalam Film Indonesia', *Prisma*, No. 7, July 1981.
— 'The Taming of The Shrew or Film in the Production of Femininity in Indonesia', collection of papers presented at the Second Women in Asia Workshop, Monash University, July, 1983.
— 'Hidden from History: Aspects of Indonesian Cinema 1955–65', *Review of Indonesian and Malaysian Affairs*, Vol. 19, No. 2, 1985.
— 'Sjumanjaya: A Film-maker as Social Critic', *Inside Indonesia*, No. 6, December 1985.
— 'Film Remaja: The Construction of Parental Power', *Asian Studies Association of Australia Review*, November 1986.
— (ed.), *Histories and Stories: Cinema in New Order Indonesia*, Centre of Southeast Asian Studies, Monash University, Clayton, 1988.
— 'Power and Poverty in Indonesian Cinema', in Paul Alexander (ed.), *Creating Indonesian Cultures*, Oceania, Sydney, 1989.
— 'Si Boy Looked at Johnny: Indonesian Screen at the Turn of the Decade', *Continuum*, 4:2, 1991.
— 'Repression and Resistance: Interpretations of Feminine in Indonesian Cinema', in Virginia Hooker (ed.), *Culture and Society in New Order Indonesia: 1965–1990*, Oxford University Press, Kuala Lumpur, 1993.
Showalter, Elaine (ed.), *Women's Liberation and Literature*, Harcourt Brace Jovanovich, New York, 1971.
Siagian, Bachtiar, *Ichtisar Sedjarah Perfilman di Indonesia*, Komite Nasional Indonesia FFAA3, Jakarta, 1964.
Siahaan, J.E., and Tony Ryanto (eds), *Berkala BSF*, n.p., Jakarta, August 1971.
*Sinematek Indonesia* (ed.), *Apa Siapa Orang Film Indonesia: 1926–1978*, Yayasan Artis Film and Sinematek Indonesia, Jakarta, 1979.
Situmorang, Sitor, 'Juri Festival Pecah', *Star News*, No. 14, 1955.
— 'Sejarah Permulaan Produksi Filem di Indonesia: Catatan Manus Franken', *Sinema Indonesia*, No. 2, 1981.
Sjumanjaya. 'Menciptakan Budaya Produser Film Indonesia Hari Ini', unpublished paper for Rapat Kerja Lokakarya PPFI, 7–8 October 1980.
Smith, Alan, 'The Integration Model of Development: A Critique', in Mortimer (ed.), 1973.
Southwood, Julie and Patrick Flanagan, *Indonesia: Law, Propaganda and Terror*, Zed Press, London, 1983.

Stivens, M. (ed.), *Why Gender Matters in Southeast Asian Politics*, Monash Papers on Southeast Asia No. 23, Clayton, 1991.

Straubhaar, J.D., 'Beyond Media Imperialism: Assymetrical Interdependence and Cultural Proximity', *Critical Studies in Mass Communication*, Vol. 8, No. 1, March 1991.

Sullivan, N., 'Gender and Politics in Indonesia', in Stivens, M. (ed.), 1991.

Sumarjo, Jacob, 'Image Indonesia dalam Film Nasional Kita', *Kompas*, 16/4/74, reprinted in Misbach Yusa Biran (ed.), 1983.

Sumarjono. 'Perjalanan dan Tujuan: Sekapursirih Ketua KFT', in *KFT Buku Anggota 1964–74*.

Susanto, Astrid, 'The Mass Communications System in Indonesia', in Jackson and Pye (eds), 1978.Sutarto, R.M., 'Sejarah Perfilman Nasional', *Almanak Pers*, Antara, 1976.

Sutarto, R.M., 'Sejarah Perfilman Nasional', *Almanak Pers*, Antara, 1976.

Sutherland, Heather, *The Making of a Bureaucratic Elite: The Colonial Transformation of the Javanese 'Priyayi'*, Heinemann, Singapore, 1979.

Suwardi, Harsono, 'Problem Komunikasi Untuk Pembangunan', *Prisma*, No. 3, June 1974.

Tanter, R. and Young, K. (eds), *The Politics of the Middle Class in Indonesia*, Centre of Southeast Asian Studies, Monash University, Clayton, 1990.

Tedjasukmana, Iskandar, *The Political Character of the Indonesian Trade Union Movement*, Monograph Series, Modern Indonesia Project, Cornell University, New York, 1958.

Teeuw, A., *Modern Indonesian Literature*, Martinus Nijhoff, The Hague, 1967.

*The Times*, 'The Cinema in the East', 18/9/1926, reproduced in *Review of Indonesian and Malaysian Affairs*, Vol. 15, No. 1, 1981.

Toer, Pramoedya Ananta, see Pramoedya Ananta Toer.

Trinh, Minh-ha, 'Not you/Like you: Post-Colonial Women and the Interlocking Questions of Identity and Difference', in *Inscriptions*, Nos 3–4.

— *Women, Native, Other: Writing Postcoloniality and Feminism*, Indiana University Press, Bloomington, 1989.

Tryman, Setiadi (ed.), *20th PPFI: Dalam Perjalanan Sejarah Perfilman*, PPFI Public Relations Unit, Jakarta, 1977.

van Rees, Michonne, 'The 1977–78 Student Movement in Indonesia', unpublished MA preliminary thesis, Melbourne University, 1981.

Wang, Y., 'Mixing Memory and Desire: *Red Sorghum*, A Chinese Vesion of Masculinity and Femininity', *Public Culture*, Vol. 2, No. 1, Fall 1989.

Wieringa, S., 'Indonesian Women's Organisations Since 1950', in Wieringa (ed.), *Women's Organisations in Historical Perspective*, Institute of Social Studies, The Hague, n.d.

Wijaya, Hussein (ed.), *Seni-Budaya Betawi*, Pustaka Jaya, Jakarta, 1976.

Wilber, Charles K. (ed.), *The Political Economy of Development and Underdevelopment*, Random House, New York, 1973.

Williams, Raymond, *Marxism and Literature*, Oxford University Press, Oxford, 1977.

Wiryani, Umi. 'The Second Sex in Indonesia', *Inside Indonesia*, No. 7, May 1986.

Wolff, Janet, *The Social Production of Art*, Macmillan, London, 1981.

Yau, E. 'Yellow Earth: Western Analysis and a Non-Western Text', *Film Quarterly*, Vol. 41, No. 2, 1987–88.

## Official Documents and Publications

Biro Hukum, *Himpunan Peraturan-Peraturan Perfilman Tahun 1964 s/d 1978*, Department of Information, Jakarta, n.d. [1979?].

BPS (Biro Pusat Statistik), *Statistik Bioskop Indonesia*, Republic of Indonesia, Jakarta, 1978.

— *Statistical Yearbook of Indonesia 1977–78*, Republic of Indonesia, Jakarta, 1978.

— *Statistik Bioskop Indonesia*, Republic of Indonesia, Jakarta, 1979.

— *Statistical Yearbook of Indonesia 1984*, Republic of Indonesia, Jakarta, 1984.

— *Statistik Bioskop Indonesia*, Republic of Indonesia, Jakarta, 1984.

*Bulletin KFT*, No. 4, Year IX, September 1981.

Department of Information, *The Second Five-Year Development Plan*, Republic of Indonesia, Vol, III, n.d.

— Selected Ministerial Decrees, Republic of Indonesia, Jakarta, 1966–82.

— *Katalog Film Indonesia: Produksi 1973–74*, Jakarta, [1974?].

— *Perfilman Indonesia 1976*, Jakarta, 1977.

— 'Lembaran Negara Hindia Belanda Tahun 1940, No. 507', *Badan Sensor Film*, Jakarta, 1978.

— *Indonesia 1979: An Official Handbook*, Republic of Indonesia, Jakarta, 1979.

— *Aneka Data Perfilman: 1969–79*, Vol. I, Jakarta, 1980.

— *Pola Dasar Pembinaan Dan Pengembangan Perfilman Nasional*, Jakarta, 1980.

Dewan Film, *Pola Dasar Pembinaan Dan Pengembangan Perfilman Nasional*, Department of Information, Jakarta, 1980.

— *Kode Etik Produksi Film Nasional*, Department of Information, Jakarta, 1981.

Dewan Juri FFI 1980, 'Pertanggungan Jawab Penilaian Oleh Dewan Juri F.F.I. 1980 Semarang', *Bulletin Karyawan Film Dan Televisi Indonesia*, No. 3, Year VIII, Special issue FFI 1980.

Joint Ministerial Decree No. 49/Kep/Menpen – No. 88A – No. 096a/U/1975 (known as SK Tiga Menteri).

*KFT Buku Anggota 1964–74*, Persatuan Karyawan Film dan Televisi Indonesia, Jakarta, [1975?].

LEKNAS-LIPI, *Laporan Penelitian: Pengaruh Sosial Budaya Dari Komunikasi Satelit*, (3 vols), Jakarta, 1976–79.

Lembaga Pers dan Pendapat Umum, *Audience Research Film*, Department of Information, Jakarta, [1972?].

PT Inscore Indonesia, *Laporan Penelitian Aspek-Aspek Perfilman Nasional*, Department of Information, Jakarta, 1977/78.

Presidential Instruction, No. 012, 5 August 1964.

Republic of Indonesia, *Berita Negara Tambahan: Perseroan-Perseroan Terbatas*, Jakarta, 1966–82.

Secretariat BSF, *Kriterium Penyensoran Film - Ordonanntie Film 1940 Dan Pengumuman Lain-lainnya*, Department of Information, Jakarta, 1978.

## Newspapers, Magazines and Journals

*Aneka, Bendera Buruh, Berita Minggu Film, Berita Buana, Bintang Timur, Citra Film, Far Eastern Economic Review, Harian Rakyat, Indonesia Raya, Kedaulatan Rakyat, Kompas, Merdeka, Patriot, Pedoman, Pelita, Perniagaan, Sinar Harapan, Sinar Pagi, Sinema Indonesia, Suara Karya Minggu, Star News, Tempo, Terbit, Vista, Warta Bakti, Yudha Minggu.*

# Index